A Foreign Affair

By

Amanda Matti

W & B Publishers
USA

W & B Publishers

For information:
W & B Publishers
9001 Ridge Hill Street
Kernersville, NC 27284

www.a-argusbooks.com

ISBN: 9781942981978

Book Cover designed by Dubya

Printed in the United States of America

Dedication

For our girls, Elise & Elaina; may you both someday experience true love.

A Note to the Reader

In order to safeguard the privacy and security of the individuals mentioned in this book, all names - save mine and Fahdi's - are pseudonyms. The incidents recounted here are based on a combination of writings from a journal I kept while in Iraq, my own memory, and Fahdi's relay of information to me regarding events I did not personally witness. All dialogue has been reconstructed to the best of Fahdi's and my memories and in some cases has been translated from Arabic. Conversations in this book are not verbatim but are accurate renderings of what was said and what occurred at the time. The views expressed in this book are mine and do not represent the views of the Department of Defense or any of its components.

A Foreign Affair

"Sometimes, right in the middle of an ordinary life, love gives us a fairytale."

.....Anonymous

Preface

You live only once. You breathe in. You breathe out. The days go by, each seeming like a replica of the one before. But you will never see the day you just lived again. It is gone forever, a speck of dust thrown upon the mounting sands of time. The sun rises each morning, but it's not the same dawn as the one you witnessed the day before. It sets each evening, but it kisses the ground in a different way each dusk. You are not the person today that you were yesterday, nor are you the person you will be tomorrow. At some point in everyone's life, they begin to realize this. They "wake up" and begin to see the world in a whole new light. The veil lifts and the rose-tinted glasses come off. Some refer to it as a rebirth or finding the meaning of life. Others say it's simply growing up. You realize your mortality, and you are able to embrace the beauty of life and the world around you. On the flip side, you are also more aware of the evils and darkness that exist in the world; for every good there must be an evil. Everything must have an opposite. The universe tends to balance itself out. For most people, it takes some kind of significant earth-shattering event to bring about their "awakening." Oftentimes it's a death or a tragedy of some sort. It can be a natural disaster like a hurricane, an earthquake, or a tsunami. Or, it can be a social disaster like the collapse of an economy or war–whether you're an active participant in one or simply find yourself involuntarily in the middle of a hostile conflict. It can also be brought about by a shock of beauty, perhaps the birth of a child.

I consider myself one of the most fortunate. I voluntarily chased my answer to the meaning of life into the jaws of a brutal war. Tragedy, death, or bloodshed could have easily brought about my awakening, but that's what I was expecting. I was poised for battle. I was ready to fight. I had hate and prejudice built up inside me. I knew what I was getting into. I'd coached my mind to be prepared for horrible sights, awful scenes. But as the saying goes, "If you want to make God laugh, just tell him your plans." I was armed and ready to slit throats when fate decided to wake me up with a love story.

Chapter 1

**Thursday, 24 March – Wednesday, 18 May
2005**

I'm never going to love you the way you want me to. Those were the words I heard my boyfriend, Shawn, say several times while we were dating. After two and a half years of this, I knew it was time to cut my losses and end the relationship. But that's a difficult thing to do when you live two miles apart and you have to see each other at work every day. Shawn was enlisted in the Air Force, and I was enlisted in the Navy. We were both Russian linguists stationed at Fort Meade, Maryland where we worked at the National Security Agency. (Yes, the infamous NSA.) The NSA is often misrepresented in Hollywood spy movies like *Enemy of the State* as the evil communications spy agency listening in on every American's phone conversations and monitoring all Internet traffic. In reality, it's a lot of overpaid government cronies who show up to work in sweatpants with no underwear and spend their time counting down the days until their retirement. Granted, there are a few hardworking, dedicated individuals sprinkled in here and there, too, who carry the load for everyone–got to give credit where credit's due.

In early 2005, I was 22 years old and I'd been in the military for nearly five years–three of them spent at the agency. Shawn was working on year number seven in the Air Force. It was a mind-numbing job. The Cold War ended when I was in grade school, and what was left of the

Eastern Block was a minimal military threat by this time; so there really wasn't much use for Russian linguists. All the action was happening in the Middle East where the war in Iraq (the second one) kicked off two years earlier in March of 2003.

I felt like I had contributed very little to my country in my five years of military service, considering I spent the first two years learning a foreign language and then nearly three years sitting in the basement of the NSA twiddling my thumbs. I'd never even left U.S. soil. But hey, it beat living at home and the money was decent, so I just rolled with it. Most people in the military would be thrilled to have a desk job in D.C., but I was young and dumb and getting bored– bored with my job, bored with my life, and bored with my emotionally empty relationship.

Shawn was never the best boyfriend, but I thought I was in love. He was older and more mature, and I followed him around like a puppy even though he treated me like crap a lot of the time. After two years together, the most thoughtful gift he'd given me was a tank top picked up in an airport gift shop on his way back from a trip to Las Vegas with his buddies. I wasn't even worth an entire t-shirt. I knew I had to get away from Shawn, but I didn't have the willpower to be able to stick to a breakup while having to see him every day at work. I knew I had to put some distance between us, and I was desperate for some excitement and adventure.

The agency was constantly posting internal adver-tisements for general intelligence volunteers to deploy to Iraq or Afghanistan for three or four months at a time in support of the war on terrorism. Even though I was a Russian translator, (yeah, not a lot of Russian being spoken in Iraq) I still held a top-secret security clearance, meaning, if nothing else, I could be a classified paper-pusher at an embassy. I figured a few months in Baghdad or Kabul would be an amazing life experience, and I wanted to contribute more directly to our military efforts in the

Middle East. It was also great fodder to put on my military resume, which would be useful when promotion time rolled around. Since I already worked in the agency, I simply had to pass a medical screening. I was a little leery of volunteering to go to a war zone, but basic statistics stated that my chances of being killed in a car accident on the interstate were higher than being killed in Iraq. I also believe in fate and figured if I was slated to die at a young age, I'd rather do it serving my country.

I preferred a deployment to Afghanistan where there was mountain scenery and bearable temperatures, but there was nothing leaving until the fall. I perused the list of open positions, picked the most intriguing option, and submitted my application. The mission was a 120-day agency deployment to Baghdad, Iraq working as an intelligence analyst and Foreign Relations Liaison Officer for the Foreign Affairs Directorate. They must have been desperate for volunteers because they were asking for officers, upper enlisted members, or experienced civilians; but I, a lowly E5, was asked to interview and subsequently offered the position two days after submitting my application. I was stunned when they offered me the job, and I immediately doubted the commitment I made when I accepted. *Holy crap, did I seriously just* volunteer *to spend 120 days in Hell?*

My deployment date was set for May 16, meaning I had less than two months to prepare to go to war. Even though I was active duty military, I was still a desk nerd and had to attend a week of weapons qualifications before I could go over and play with the other soldiers in Iraq. I qualified on the Beretta 9mm pistol and the M-4 rifle, which is just a smaller scale version of the infamous M-16. I did just well enough to pass–which means I could load the bullets into the gun and pull the trigger.

During the weapons training, the instructor called out down the line, "Fire three rounds into the target then return weapons to safe position. Ready. Fire!"

When the shooting ceased, we were instructed to place our weapons on the ground and walk out to retrieve our targets. Mine was completely untouched.

"Well isn't that something," the Marine next to me said as he pulled down his target. "I fired three rounds and hit the target five times."

Crap.

Yep, two of my rounds actually hit the target of the dude next to me and God only knows where my third round went. But in my defense, I think I was actually aiming for his target instead of mine–my bad. When the instructor started coming down the line to check everyone's targets, I discreetly poked a hole in mine with my little finger so I didn't look like a complete loser

*****

I was scheduled to fly a commercial airline out of D.C.'s Dulles International Airport to Amman, Jordan with a brief layover in Frankfurt, Germany then continue on to Baghdad via military aircraft after spending a night in Jordan. Shawn offered to give me a ride to the airport and I accepted.

"Oh crap!" I shouted as we merged onto the I-495 outer beltway of D.C.

"What?" Shawn asked.

"I forgot the damn power supply for my laptop. I left it plugged into the wall in the living room!"

"Do you want to go back?"

"Yes, we have to." I knew it wasn't something I could replace at an airport gift shop, and I was sure I'd have a hard time finding a RadioShack in Baghdad. So we turned around and sped back to my house. We lost about forty minutes, but thankfully we left extra early for the airport. I had a little over an hour to catch my flight by the time we finally made it there.

When we parked, we made a mad dash for the international terminal. I carried my briefcase containing my laptop and left Shawn to battle with my two larger bags loaded with body armor and military gear. We made it to the United Airlines check-in counter with time to spare, but I knew I was in for a fight with the guy at the counter over the weight of my luggage.

"Ma'am, your luggage is not within the weight limit," the young man with no personality behind the counter informed me dryly. "You will have to remove some items before I can check your baggage or you can pay the $400.00 overweight fee."

Damn. I could just charge the overweight fees to the super-sweet government credit card I was issued (specifically for such expenses), but considering the reason my luggage was overweight had a lot to do with the dozen family-sized bottles of Pantene shampoo and conditioner I had stuffed between the body armor, I was reluctant to immediately jump to this route. There was no way I was going to spend 120 days in the desert sun and sand with army PX all-in-one shampoo and conditioner–hell no.

"You take Visa, right?" I replied with a big smile and slid him my government credit card. Yes, your tax dollars hard at work. Don't judge me–I'm not proud of it.

Once the bags were checked, we continued on to security where I had to leave Shawn behind. It was only a four-month deployment but we both knew it was a soft breakup. It reminded me of a scene from one of those sappy romantic movies where the lovers part for what's supposed to be a simple summer abroad, but they ultimately fall out of touch and never see each other again.

"Kick some ass over there, girl," Shawn said as he hugged me. "Take care of yourself and remember: shoot first and ask for forgiveness later."

"I'll call or email when I can to let you know I made it there, okay," I replied, and then I walked away.

When I arrived at my boarding gate, it was already packed with people. A quick scan confirmed my fear that unless there were two planes departing from this gate, some of us were getting cut from the flight. As if reading my mind, an airline employee got on the intercom and read off a list of names with instructions for those individuals to approach the ticket counter. Mine was one of the names called. While waiting in line with the other unfortunate few to be rebooked, I learned the guy in front of me was active duty Army stationed in Germany and the guy behind me was in the Air Force and trying to get back to Ramstein. I sensed a pattern. Anyone on a government ticket was getting bumped.

Once I had my new tickets in hand, I picked out a quiet little corner of the airport terminal, dropped my carryon bags, and settled down for the night. The airline offered to put me up in a hotel, but it was already after midnight and I was more than happy to pocket the $75 cash they provided me with for hotel accommodations. After five years in the Navy and working a rotating shift schedule, I'd learned to sleep just about anywhere.

My flight the next afternoon left relatively on time, bound for Amsterdam instead of Frankfurt due to the rebooking. I was quite relieved to discover my neighbor was a young woman instead of a 300-pound angry traveling businessman with a drinking problem. When I sat down, we exchanged brief sideways smiles. She, too, was obviously relieved at the sight of me.

I soon learned she had just graduated from high school and was on her way to spend the summer in Amsterdam with her older sister who was there attending college. I was immediately jealous and remembered my awesome high school graduation trip to Europe five years earlier. I smiled and mentioned how cute Dutch boys are. I had a mind-blowing weekend with a group of Dutch Marines visiting D.C. a couple of years prior (one Dutch Marine in particular), but that's another story.

A couple of hours into our seven-hour flight, I began feeling a little funny. Half an hour later, it turned into a full-scale attack of flu-like symptoms. I was nauseated, I broke out in a feverish sweat, my body started aching, and I could hardly keep still in my seat. I contemplated getting right back on a plane for the U.S. when I arrived in Amsterdam, knowing I'd be useless to them in Baghdad in this condition. But once I arrived in Amsterdam my symptoms subsided and I realized I'd probably simply suffered some sort of panic attack, so I decided to push on through to Jordan.

My flight from Amsterdam to Amman was nearly five hours, so I had time to recover from my anxiety, and by the time I landed in Amman, I felt pretty much myself again. When I stepped off the plane in Jordan, reality sunk in and I realized just how far away I was from everything I knew.

While stuck in D.C. I sent a message to the U.S. Embassy that I was going to be a day late, so I prayed there would be a representative waiting to meet me and give me a ride to my hotel. When I made it to customs. I scanned the area for my escort. I was told someone would be waiting with a sign that had my name on it. I spotted several people with signs but none of them had my name, so I began to freak out a little. After roaming around customs for about fifteen minutes, double-checking every person with a sign, I decided to go on through customs and try to find a phone on the other side to call the embassy.

While getting my passport stamped, I asked the man behind the counter if he could tell me where I could find a phone, but his English wasn't advanced enough to understand my question and he got flustered.

"I…I…sorry, Ma'am," the customs man stuttered. "I no speak English."

I just smiled and was about to continue on in the direction of the crowd when a man leaning against the wall in the hallway behind the customs area walked over to the flustered agent and me.

"I speak English," the man announced. "What can I help you with?"

"Oh, thank you," I said. I had just begun to tell him about the people that were supposed to meet me when another man came jogging up to the counter and breathlessly blurted out, "Are you Ms. McEwen?"

"Yes," I answered as relief washed over me.

"I am here to take you to your hotel," he informed me in a heavily-accented voice. "Please follow me and we will go get your bags."

Chapter 2

Wednesday, 18 May–Friday, 20 May 2005

I followed my escort, obviously a local Jordanian, to the baggage claim area where he stuck me with a group of four other U.S. government employees who'd also just arrived. Surprisingly, both of my jumbo suitcases actually made it to Jordan. I was sure they were lost due to the flight delay and route changes. I was the last arrival of the evening for our escort, so once I had my luggage in hand, we all headed out to the commuter van.

It was about a 30-minute drive from Queen Aliyah Airport to the hotel district in downtown Amman. Even though it was after dark, I still stared out the window of the van trying to take in all I could. I kept trying to wrap my head around the reality that I was now in an Arab country 10,000 miles away from home, would soon be in the middle of a war zone, and I was on my own. It gave me a rush of excitement with a taste of fear unlike any I had ever known.

Amman was a beautiful city and much more modern and westernized than I had expected. Of course they put us up in the ritzy part of town, but I was still pleasantly surprised. Everyone in the van was booked in separate hotels and mine was the last stop. I checked into my room, threw all of my stuff down, and collapsed on the bed. Once I peeled myself off the bed and splashed some water in my face, I pulled out my laptop and composed a safe-arrival email to send to family and friends.

I was told to be waiting in the lobby the next morning at 0800 for the escorts to take me to a private airport to catch a cargo plane to Baghdad. I waited in front of my hotel for over an hour the next morning and by 0900, I began to worry. Just as I was about to go back inside to track down a phone, one of the bellboys told me my ride had arrived. He pointed me in the direction of a luxury sedan with a single male driver. I was a little confused since I'd been dropped off in a van the previous night. I went over and the man asked me in very broken English if I was Miss McEwen. His English was so broken he totally butchered the pronunciation of my last name and I only understood that it started with the letter "M." Considering my last name was difficult for Americans to get right, I figured he was talking about me and I jumped in the car.

I felt something was off when I got in the car. When the driver asked me where I wanted to go, I knew something was definitely wrong. I didn't know the name of the airport I was supposed to be going to, he was supposed to just take me.

"Are you sure I am the person you were supposed to pick up?"

"Yes," he replied as he pulled a paper from his coat pocket. I quickly snatched the paper to read what it said, but a lot of good that did me. Welcome to the world of squiggles and backwards writing. I began to panic.

"Stop the car," I told him. I asked him to read the name on the paper very slowly.

"It says here I am supposed to pick up a Miss Marcum at 9 a.m."

My heart jumped into my throat and I demanded he turn the car around and return to the hotel. The people who were supposed to pick me up had probably come and gone already while I was away. When we pulled up to the hotel I noticed the van that had dropped me off last night beginning to pull out of the hotel drive. I leapt out of the car before it had even stopped and yelled to the driver of the van to wait.

The hotel door staff apologized repeatedly for the mix-up and helped me transfer my luggage from the car to the van. I crawled into the van to discover six other very quiet and serious-looking passengers. It was an excruciatingly long and silent 15-minute ride to the airport.

When we arrived at the airport, we were shuffled into a small prefab trailer with some chairs, magazines, and, most importantly, an air-conditioner. Twenty minutes later, we were instructed to remove our luggage from the van and place it on the wooden pallet out front so that it could be fork lifted and loaded onto the aircraft. Once everyone's luggage was on the pallet, the airport crew (of which there were only about five and all were wearing civilian clothes) conducted a quick roll call and instructed us to board the waiting cargo plane.

Toward the front of the plane, both walls were lined with netted seats. There were slots for twenty people, and we had exactly twenty people on our flight so it was a little tight. There was only one other female aside from myself, so she and I sat next to each other. As soon as I sat down I knew I was going to have a problem because it was stifling hot. I have severe issues with motion sickness and this situation had puke-filled barf bag written all over it. I immediately whipped out the sacred Dramamine, swallowed a couple, and then offered some to the girl next to me. She was obviously having the same thoughts and thanked me graciously as she took two for herself. None of the guys wanted any, and I was glad to save the rest for any other air travel I would have to endure over the next four months.

After takeoff, I tried to get comfortable for the two-hour trip, but a cargo plane isn't exactly a luxury jet. Luckily, Dramamine has an extremely sedative effect on me, so about twenty minutes into the flight, I nodded off. I woke up a little while later freezing my ass off. I was dressed for 100-degree heat, and at 30,000 feet, a cargo plane turns into a flying metal freezer. I soon discovered enduring the subzero temperature was the least of my issues as the plane banked sharply and began a spiral decent. Dramamine is a great drug, but it's no competition for a corkscrew. I turned green in about thirty seconds and the only thing keeping me from spewing all over the inside of the plane was sheer willpower. When we finally landed, I managed to make it off the plane, but as soon as I stepped onto solid ground I puked my guts up right onto the tarmac of Baghdad International Airport. Welcome to Iraq! Once I finished, I was mortified but felt much better and made my way to a line of waiting SUVs that drove us to the Welcome Center.

The Welcome Center was formerly one of Saddam's small palaces, which the U.S. government took over and transformed into a makeshift hostel for government personnel traveling into and out of Iraq. It was set up to temporarily house personnel while they awaited transportation to their specific location within the country. It had a small cafeteria, transient rooms with showers, televisions tuned to AFN (Armed Forces Network), a gym, a computer room, and free stateside service telephones. All incoming personnel were also briefed here and received a photo ID badge to wear around their necks for the duration of their time in country.

Fortunately, I was stuck at the Welcome Center for only a few hours. I arrived at 2 p.m. and managed to get a seat on the next chopper for the Green Zone scheduled to leave at midnight. I napped until early evening and then made my way to the cafeteria to see if I could scare up some dinner. Still feeling a little queasy from my bout of motion sickness, I grabbed some fruit and returned to my couch to watch TV. The Armed Forces Network was nice for only half an hour. The shows were five-year-old reruns, and the movies were so edited they bleeped out the word *crap.* Every five minutes, there was a news break starring the U.S. Air Force's finest reporter, Stevie the stuttering Staff Sergeant. I decided to pull out the trusty laptop and watched a DVD until it was time to head back out to the tarmac and board the chopper for my final destination.

Before boarding the chopper, I and six other new arrivals were instructed to don our body armor and helmets. I'm sure my 5'2" frame enveloped in thirty pounds of body armor and wrestling two 75-pound bags was an amusing sight. At midnight, we arrived at the unlit landing zone (referred to as the LZ) where the chopper was waiting. We unloaded from two black SUVs and walked single file across the LZ to the awaiting chopper. I was the last to board and found the chopper completely packed with passengers and luggage and no open seats. The chopper's door gunner told me to "wait one," took a cooler from the cockpit, and placed it on the last bit of open floor space next to the doorway. I sat on top of the slippery cooler lid and the Gunner stretched a single bungee cord across the open doorway. As the chopper took off into the night sky, I clung to anything within reach that was bolted to the wall, knowing that one swift bank could send me flying out the door.

A bright moon hung in the clear night sky and cast an eerie illumination upon the passing city below, which seemed to fade into an endless black horizon. As the warm desert wind whipped across my face, I felt a strange sense of peace and comfort; it was hard to believe there was a war being waged below. The moon was just bright enough to silhouette the expressions on the faces of my fellow passengers. They reminded me of mice in a snake cage. Aside from the crew, everyone looked extremely apprehensive. Oddly, I didn't match my fellow travelers' apprehension, but perhaps I was too exhausted to acknowledge its existence. I just desperately longed for a hot shower and a real bed.

When we landed in the Green Zone, we filed off the chopper and jogged across the LZ to another group of waiting SUVs while the ground crew loaded our luggage into the vehicles. We were shuttled to our base, also on the grounds of another former palace. (Seriously, how many did the guy need?) The base was composed of a few buildings that served as office space, a chow hall, a nice swimming pool, and numerous small prefab trailers (pods) that served as living quarters. Each pod also had a cable TV, DVD player, and high-speed Internet access. I wasn't sure if this was war or summer camp.

When we pulled up to the gate, the guard checked our badges and did a quick walk around the car with a mirror to check for bombs in the undercarriage of our vehicle. Once we were given the all clear, we continued on to a small building with a sign out in front that said "Processing." A friendly woman greeted and provided us with the number and keys to our assigned pods. We were also provided with a laundry bag containing a pillow and linens. Once I had my gear in hand, a small middle-aged man of Japanese descent approached me. He introduced himself as Tom Takaki, director of the small intel team detachment and my new boss.

Tom and one of the guys on our team helped me gather my luggage and escorted me to my room. It was a bit of a walk from the chow hall and main office area, but close to the swimming pool. Considering it was well after 1 a.m., I was surprised to see the light inside the pod was on. I knocked on the door and a small blond woman, who looked to be in her mid-thirties, answered. I introduced myself and told her I was her new roommate. She gave me a kind smile, told me her name was Elaina, and welcomed me inside. Tom told me to be at the chow hall the next morning at 0700 to meet the other members of the team over breakfast. He then handed me a mobile phone and informed me that each member of our team had one. He gave me his number in case I needed anything before morning and told me I could also use the phone to call the U.S. I simply had to dial the area code and number.

Once inside, I noticed the room was about 12- by-16 feet and had a small attached bath with shower. There were two sets of bunk beds and four wall closets. I shuddered at the thought of four people cramming into this small space. I was relieved to discover that Elaina's was the only bed made up and I found that three of the closets were empty. She had one of the bottom bunks and I claimed the other. Elaina crawled in bed soon after I arrived, so I didn't want to bother her by taking a shower. I just brushed my teeth and took a quick baby wipe bath–something I still affectionately refer to as the Baghdad shower. Then I fell into bed and tried desperately to get some sleep. Although it was the middle of the night, I lay there wide-awake. I was severely jet lagged (my internal clock thought it was only five o'clock in the afternoon), and my mind was racing. I felt very alone and very far from the world I knew. It was one of the most restless nights of my life. I managed to get less than an hour of sleep before my alarm rang at 0615 and I awoke to my first morning in Iraq.

Chapter 3

Friday, 20 May–Saturday, 21 May 2005

When I opened my eyes, I saw sunlight streaming in through the single window over Elaina's bed and noticed that she was already gone. I rolled out of bed feeling like I'd been hit by a truck and began rummaging through my luggage for some clothes. One of the guys from my new team knocked on my door around quarter to seven and offered to walk me to the chow hall, a gesture I was thankful for since everything looked totally different in the daylight and I had no clue how to get to the chow hall. He introduced himself as Kyle, and as we made our way to the chow hall he told me he'd arrived in Iraq three months ago. We met up with the rest of the team and Tom introduced me to everyone. Aside from Tom, who was a Lieutenant Colonel in the Air Force, and Kyle, who was a Sergeant in the Marine Corps, there were four other guys on the team: Seth, an Army Sergeant; Kevin, an Air Force Sergeant; Robert, a retired Naval Reserve Captain; and Josh, a young NSA civilian employee. I was not only the token female, but also the only one on active duty in the Navy. It was also at this first meeting that Tom explained to me what our mission was in Baghdad: our team worked within the Iraqi National Intelligence Service (INIS) on the far side of the Green Zone where members of various U.S. government agencies and branches of the military assisted in the reestablishment of an Iraqi intelligence agency. The new

Iraqi employees were recruited, vetted, and trained by U.S. and coalition government agencies, and our team was one of the small U.S. contingencies within the INIS lending a hand. Our main mission was to help the Iraqis become self-sufficient in conducting intelligence operations to support their own free government. Our secondary goal was a simple public relations mission to prove we didn't invade only to kick Saddam's ass and then leave, but that we were genuinely interested in helping Iraq establish a functioning democratic government.

Our team worked in three shifts and had at least two members on duty at the building at all times. However, the week I arrived, Tom decided we no longer needed a night shift. He felt the Iraqi employees were now capable of handling the nights on their own and were given a phone number each night to reach the on-call team member.

Following breakfast on my first day, Tom showed me around our team's private office at the base, which was two pods put together and wired so we could communicate with agency headquarters in the U.S. via computers and phones. He set me up with a computer account so that I could use any computer at the base and issued me a two-way radio. Each member of the team had a radio and call-sign—I'm not sure how, but mine ended up being "Triscuit." I think Seth came up with it. This office space was also where we stored our weapons and equipment. We were all issued a personal 9mm pistol with three 15-round clips that we kept on us at all times. The team also shared several M-4 and M-16 rifles that we carried when we left the base to go to work at the building. Those we kept locked in the office while we were at the base.

We each worked eight-hour shifts six days a week, and Tom decided to start me off on the evening shift, which ran from 3 p.m. to 11 p.m. After my tour of the office, Tom informed me that my first shift at the building would be the following evening with Kyle.

"Kyle's been here the longest and knows everyone up there the best, so he'll introduce you to all the department employees." He then gave me the rest of the day to myself to unpack, get settled in, and explore the base grounds.

Kyle asked me to meet him back at the office at quarter to three the next afternoon with my body armor, pistol, radio, and phone. "Anything else I should bring?" I asked.

"Just a smile," he replied. "Be prepared to meet a lot of Iraqis."

I returned to my room and began unpacking. The first thing I dug out was my MP3 player so I could listen to some music while getting the job done. About an hour later, Elaina came home. She was a freak. I really don't know how else to describe her. She was one of the weird government "lifers." She was in her late thirties, had been working in the federal government intelligence ring since she was a teenager, and could no longer properly socialize with the rest of humanity–a typical occurrence in this business.

She struck up a conversation soon after walking in the room. At first, I thought she was being nice, but I soon realized she was simply exercising her interrogation skills. "So, Mandy, where are you from?" she asked as she dragged an exercise mat to the center of our room. I told her I grew up in Florida, joined the Navy when I was 17, and was currently stationed in Maryland.

"Wow, that's exciting," she replied with feigned interest. "How often do you get to see your family?"

"Not very often, which is plenty." By now, Elaina was well into her yoga and had one leg hooked over her neck behind her head. "I drive out to Ohio to visit my mom every few months," I added.

After I said this, Elaina scrunched her face into an overly-dramatic confused look and said, "Hmmm, I thought you said you were from Florida." Her eyes screamed, *Aha! I've caught you in a lie!*

I was going to explain that my mom moved from Florida to Ohio a couple of years after I joined the Navy to be close to her family, but I decided she could hone her interrogation skills on someone else.

"I did," I said flatly. I put my headphones back on and continued unpacking.

When I finished, I decided to try my first shower in my new place. By that point I'd have been happy with a hose and a bar of soap since I hadn't had a real shower in four days. One good thing about showering in Baghdad in the summer is you never have to wait for the hot water. Thanks to the 120-degree daytime temperatures, I had the faucet laid over on the cold side and the water still came out nearly scalding.

After my shower, I walked over to check out the swimming pool. It was a good size and the sparkling blue water indicated it was well-maintained. It even had a swim-up bar and plenty of lounge chairs surrounding it on the deck. *Oh yeah, this is going to be a* rough *four months.*

Although I didn't have to report for work until the next afternoon, I tried to go to bed early to get over my jet lag and adjust to the new time. I tossed and turned for hours and didn't manage to fall asleep until around 4 a.m. I slept until midmorning and hoped I'd have more success the next night. I just prayed Tom didn't switch me to the day shift any time soon and I'd have to report before 7 a.m. After throwing on some clothes, I headed up to the chow hall to get some food. Although it was between meal times, they always had snacks and drinks available. I didn't cook at home and often subsisted on one of man's greatest inventions: cereal with milk. I was happy to find the chow hall had a fairly good selection of American cereals. We had a small refrigerator in our room, so I returned to my room with a box of cereal and a couple cartons of milk.

The milk in Iraq was an interesting experience. It came in a rectangular carton and sat out on the shelf at room temperature until it was opened, then it required refrigeration. It was called UHT (Ultra-High Temperature) milk and, as its name suggests, was able to withstand the Iraqi heat for travel. Unfortunately, my stomach couldn't stand the UHT milk. It took two weeks of battling daily stomach cramps and diarrhea to finally adjust to the UHT milk, but I refused to give up cereal. After a couple of weeks, the cramps stopped and I was able to tolerate the milk just fine. I learned that I was one of the few on the base who could adapt so I had it and the cereal pretty much all to myself.

After another scalding shower, I dressed and geared up for my first day of work.

I stepped out the door into the merciless Iraqi heat and was drenched with sweat after the short 5-minute walk to the office. When I arrived, Kyle tossed me an M-4 rifle and said, "Let's head out." We walked to the vehicle corral and were picked up by our security escorts in our team's vehicle, which was a massive, white armored SUV that we affectionately referred to as the White Elephant. It was so heavy due to all the armor plating that it only got about four miles to the gallon. According to protocol, all team members were supposed to be escorted to and from the building by a security team, but since we didn't officially exit the Green Zone, we eventually just drove ourselves back and forth so the security teams could be available to escort those traveling into more dangerous areas. When I climbed up into the back seat, I noticed the thermometer on the rearview mirror read 109 degrees Fahrenheit. It was only May and I shuddered at the thought of how ungodly hot it would be in July and August.

The base was fenced in with high concrete walls so the drive to work was my first opportunity to see what was beyond the borders of it. As we rolled outside the main gate, I plastered my face to the window and soaked in as much of the scene as possible. The Green Zone was a concrete jungle of barricades with concertina wire and checkpoints on practically every corner. Since arriving in Iraq, I'd been relatively isolated from the local population. Only Americans were allowed on the base and I'd seen only Americans at the transient house after arriving at the airport. Although the Green Zone (also referred to as the International Zone or IZ) was a secured area, there were still many Iraqis who lived and worked within the perimeter. The traffic was very heavy and the streets bustled with women in burkas and kids kicking soccer balls in empty lots. As we crept along the IZ's major thoroughfare in bumper-to-bumper traffic, I felt nervous for the first time. We were soon surrounded by local traffic and I realized the possibility that any of these vehicles could be a car bomb and, in a booming flash, I could be dead. But I just figured when your number is up, it's up, and if I was meant to die in a car bomb in Iraq then there was nothing I could do about it. I don't know how rational this thinking was, but I immediately relaxed and never felt particularly nervous again while traveling around Iraq. I just couldn't think like that or I'd go crazy–it was my way of detaching myself from the fear.

I realized how truly international the Green Zone was on this first outing. It was like Epcot Center at Disney World. Each country seemed to have their own sections and their own checkpoints. I saw Japanese, Georgian, British, and Australian, military personnel, as well as a lot of Gurkhas. The Gurkhas were my favorite. They were soldiers from Nepal and the northern regions of India who had served in the British Indian Army since the 1800s and were well known for their combat skills and military strategy. They carried long, curved knives that customarily were not to be removed from their sheaths except to draw blood. Gurkha regiments continued to be employed by both British and U.S. forces in several areas of the world. They were consistently very nice to us, and I always felt safe when they were nearby.

Our security escorts dropped us off in the rear parking lot of the INIS building and we had to walk around to the front gate, which was technically beyond the Green Zone, to access the building. Four Iraqi civilian sentries armed with AK-47s guarded the main entrance to the building. Once inside, I noticed several more stationed in the main hallway right outside a pair of large cherry wooden doors with the title "Director General" posted above. The director general of the INIS was basically the Iraqi version of the director of the CIA. I later learned that the director general at the time, who we referred to as the DG, was a former Special Forces general under Saddam and was actually trained in the U.S. by the Army Rangers during the Iraq-Iran War. He was also a helicopter pilot who made a name for himself when he defeated an entrenched Iranian force that numbered in the thousands via an air assault. He turned dissident against Saddam's regime in the late 1980s and started assisting the U.S. government in plotting an overthrow in the early 1990s. He was one of the masterminds of an elaborate coup in 1996, but unfortunately, the coup failed. Three of the general's sons were murdered by the regime, and the DG fled to the United States. Following Saddam's ousting, the CIA appointed the DG as head of the new INIS.

Kyle and I continued on to a pair of tiny elevators near the center of the building. The building had nine stories and resembled a large Holiday Inn–almost a perfect rectangle with one main hallway on each floor and offices on either side. We took an elevator up to our department, which was located in the east wing on the ninth floor. As soon as we entered through the department's large double doors, Kyle was heartily greeted by a group of Iraqi employees gathered in the main hallway for a smoke break. They waved and shouted hellos to Kyle. Kyle greeted and shook hands with each of them and then introduced me.

They spoke no English beyond saying hello, but each smiled brightly and happily offered his hand for me to shake. Typically, this was a culturally uncomfortable gesture for Arab men, but these guys were obviously beyond that. Before coming to Iraq, my small-minded, media-shaped outlook had me expecting most Iraqis to be ignorant heathens clinging to ancient customs, but I was pleasantly surprised by the outpouring of warm welcomes I received on my first day.

After making it past the group in the hallway, Kyle shuffled me into a small office reserved exclusively for the U.S. liaisons assigned to the department. Two other guys from our team, Sam and Jeff, were sitting at the two desks in our office when we walked in. They were obviously happy to see us because it meant their workday was over and they were free to head back to the base.

The office had a couple of computers, one connected to the Internet and one on a closed network for our work stuff. You could definitely tell the place was used by a bunch of guys, especially when I noticed the TV with a Sony PlayStation 2 connected to it. There were also a few storage cabinets and a rack with a mainframe computer, which was basically the brain system for all the computers in the department. Once inside the office, I was able to drop my body armor and M-4 rifle, but I kept my 9-mm on my hip–after all, I was in a building with over 1,000 Iraqis and just a handful of Americans.

Once I had been shown around our office, Kyle asked if I was ready to tour the rest of the department and meet all the employees. There were approximately fifty Iraqi nationals working in our department and I was going to get to meet most of them in the next half hour. Because of the whirlwind of activity over the past few days, I hadn't given much thought to starting work; but now that I was in the building, I was nervous and did my best to smile my way through the introductions.

Our first stop was to meet the Iraqi head of the department. His name was Abu Zaid and he had his own office at the end of the hall. He was a big guy who looked to be in his mid-forties. He spoke a limited amount of broken English but was very nice. He welcomed me to Iraq and to the department. Like the first group of Iraqis, Abu Zaid did not hesitate to shake my hand and flashed me a sincere smile. I instantly liked and respected him.

After a few minutes of chatting with Abu Zaid, Kyle and I continued on to the next office across the hall. This was the translators' office. There were typically two translators on duty at all times to help us communicate with the non-English speaking employees and translate work documents between English and Arabic. When we walked in, an Iraqi man who looked to be in his late thirties quickly approached us. He said hello to Kyle and then introduced himself as Ihab while he shook my hand. Ihab's English was quite good. His thick British accent made it obvious he spent time in the UK.

The other translator came over and my life changed forever. He looked at me with strikingly hypnotic green eyes and extended his hand as he introduced himself. His name was Fahdi. He was in his early twenties, about 5'9", and had olive skin and black hair. He had a slender build and I noticed a hint of stubble on his angular face. He did not have the typical Arab facial features and I figured he was possibly a hybrid with a European parent. He smiled as he gently shook my hand. I managed to squeak out my name but couldn't stop staring at his eyes. Kyle chatted with Ihab for a couple of minutes and Fahdi returned to his desk while I continued to ogle him out the corner of my eye. Kyle then shuffled me down the hallway to meet the rest of the employees, but I didn't remember anyone after Fahdi.

When we returned to our office, Kyle sat at the secure computer, which was linked with another computer at the office on base, and started typing. I checked my emails on the internet computer. I noticed that every few minutes Ihab would come in and hand Kyle a small piece of paper with information that Kyle would type into the computer. I was about to ask him what he was doing when he turned to me and said, "I'll show you what this is tomorrow so you can start doing it too, but for tonight just relax, roam around the building a little to get your bearings, and interact with the people here."

I was still feeling a little shy and uncomfortable with walking around the building alone, so I tried to make myself look busy on the computer. A few minutes later, Fahdi entered to give Kyle another one of those small papers. I tried not to stare, but I couldn't help myself. He and Kyle chatted for a few minutes while I did my best to gaze discreetly at Fahdi from behind my computer monitor. I overheard him mention he was in the process of applying for a visa to visit the U.S. and ask how he could apply to immigrate to the U.S. to live.

"The easiest way to get over there is to just marry an American girl," Kyle informed Fahdi with a sideways smile. Then he turned in my direction and said jokingly, "Mandy over here is single, maybe she'll help you out." Even though Kyle was kidding, my face turned beet red and I did my best to hide behind my computer.

Fahdi smiled and said, "Well I don't want to use anyone." All I could think was *Use me, use me!* "I'll do some more research and see if I can come up with anything," Fahdi added and then returned to his office.

After Fahdi left, Kyle was giving me the well-get-out-there-and-mingle look, and I realized I couldn't stall any longer. Instead of aimlessly roaming around, I decided to venture out and try to find the bathroom. I headed over to the translator room for directions, mainly in hopes of catching another glimpse of Fahdi. When I walked in, Fahdi and Ihab were at their desks and two other men were also seated in the office.

Fahdi gave me a passing glance from behind his computer and, as if he was expecting me, said, "Hi, come on in and have a seat." I decided to hold off on getting bathroom directions until I needed to use it to break the ice or as an escape subject. Fahdi continued to type on his computer but asked, "So, how do you like Iraq so far?"

Things are definitely looking up, I thought to myself, but I simply replied, "I like it a lot. It's a little hot, but everyone has been very nice. I just wish I could speak some Arabic so I could communicate a little easier."

"If you want, I can work with you on some basics," Fahdi offered.

Score.

"That would be great, if you have time. I don't want to put you out or anything," I replied.

"Trust me, I have time. I sit here most of the night playing online poker. I'm usually here from 4 p.m. to midnight. Are you going to work the evening shift regularly?"

"So far, the plan is for me to work 3 p.m. to 11 p.m. until Tom tells me otherwise."

We made plans to meet the following evening at 6 p.m. in his office and start an informal language class.

I hung out in the translator room for most of the evening and successfully fulfilled my duty of mingling with the employees as they floated in and out of the office to chitchat with Fahdi and the others. As the shift wound down, Kyle said he'd give me a break for my first night and decided we'd leave a little early. As I reluctantly donned all my equipment, body armor, and rifle, excitement tickled the pit of my stomach as I thought of language classes with Fahdi the next day.

Chapter 4

Sunday, 22 May–Friday, 27 May 2005

My first week of work was laid back and I realized just how easy our job really was. All we did was make nice with the Iraqi INIS employees, focusing on upper-level department heads and executives, and babysit the computers and equipment within our department since a combination of U.S. intelligence agencies "generously" provided them. American technicians and personnel were responsible for the installation and maintenance of all of the equipment. If anyone in our department had issues with the equipment, we served as embassy liaisons and arranged for IT specialists to resolve the problems.

I met with Fahdi every evening at 6 p.m. during my first week for Arabic tutoring, and started picking up the basics. During our "class", other employees would float in and out of Fahdi's office. I chatted with the other employees about various topics, but Fahdi remained relatively silent and kept things almost rigidly professional between us. He sat back and simply observed while the others and I discussed the war and reconstruction efforts. Several, especially the younger ones, wanted to know all about life in the U.S. Most of them looked favorably upon America's removal of Saddam's regime, while others blatantly declared life was better under Saddam. But, they acknowledged that those days were over and that they could only move forward and try to make a better future for their country and families. Almost all of them had difficulty pronouncing my name, Mandy. The "M" at the beginning threw them off, and I ended up being called Sandy by many of the employees. I tried correcting them at first, but soon gave up and simply embraced my new name. Everyone treated me respectfully and I felt revered simply because I was American.

Thanks to my celebrity status, on my fifth evening of work, a couple of the employees in our department invited me to eat dinner with them and several of the other workers. The Americans who worked within the INIS typically ate at the U.S. run chow hall across the street from the building inside the Al Rasheed Hotel, but the Iraqi employees usually brought their meals from home and ate lunch or dinner in our department's small break room across the hall from my office. I was already familiar with Iraqi food and enjoyed the cuisine, so I was delighted to accept the invitation and happy that I wouldn't have to make the long walk to the Al Rasheed to get my dinner. However, my first experience eating dinner with the crew was a little unsettling. Until then, the few meals I had eaten in the building were with Fahdi or some senior-level employees who dined in the western style–i.e. with utensils. But when I arrived for dinner with the crew, eight guys were gathered around a table that had one large pot of lamb, rice, and veggies in the center and some flat bread scattered around–and nothing else. Each guy just dipped into the pot with his hand and pulled out some rice and meat. Some would transfer it to a plate if they weren't within arm's-reach of the pot, while those who were closest to the food simply took it straight from the pot and rolled it into some bread or ate it out of their hand. The worst part was that they would lean over the pot while doing this so that the particles that fell from their hand or off their mouths would drop back into the pot. Waste not want not, I guess.

One of the guys offered me a seat and then filled his bare hand with food from the pot into which I just watched rice drop from another guy's mustache. He then put his handful of food onto the paper plate in front of me. All I could think was, *Oh God, I'm on Iraqi Fear Factor!* I kept having flashes of the dinner scene from *Indiana Jones and the Temple of Doom* with the snakes crawling on the table and bug guts for appetizers and monkey brains for dessert. *What? You are not eating? No thanks. I had regurgitated lamb and rice for lunch.*

I managed to push the food around on my plate for a few minutes without drawing too much suspicion, but knew that wouldn't last much longer. I reasoned with myself that it was my duty to acceptingly take part. I was going to eat it for my country! I was going to eat it for peace! Thank God Fahdi walked in and rescued me before I had to put anything in my mouth. He gave me a sinister knowing smile and then announced that I was needed in the office so that I could make a quick escape and also save face. Fahdi did his best to suppress his laughter as we made our way down the hall toward his office, but he couldn't hide the smirk on his face.

"You think this is just hilarious, don't you?" I said.

No longer able to hold it in, Fahdi started laughing and said, "Oh. it was great, you looked like you were about to pass out. Your face was completely white."

"You could have at least warned me," I moaned.

"But then you wouldn't have gotten the *complete* Iraq experience," he replied sardonically and flashed me the smile I couldn't resist.

Soon after I arrived home to my trailer that night, my cell phone rang–it was Shawn. I had included my new phone number in a mass email to family and friends soon after my arrival in Iraq, and Shawn was one of the recipients. I expected an official breakup conversation, so I figured he was now calling to get it over with.

Unfortunately, the conversation turned into a two-hour emotional rollercoaster.

"Look, things are most likely going to be completely over between us when I get back," I told him.

"You're throwing away something special," he countered. "We can make this work."

His words surprised me because he never seemed this crazy about me at any point in our relationship before; but I knew that if I went back to him, things would just resume as usual and I'd be miserable.

"No. It never really worked and it never will," I said more to myself than him, and hung up the phone.

The next morning, I indulged in another bowl of cereal topped with UHT milk and paid the price of some more searing stomach cramps. I curled up on my bed in the fetal position for the next thirty minutes until the cramps passed and declared that if these episodes didn't cease within the next couple of days, I'd have to contemplate the unthinkable–four months without cereal.

Luckily, by 3 p.m. I was feeling fine and ready for another evening at the building. It was Kyle's day off, so I was going to work with Kevin, another member of our team. Kevin was a big, jovial black guy and I immediately liked him. He was laid back and got along really well with the Iraqis. He didn't treat them like they were a lesser species like a lot of the Americans subconsciously did. When I arrived at the base office, Kevin informed me that our security escorts for the evening were a couple of shell-shocked nut jobs. Pancho and Geronimo, as they referred to themselves, were great guys and I trusted them with my life, but they had endured one too many roadside bombs, if you know what I mean. They had seen and been through a lot of shit in Iraq and were slightly over the edge, but I respected the hell out of them.

Fun with Pancho and Geronimo began when we approached our first checkpoint on the way to the building that was manned by some unsuspecting Georgian soldiers.

Since the rear passenger windows of our SUV were darkly tinted and the windows in the armored vehicle didn't roll down, those of us in the backseat usually just leaned forward and put our badges up to the glass of the front windows for the checkpoint guards to see. But the guys on duty that afternoon kept gesturing for us to roll down the window. Pancho tried to make it clear that we were unable to comply, screaming, "The windows don't roll down, asshole! It's an armored vehicle!"

Of course, the seven layers of armor were not only bulletproof but also soundproof. The guard then motioned for Pancho to open the door. As Pancho fumbled for the door handle, he became slightly more belligerent, "Ugh, you little mouth-breather, you are really starting to tick me off!"

As soon as the door opened, the guard sputtered in broken English, "Sir, I need to clearly see the badges of everyone in…" but Pancho cut him off.

"You don't break the seal man! What is the point of an armored vehicle if the door is open, huh!?"

The poor guard was just trying to do his job, but Pancho did have a point. The guard quickly glanced at our badges and waved us through. Crisis averted. We continued on to the building without further incident. The area where we parked the vehicles was about a block from the building and the security guys were responsible for escorting us the several hundred meters to the front entrance. The street was full of Iraqis because we arrived for our shift when most of the locals were heading home from work. Making his way down a crowded street of Iraqis always triggered Pancho's paranoid-commando mode. As we walked along, he would eyeball everyone we passed and whisper under his breath, "Try it Iraqi, I dare you. Go ahead, reach for that 45 I know you've got in your pants." Then, every few minutes, he would affectionately pat his M-4 rifle and say, "See this, this is my Iraqi-be-cool stick." I just prayed none of them spoke enough English to understand what he was saying.

Geronimo was a little less extreme and tried to explain Pancho's condition. "Yeah, Pancho's a little shell-shocked," he said. I simply nodded but thought, *Gee, I didn't notice.* "Last week, he unloaded his rifle into a fifth-story balcony because he thought he 'saw' something," Geronimo continued. "God only knows what it was. The captain asked him why he showered fifty rounds into a balcony of an apartment building, and his reply was because that was all the ammo he had." I'm pretty sure he was pulling my leg, but I laughed for him anyway.

Kevin and I made our way up to the office, and while we were removing our body armor, Fahdi knocked on the door. Kevin smiled broadly and said, "Hey man, what's going on?" while giving Fahdi a friendly handshake. I soon realized the two were good friends. Kevin was one of the first volunteers for the program when it started the year before, and he and Fahdi had met on Kevin's first tour.

The air conditioner in our office wasn't working well, so we went next door to Fahdi's office to hang out. Fahdi had a cot and a locker since he often pulled 24-hour shifts. He was busy translating a document on his computer, so in our boredom, Kevin and I decided to be nosy and raid Fahdi's locker, which he could clearly see us doing. The first item we noticed was his wallet lying on the main shelf.

"Nice wallet man," Kevin called across the room. "Can I look at it?"

"Sure," Fahdi answered, "but there's not much to look at."

"I'm just bored and this way I can look at the pictures of all your girlfriends you have in here," Kevin said teasingly.

"Well, I hate to disappoint you, but I don't have any pictures of girls in there."

My mind immediately began to churn. *Cha-ching. This most likely means he doesn't have a girlfriend. Unless carrying pictures of your significant other around isn't typical over here. Or maybe he's gay. Damn, that would be my luck.*

As Kevin flipped through the wallet, we found nothing exciting. Then Kevin pulled out a small envelope that had several copies of passport-sized professional photographs of Fahdi. Kevin frowned and said, "Dude, you've got pictures of yourself in here. What the hell? Where are all the chicks?"

"I need pictures for IDs and badges," Fahdi answered. "I told you I didn't have any girls in there." I took the pictures from Kevin so that I could get a closer look, and of course, they were beautiful. His bright green eyes practically glowed off of the paper.

"Damn that's one fine man," I muttered to myself.

When Fahdi was done with his work, he flipped on the TV in his office and I got to watch my first Arab music video. It reminded me a lot of old school MTV–shaking cameras, bad effects, the whole nine yards. There were, however, a couple of songs that were catchy. Kevin eventually left to make the rounds and left Fahdi and me alone. I noticed on Fahdi's computer he had *Yahoo!* instant messenger up and had been chatting with someone. It may be incredibly juvenile, but I sat there for the next ten minutes trying to work up the courage to ask him for his screen name so I could chat with him online from my room at the base. Finally, I took a deep breath and blurted out, "So, when are you going to give me your screen name so I can add you to my friends list on instant messenger?"

He smiled and said, "Well, what are *you* going to give me in return?"

"Um, *my* screen name?" I answered, unsure. I'm not very good at games like this.

Before he could say anything, one of the operators came in and handed Fahdi a report that needed to be translated, so he turned back to his computer and got to work. I continued to watch TV while he typed, figuring he'd give me his instant messenger info when he was done. He didn't.

As the night went on, I bounced back and forth between my office and Fahdi's with some tours of the department in between to talk with some of the other employees. But I made sure to avoid being caught outside my office at dinnertime, something I noticed Kevin was careful to do as well. As the end of the shift approached, I grew impatient that Fahdi still hadn't given me his instant messenger information, but I refused to mention it again. The ball was in his court. I went over everything in my head. *I know I've been getting some vibes over the past few days that he's interested in me at least a little. Maybe I misread him. It is a different culture, maybe I was totally wrong? Crap, I look like an idiot.*

Pancho and Geronimo showed up a little early to pick us up that night, which was fine with me. I was sure I had made an ass out of myself and just wanted to get out of there pronto. I threw on my gear in record time and bolted out of the department ahead of Kevin and the security guys. I made a beeline for the elevators, rode down to the first floor, and made my way through the lobby, waving goodnight to the Kurdish door guards. When I stepped out of the building's front entrance and into the balmy desert night, I realized just how far ahead of the team my hurry to escape put me. *Damn, I should probably chill in the lobby until they catch up.* I turned around and tried to nonchalantly return to the building's lobby. I heard the elevator *ding* and then the shuffle of booted feet coming around the corner followed by Pancho's unmistakable voice calling out to me, "Hey, Princess! If I'm going to keep your little ass alive, you probably shouldn't be running off all by your lonesome."

"Sorry, I thought you guys were right behind me."

"Do it again and I'll be walking you to and from work on a leash," Pancho informed me with a smile on his face.

I gave a little smirk and Geronimo bent toward me and said, "He's dead serious, Cupcake."

The next day was my day off and I was just thankful to not have to face Fahdi. When I woke up, I discovered my roommate's locker and bunk was cleaned out. She left a note on the desk telling me she was headed to another base and wished me luck in the rest of my deployment. *Sweet. I've got the place all to myself.*

After breakfast (which I enjoyed around 10 a.m.) I tried out the swimming pool. I threw on my swimsuit, bathed myself in suntan lotion, grabbed the Cosmopolitan Magazine I brought with me from the States, and headed for the pool. Since it was midmorning on a regular workday, there were only two other girls at the pool. I spread my towel over one of the lounge chairs and settled down to read my magazine. I lasted about six minutes in the blazing sun and 112-degree heat before I decided to take a dip to cool off and then moved my chair to a shaded spot. I had no idea how the other girls were lasting so long laying in the direct sun in bikinis. *Yeah, your skin is not tanning, it's actually dying.* It wasn't much longer before I decided to head back to my room because I could feel my skin burning even in the shade. I spent the rest of the day surfing the Internet and playing video games. (I'd had the foresight to stick my Playstation 2 in my bag at the last minute before leaving my house. I was addicted to the SSX Tricky Snowboarding game.)

Tom told me I'd have the day shift the next week, so I forced myself to go to bed early. I'd have to be ready and on the way out at 0730 but had yet to recover from jet lag due to working the evening shift. Luckily, I brought along some sleeping pills, so I popped a couple and was able to pass out sometime before midnight.

Chapter 5

Saturday, 28 May–Thursday, 2 June 2005

I worked my first day shift with Josh. On our way to the building he explained that there were not only more people in the building during the day, but more important ones. But, since the standard Iraqi weekend was Friday and Saturday and today was Saturday, this wouldn't be different from the usual evening shift.

I immediately wondered if Fahdi also had the day off. I was still embarrassed about the blatant flirtation I'd conducted with him two days before and what I interpreted as his rejection. I just hoped he was still on the evening shift and wouldn't show up for work until after I was gone. No such luck.

Within ten minutes of our arrival at the office there was a knock on the door. Guess who.

"Hey Fahdi, how's it going?" Josh asked after Fahdi entered the room.

I rolled my eyes. *Doesn't he have a friggin' home?* I tried to look busy on my computer and avoided looking in their direction. Fahdi was giving Josh a rundown on what went on with operations during the night, and I noticed that every so often he'd shoot a glance my way.

Josh noticed one of these glances and jumped in, "Hey, have you met Mandy yet?"

Fahdi smiled and simply said, "Yes, we've met." Then he nodded in my direction and left our office. I could tell Josh thought I was being a little standoffish and I knew I couldn't avoid Fahdi forever, so I decided to head over to his office and try to see where things stood between us.

When I walked in, Fahdi was alone. He was sitting behind his desk lounged back in the big leather chair with a lit cigarette in his hand. The morning sun was shining in through the floor-to-ceiling windows behind him, silhouetting his figure and the smoke as it swirled over his head. His gaze fell on me as soon as I entered the room but he didn't move.

All I managed to squeak out was, "Hi."

I felt his gaze upon me, studying me intently for a few seconds. Then, he put the cigarette back to his lips, inhaled deeply, and stubbed it out in the glass ashtray beside his computer. His green eyes never left mine.

Finally, he smiled and said, "How's it going?"

"Good," I answered. Then I blurted out, "Why are you here?"

Okay, that came out wrong.

He leaned forward and turned the question back on me, "Why are *you* here?"

I could tell his question went deeper than mine, so I just avoided it. "I meant, why are you working during the day? I thought you worked the evening shift."

"I work all different times. Sometimes I am here for several days at a time. It's not always easy to go home." He shifted in his seat and added in a facetious tone, "It's like a warzone out there."

I felt my cheeks flush and I looked at the floor.

"And there's not much to do anyway, so I'd rather be here working than sitting bored at my house," he added.

Before I could say any more, he invited me to have a seat in what was now my usual chair beside his desk. Since Fahdi hadn't been real chatty the first week we worked together, I had been afraid to ask him the slew of burning questions I had for him. Today, it seemed the air had changed. We both knew we were entering territory beyond last week's working relationship.

I started off with a relatively innocuous question: "So where did you learn English?"

"Mostly from movies, music, and watching TV," he answered smoothly. "But I also majored in English at Baghdad University. And, of course, I learned all the American slang and bad words when I worked with the Marines."

He went on to explain that he had worked as a local translator for the U.S. Army and Marines since the beginning of the war, before coming to work at the INIS. "A few days after the Americans made it into Baghdad, a U.S. Army convoy came though my neighborhood. They stopped, and a couple of officers were trying to talk to one of my neighbors but he didn't speak English and they didn't know any Arabic. I was watching from my porch and when I saw the issue they were having I decided to go over and translate for them. When we were done, one of the officers asked me if I wanted to work for them regularly as a local interpreter. I liked doing it and it was a way to make money, so I agreed. I started with the Army and then went to work for the Marines because I was one of the few local translators that agreed to go out on combat raids with the tactical teams. It was fun and I got to carry a gun," he added with a broad smile.

"Did you ever get hurt?" I asked.

"Yeah. I broke my arm," he said and pointed to the middle of his right forearm. "We were driving in a convoy near Ramadi when an RPG slammed into the road under us. Although we didn't get hit directly, the driver panicked and ended up flipping our Humvee. I broke my arm when I slammed up against a metal box in the Humvee. A couple of months later, I got shot in the chest right above the heart with an AK round while doing a raid with the Marines. Luckily, I had body armor on, but it knocked me on my ass and hurt like hell. I thought I was dead. I just remember lying on the ground looking up at the sky and not being able to breathe. A couple of the Marines came over to me, ripped off my vest and helmet, and kept telling me that I was going to be okay."

"Holy crap, Dude. I know that can break some ribs. Did it?"

"No. The doctors did some x-rays when I got back to the base, but nothing was broken. But my entire chest and all the way down to my stomach was black and blue for a week."

"You were actually really lucky."

"Yeah, they told me that if it were an inch higher, it would have gone above the vest and gotten me in the neck and I probably wouldn't be alive."

"So how did it happen? Were you on a raid?"

"Yeah, we were after some guys we heard had planted an IED. They were hiding out in a house, and when we entered the neighborhood, they attacked us with AK-47s and RPGs. The Marine officer in charge of the team I was on, Major Weiss, told me to stay by the Humvee while he and the other guys tried to get to the house. But I was afraid they would aim for the vehicles with the RPGs, so I figured I'd be safe further away from it. I began running towards the fighting. I heard the major yell to me to stop and get down, and then I got shot. But it's still a good thing that I ran from the Humvee because right after that, it did get hit with an RPG, and I would have probably been dead."

"Did they let you stay on the base to recover?" I asked.

"Yeah, they gave me a week off for both injuries, but I already lived on the base anyway–it was safer. When I first started working for the Americans, I went home every few days, but later it was just too dangerous and I didn't want to put my family at risk by going home."

"What do you mean?"

"About a year ago, I worked at an Army camp translating for U.S. drill sergeants training the new Iraqi

Army recruits. The U.S. Army unit I worked for had one of their contracted translators, who came with them from the U.S., in charge of us local translators. He was originally from Palestine and immigrated to the U.S. in the 1990s and became a U.S. citizen. When the local translators arrived for work every day, he was in charge of checking our IDs when we entered the base. Well, the asshole photocopied our IDs and made a small fortune for himself on the side by selling our photos and personal information to the insurgency. To them, we were even worse than the Americans because we were traitors and a dishonor to the Iraqi people for working for the U.S. forces. They turned our pictures and info into wanted posters and distributed them throughout northern Baghdad, posting them in mosques and other places. I found out when one of my friends called me and said he'd seen one of the posters in a marketplace. I didn't believe him until he actually tore it down and brought me the poster."

"Holy cow, Dude. Did you tell the Americans?"

"Hell yes! They conducted an investigation and discovered the Palestinian guy had sold information on over twenty local translators. They arrested him and apologized about what happened but said there was nothing they could do to protect us aside from allowing us to live on the base 24/7–as long as we agreed to continue working for them. They knew they had us then. If any of us ever refused a mission they could just threaten to kick us off the base, basically feeding us to the wolves. I stayed on the base as long as I could, hoping things would blow over, but these guys don't give up easily and I eventually had to start leaving the base and going home sometimes. They did their homework on us and managed to get some of our phone numbers and home addresses, including mine. I got a lovely call from someone telling me to 'start counting down my days,' and then they started tossing dummy grenades in my front yard with notes wrapped around them saying they would kill me if I didn't stop working for the Americans."

"Why didn't you quit?"

"I don't like being bullied. It's a matter of principle. I'll quit on my terms. And anyway, things have gotten better since I started working here. I no longer officially work for the Americans, and, obviously, it's a lot safer working here. It's an easy desk job and no more midnight raids," he added with a smile and lit up another cigarette.

"Not to sound too judgmental here, but exactly how many packs of cigarettes do you go through a day?"

"About four," he answered immediately.

"Good God! When did you start smoking?"

"The day I found out that son of a bitch sold my information to the insurgency." He exhaled a cloud of smoke over his head. "And it was a good way to kill time while stuck on the bases when there was nothing to do."

"So who did you like working with more, the Marines or the Army?"

"Definitely the Marines. They are crazy and a lot of fun to hang out with. Let's just say I learned a lot," he added with a giggle.

"Oh, I bet," I interjected.

"Yeah, every conversation was either about sex, girls, or porn. For fun, they would make bets to see who could make someone cry first by making fun of him and picking on him. But overall, it was fun hanging out with them in the camp."

"So were any of them ever mean to you or treat you badly because you were Iraqi?" I asked.

"There were a couple of minor incidents, but nothing serious," he answered.

I could tell he wasn't being completely truthful with me.

"And most of them didn't even know I was Iraqi. I always wore a Marine or Army uniform or PT gear, so I blended in. Unless they personally knew me, they thought I was just another soldier or Marine."

As soon as the words were out of his mouth I heard a loud bang that sounded like someone slamming one of the office doors in our department, followed by another slam.

"Somebody must be pissed off," I said as I rose from my chair and headed for the hallway. "Who the hell is slamming doors?" I turned back toward Fahdi before I reached the door and saw he was smiling and shaking his head.

"What?"

"Yeah, those noises weren't slamming doors. Welcome to Iraq. They were mortars."

My eyes turned into saucers and I gasped, "Seriously?! I think this is the first time I've heard any explosions since I got here."

"It's been pretty quiet here the past week or so. Sometimes we will get several attacks a day and then it will be quiet for two weeks. They lob them into the Green Zone from the other side of the river. They are shooting blind so the damage is usually minimal, but sometimes they get lucky. This building has been hit several times, mainly because we are the tallest structure this close to the edge of the Green Zone. Last month, we had a close call that blew out all the front windows of our department."

"Then why the hell do you have your desk so close to the window?" I asked in amazement.

"I like the light," he said nonchalantly.

Fahdi and I sat and talked about his experiences with the U.S military nearly the entire shift. He shared many of his war stories from his time with the Marines and I hung onto every word. He made a lot of good friends and still kept in touch with many of them via instant messenger and email. He told me he planned on applying for a visitor visa and spending a month in the States to visit some of his buddies. He also hoped to land a job as a translator with one of the stateside military contractors and switch over to a work visa. He had no idea how ridiculously complicated it was to get a visa of any type to the U.S., especially since he was Iraqi, but I told him I'd help him research the process and with the paperwork.

Tom called an impromptu team meeting at the base office and informed us that a British intelligence officer would be joining our team. We were to pick him up at the U.K. camp the next morning before our day shift and take him with us to the building. Exhausted from the change in schedule, I barely kept my eyes open during the meeting and headed straight for my room once we were done. I did everything short of putting splinters in my eyes to stay awake for a few more hours because I knew if I fell asleep at 6 p.m. my sleep schedule would become even more messed up. I held out until around nine and then fell into such a deep sleep I didn't even wake up when a car bomb went off at our south gate at dawn. It rendered enough force to knock my belongings off my bathroom shelf, but I didn't find out about the attack until I arrived for breakfast at the chow hall and everyone was talking about it.

The one good thing about working the day shift was how nice the weather was in the early morning hours. It was actually refreshing and bearable to be outside until about 10 a.m. During the summer in Iraq, the sky was always crystal clear without a single cloud and it was the most beautiful blue. When you looked up it seemed like a big, blue blanket that you could almost reach up and touch. From May to September, every day was basically a carbon copy of the last. Oh to be a Baghdad weatherman in the summer: *Conditions will be clear and hot with lows in the 90s and highs in the 120s with a 0% chance of rain. I'll be back with an update in October. Back to you, Steve!*

On my walk to the base office, my cell phone rang. It was Shawn. Not in the mood to deal with more relationship talk, I ignored it. But he tried back a few minutes later, so I answered and told him I was at work and couldn't talk. He apologized profusely in his most endearing tone and kindly asked me to call him back whenever it was convenient for me.

Seth was my partner at the building for the day, and on our way to work, we swung by the U.K. camp and picked up our new British team member, Paul. He was tall, lanky, and a ball of energy. He was really nice and a lot of fun to hang around with, but I'm pretty sure the only reason we accepted a British guy onto our team was to prove the U.S.'s willingness to cooperate with the international community in our intelligence efforts. (Allowing a British guy on our team wasn't a huge gesture of international cooperation–they'd let a Brit on the team long before a U.S. citizen who worked for The New York Times.)

When we arrived, we were inundated with work. Obviously, it had been a pretty busy night for our department. Seth and I got right to work while Paul observed what we did to learn the ropes. After only a few minutes, I came across a translated report that made no sense so I headed over to the translator office for some clarification. The door to the translator room was closed, which was unusual, but I just gave a quick rap on the door and opened it before hearing any response. I thought the room was empty at first because no one was sitting at any of the three desks and all the computers and TV were off. Then I heard a sound to my right and looked to see a form lying on the small bed between the lockers and the far wall. It was Fahdi and he was half naked and obviously just waking up. I threw my hands up over my eyes and blurted out, "Oh my God. I'm so sorry," and bolted for the door.

When I came back into our office Seth looked up and asked, "Did you get an answer to your question?"

"I…um…no, there was no one over there. Maybe they went to get some breakfast or something. I'll try later." And I sat back down at my computer.

A few minutes later, there was a knock on our door and my face turned bright red because I knew who it was. "Good morning, Fahdi, how's it going?" Seth called out.

"Sorry, I got a late start this morning. We had a really busy night and I didn't get to sleep until around 6 a.m.," Fahdi explained.

"Don't worry about it, Man. We picked up a new addition to our team this morning, so we were late getting in here anyway." Seth then introduced Fahdi to Paul.

"So, was there anything you guys needed?" Fahdi asked and looked directly at me.

I remained silent but Seth jumped in. "Didn't you have a question about something, Mandy?"

"No I figured it out," I answered curtly. "Thanks anyway." And to my relief, Fahdi left without another word.

Over the next couple of days, things between Fahdi and me loosened back up and we just let the whole me-walking-in-on-him-in-nothing-but-his-underwear-incident slide without mentioning it. I walked into his office a couple of days later around lunchtime and saw that he had snuck off to the newly opened Green Zone Burger King and was halfway through a double-bacon cheeseburger. I feigned a gasp and said in mock disapproval, "You cheater! You went to BK and didn't get me anything?"

"A few of the analysts went for lunch and stopped by before leaving to see if I wanted them to bring me back anything," Fahdi quickly explained. "I'm sorry. I can get someone to go back and get you something if you want."

"No, no, I'm just messing with you. But you have the power to make someone go get me food?" I asked, intrigued.

"Well," he said with a smile. "I wouldn't say 'power', but they like me."

I sat down on the other side of his desk and was hit by a thought. "Now, I'm no religious scholar," I said eyeballing his sandwich, "but I'm pretty sure Muslims aren't supposed to eat bacon."

"They're not," he said without missing a bite.

"So are you cheating or is the bacon on that burger not really pork?"

He stopped chewing and looked up at me. "I'm not Muslim," he replied with a cheek-full of burger and in a tone that said *duh*. "I'm Catholic."

Oops. "So, did you convert or were you born Christian?" I knew there was a small minority of Christians in Iraq, but chances of running across one were pretty slim. And although I had never seen Fahdi practicing any of the Muslim rituals, a lot of the employees, most of whom were in fact Muslim, didn't pray at work–especially the younger ones.

"I was born Christian," he explained. "But I'm not a very good Catholic. I haven't been to church since high school."

"Did you or your family have to deal with any kind of persecution because you were Christian?"

"No, not really. My brother, sister, and I got teased at school sometimes by other kids, but nothing serious. They'd say stuff like we're going to hell because we aren't Muslim and stupid stuff like that. But adults knew better. Saddam was a secular guy and the regime didn't tolerate religious persecution. Saddam even protected the Christian community because he knew we were such a small group we would never pose any revolutionary threat against him. So he would punish anyone who even thought about picking on us. He actually specifically hired Christians to work in his palaces as the cooks and cleaning staff because he trusted them more than anyone else. So no one messed with us."

I wanted to find out more about his childhood, but Kevin walked in and said we were going to head back a little early for a team meeting at the base. "Well, I guess I'll see you tomorrow," I said to Fahdi as I stood up.

"Actually you won't," he replied and reached for a pen. He began writing on a post-it note and said, "I'm going to take a couple of days off to get some stuff done."

He slid the note over to me. "Here's that information you asked for the other day." I picked up the note and saw that it was his instant messenger ID. We exchanged smiles and I left for the day.

Back at the base, the entire team, including our new British addition, gathered in the small office. Tom informed Paul and me (the two newest members) that we gathered every few weeks for a team meeting to discuss how the mission was going and address any issues or questions any of the team members may have. "So, Mandy, how have your first couple of weeks been? Any questions? Concerns? You getting along well with everyone at the building?"

"Everything is going great," I said with a shrug. "No problems or issues. So far, so good."

"Are the INIS employees responding well to you?" Tom asked.

"Everyone's been very professional and really nice to me so far. I haven't felt uncomfortable at all, if that's what you mean."

"Well good, sounds like things are going well for you then. The feedback I've gotten from some of the senior employees regarding you has all been positive as well. Just make sure you continue to be sociable, which goes for everyone," Tom said, addressing the entire room again. "Remember, our main mission here is to make a good impression so they feel comfortable having us around and helping them out. When the troops pull out, our goal is for the new government to ask us to stay and continue assisting in the organization of their new intelligence service. So smile, be nice, and socialize. Now on to the next order of business, next week we are going to start giving some classes to the employees on the basics of safeguarding classified and sensitive information. We need to go over things like the levels of classification, the proper way to mark classified documents, and how to handle classified computer equipment and portable devices such as thumb drives, memory sticks, and disks. Also, as I'm sure you've all noticed, practically every employee has a cell phone with them at work. As you all well know, this is a big no-no in the type of environment we're operating in, especially considering the fact that the majority of these phones also have built-in cameras. I've got some meetings with upper-management lined up for next week to see if we can get some policies in place to ban cell phones and other electronic devices from the building. Information security is practically non-existent at that place right now, and we need to start implementing some measures to safeguard classified materials. Seth has been putting together some PowerPoint presentations on this topic, and we'll get the translators at the building to start putting them into Arabic for the class presentations. So if everyone could start mentoring the employees on proper marking, handling, transfer, and disposal of classified documents and information mediums, we can start to get a handle on this situation. That's pretty much all I've got for now. You all have my number, you know where I sleep, and you can usually track me down either here or somewhere in the building during the day. Please don't hesitate to come to me with any issues, questions, concerns, anything–I'm here to support you guys." And with that, we were dismissed.

As soon as I got to my trailer I jumped online and added Fahdi to my instant messenger friends list. Once he was added, it showed that he was currently online and logged into messenger. I stared at the screen for a few minutes debating whether or not to send him a message. Finally, I got up the nerve to send him a simple "Hello," which he swiftly responded to with "Hello back at you." We then proceeded to chat online until nearly 3 a.m. We talked about everything from our favorite foods and movies to what world sights we want to someday visit. Since I, like most people, have ten times the courage when talking to someone via instant messenger than face-to-face, I pulled off some casual flirting to feel him out. His responses were positive, so I was stoked. Before we called it a night, he told me he had a surprise for me and would give it to me the next time we worked together. By the time I crawled in bed I was on such a high I couldn't fall asleep, which sucked because I had to be up in four hours for another day shift—my first workday without Fahdi.

Chapter 6

**Friday, 3 June–Friday, 10 June
2005**

I worked the next day with Josh, but we were taking a small team field trip to visit some of the common sights around the Green Zone that afternoon. I was excited to get out and do some exploring, but I was also relieved that I wouldn't have to sit in the building all day thinking about Fahdi. After lunch, Tom and the rest of the team picked Josh and me up from the building in the White Elephant, and we all drove out to one of the Iraqi Military's former parade grounds. The sight was one of the most famous photo op spots for the U.S. military members inside the Green Zone. It was where the famous giant statues of two outstretched arms (supposed to be modeled after Saddam's) holding crisscrossed swords are located. The parade grounds were lined with a row of grandstands and were a popular spot for Saddam's military reviews. In full body armor with weapons slung across our backs and digital cameras in hand, our motley crew piled out of the White Elephant. We all took turns taking photos of each other standing under the sword statues. When we were done, Tom told us about a ladder inside one of the statue's arms that we could climb up to the top and then look out over Baghdad through a small window. Since it was 112 degrees, no one was too keen on the idea of climbing the equivalent of about five stories up a ladder inside a cramped metal statue. We decided to go up into the grandstands and check out the Presidential Box where Saddam used to stand on a platform to give speeches and observe the troops as they marched in formation on the parade grounds below. Once again, we all took turns taking pictures of each other and by the time we were done there, everyone was ready to head out.

By the time we were done with the field trip, our shift at the building was over, so Josh and I went on back to the base with the team after dropping Seth and Kevin off at the building for the evening shift. I jumped online and sent Fahdi a short email. He'd told me the day before that he was going to take his college final exam Saturday morning (tomorrow), so I wished him luck. When the war started in March 2003, he had just started his senior year in college. Needless to say, his education was put on hold for a little while, but Baghdad University resumed classes in mid-2004 and Fahdi managed to finish out his senior year. All he had left to do was pass his final and he'd earn his bachelor's in English.

Fahdi didn't respond to my email and I didn't see or hear from him until I arrived at work Sunday afternoon for the evening shift. In the past 48 hours, I'd gotten myself all worked up. At first, I thought he was just really busy, then I wondered if he just wasn't interested in me, and then I imagined something really bad happened to him. I even had a nightmare Saturday night that he'd been shot and stuffed into a car trunk. I was losing it. But when I walked into his office Sunday afternoon, he was seated in his usual spot engaging in his usual activity–smoking a cigarette. I guess he could see by my expression that I was upset because almost immediately he mentioned that he'd received my email but just didn't have time to write back. Okay, whatever, but I'd have made time to write *him* back.

"Oh, I have your surprise I told you about," he said, snapping his fingers and heading over to his locker. He pulled out a towel with an 8x10-framed painting wrapped inside. He handed me the painting and said, "It's a painting of the gardens of ancient Babylon. I bought it from a local artist while I was at one of the downtown markets this weekend."

The painting was beautiful. It was oil on canvas and depicted a setting sun behind the lush hanging gardens of ancient Babylon, which were said to have been located about ninety kilometers south of Baghdad. On the bottom portion of the frame was an inscription in Arabic. Fahdi noticed my confusion and jumped in to translate.

"It says, 'Babylon has fallen, yet Babylon endures.' It's from an old poem. When I came across this painting the other day, I immediately thought of you. Iraq doesn't look so good right now. I wanted you to see that it can be beautiful, too. It used to be, and I hope it is again someday soon."

"I love it," I said, gazing at the painting. "Thank you so much for this."

A couple of days after Fahdi gave me the painting, I decided I'd received enough signals to take things between us a step further. Blinded by my infatuation, I didn't even realize I was about to set in motion a series of events that would test every aspect of my being. I desperately wanted to broach the subject of his personal life and feel out if he was in any way attached to a significant other. I hadn't picked up on any signs that he was involved with anyone and he never wore a wedding ring, but that didn't mean anything. My information on him was so limited he could have had a wife and three kids for all I knew.

While working an evening shift with Kevin, I headed into Fahdi's office and started my interrogation. I plopped down in the chair in front of his desk where he was working on his computer. "So, tell me more about yourself."

"What do you want to know?"

I didn't want to tip my hand too much by jumping right in and asking if he was married or involved, so I said,

"Tell me about your childhood. What are your parents like?"

"My childhood was good until my father died when I was ten, then the rest of it pretty much sucked."

"Okay. Moving on. So how old are you?"

"I'll be 24 in a couple of months."

He was younger than I'd assumed. "In August?"

"Yes, August 2nd ."

"My birthday is August 17th, I'll be 23," I added.

Finally, I was tired of tiptoeing around and decided to just buck up and ask the burning question. "So," I said with an inquiring smile, "do you have a girlfriend?"

"No," he answered with a slight giggle. "There is no dating in Iraq. You are either single, engaged, or married," he explained. "But I guess to answer your question, no, I'm not engaged or married or involved in any way."

"Have you ever been engaged, or involved?"

"There have been a few times that I've come close to becoming involved, and I was engaged once. It just didn't work out. I discovered she was I guess what you call a gold digger."

"Ooh, so you're rich," I said playfully.

"We're not rich, but my family owns a veterinary supply business and we're well off. My dad started up the factory a couple of years before he died. The first few years it struggled, especially after he died, but we all worked to keep it going and by the time I was about sixteen or seventeen, it was making us good money."

After a brief silence, he turned the gun on me and our flirting was in high gear. "So what about you? Are you involved?"

I told him I'd actually been married once when I was 18, but it lasted less than two years. Luckily, we didn't have any kids. Then I told him the story about Shawn. Finally, I concluded in a hint-hint tone, "So technically, I'm currently unattached."

"Well, that makes two of us," he said with a smile and he lit a cigarette.

*****

The next day, I worked another evening shift with Kevin. The night was slow so I decided to get out of the department for a little while. Sometimes when I got bored I would go up to the roof of the building to get some fresh air and take in the view. At nine stories up, I had a good view of Baghdad and the Tigris River. I told Kevin I was going stir crazy sitting with nothing do, so I was going to get some air on the roof for a few minutes. I'd only been up there during the day and was excited to see the night view. On my way to the elevator, I passed Fahdi in the hall coming back from dinner. "Hey, where you going?" he asked.

"I'm bored so I'm going to hang out up on the roof for a little while–get some fresh air."

"That sounds cool. Is it okay if I come with you or did you want to be alone?"

"No sure, come on. The more the merrier," I added with a smile.

When we emerged from the stairwell into the open night on the roof, it was like a breath of fresh air. At nearly 10 p.m., the conditions were finally bearable. The air was warm and dry, and there was a slight breeze up on the roof that made it the perfect temperature. The night sky was clear and blanketed with millions of stars. Visibility was excellent and we could see the city lights dancing across the surface of the Tigris River for miles as it snaked through Baghdad. "I think I can see the lights from the base and the embassy," I said, pointing to the east.

"If you look a little to the right of there, you'll see the giant mosque Saddam was building," Fahdi said as he leaned close to me to show me where to look.

My body went rigid at the exhilaration of being so close to him. I felt his breath on my neck and could smell his cologne. A shiver ran down my spine as every sensory receptor in my body stood on end in nervous anticipation.

"It was to be the largest mosque in the Middle East," Fahdi continued. "Saddam's testament of devotion to Islam, which was pretty much just a pretense for neighboring countries." Fahdi scrunched his nose and continued, "Saddam cared about money and power. Religious devotion was a distant third, if even that high on the list." At that point, he must have noticed I was practically a breathing statue and hadn't so much as flinched in several minutes. "Are you okay?" he whispered in my ear. "Am I boring you?"

"No, not at all," I responded in little more than a whisper and turned to face him. Our eyes locked for a few brief seconds and we both knew what was coming next. He placed his hands on either side of my face and slowly leaned down. My heart raced and I felt my face flush as our lips touched in a brief kiss. He then pulled back for a brief pause to study my reaction. The lights from the street below converged with the moonlight, giving his face a surreal glow and highlighting the radiance of his green eyes.

"Is this okay?" he asked in a tender voice.

Unable to vocalize an answer, I simply nodded. He moved his hands down to my hips and pulled me in for another kiss. The next kiss was deeper and longer, and it was obvious he was no amateur–he definitely knew what he was doing.

A few seconds later, the night sky was illuminated by bright green and red tracer rounds followed by the sound of several loud explosions and distant gunfire. I jumped at the explosions and tried to get to the ground but Fahdi held me tight.

"Don't worry," he said calmly. "It's your guys. They're cleaning out a neighborhood in the Al-Du'ra area tonight. They won't meet much resistance. It should be over pretty quickly."

As I stood there in his arms at the top of the building, my body felt like it was on fire. I felt a rush of immense anxiety and sheer happiness at the same time. It was as if we were suspended in our own world somewhere between heaven and war.

Chapter 7

Saturday, 11 June–Thursday, 16 June 2005

The following evening, Fahdi and I stole a few more minutes for ourselves and returned to our rooftop sanctuary. As soon as we stepped out of the stairwell and into the desert evening, we were locked in each other's arms in a passionate kiss while the last rays of the setting sun danced on our skin. When we finally pulled away from each other, Fahdi held my face in his hands and gazed intently into my eyes.

"I've never felt anything like this before in my life," he said with a slight gasp in his voice. "When I first met you, it stirred something inside me, something I can't explain, but I know it's amazing. You make me feel safe, completely safe for the first time in my life. I've spent the last several years in constant fear–fear for my life, worried for my family, fear of losing my home, fear of losing my country. It's like the entire world has been falling down around me for so long, but when you came here, all that fear disappeared. I don't feel like you are something new that has come into my life. You are like a piece of me that has been missing and is now back. I feel you are a part of me, moving in my blood. I don't want to stand here and tell you I love you because I'm afraid it will scare you, but I do, I already know I love you with everything I am."

I reached up on my toes and gave him another long kiss and whispered, "I love you, too." Then we both sat on the ledge of the roof and watched the sun set out over the Euphrates River.

A few days later, I arrived at work and discovered Fahdi was not there. After anxiously awaiting his arrival for several hours, one of his friends, Harath, came into my office and told me why Fahdi was absent. Fahdi was stuck at home because his neighborhood was on lockdown.

"All of the roads around his house are blocked right now because of some insurgent activity in the area. Some houses in the neighborhood were bombed and there was some fighting between the U.S. and some insurgents this afternoon." As the color drained from my face and my eyes grew to the size of hubcaps, Harath realized what I was thinking. "Don't worry," he said quickly taking a few steps closer, "Fahdi is fine. He just can't leave home tonight. He just called me and asked me to tell you. This is quite common these days. A lot of people in Fahdi's neighborhood work to help the U.S. and this makes the area a target. But don't worry, he is fine and he knows how to take care of himself." And with that, Harath left the office and disappeared down the hall while dozens of horrible scenarios swarmed my head.

Shortly after I arrived back at the base that night, my phone rang. *Shawn* flashed across the caller ID screen. I couldn't ignore him forever so I reluctantly answered the phone.

"So, are you just never going to call me again?" Shawn erupted in a condescending tone.

"Well, hello to you, too," I responded sarcastically.

"What do you expect? I've been worried sick about you."

Bullshit. "Look, I'm fine and I'm trying to move on. I spent two and a half years trying to get you to love me and want me. Hell, trying to get you to take as much interest in me and pay as much attention to me as you are now that I'm 10,000 miles away! You treated me like dirt and made me feel worthless. I can't go through that again. I won't. It ends here. It stops now."

"Well, I guess that's it then."

"Yeah."

"Well, will you at least call me when you get back so I know you're alive?"

"Yes, Shawn. I'll call you. Goodbye."

Shortly after arriving at work the next afternoon, I headed over to Fahdi's office and discovered he had not yet arrived. I sat down at his desk and just hoped everything was okay. I spotted a stack of post-it notes and decided to leave him a note. I wrote "Guess what...I love u" on the top note and then stuck it to his computer screen. About half an hour later, I looked up from my computer and Fahdi was leaning on the doorframe of my office silently gazing at me and smoking a cigarette. I smiled and asked, "So, did you get my note?"

"You'll have to be more careful than that," he replied as if he was softly scolding a child. "There aren't going to be many people on your side or mine who will be supportive of our relationship."

"What do you mean *your side or mine*? We're on the same side," I said with a naïve chuckle.

He walked over and gave me a tender kiss on the cheek. "There is something you must understand. Our governments may cooperate, but they'll never be on the same side. We have to be careful. What we are doing could be dangerous for both of us; and I don't just mean losing our jobs."

He didn't elaborate, so I just nodded that I understood what he meant even though I still felt like he was seriously overreacting. *Military members fall in love overseas all the time. War brides are commonplace, especially in the Navy.* What could be so earth-shattering about a war husband?

He stood up and walked back over to the door. "What I came to tell you is that I'll be gone for a few days."

"What?" I quickly stood up and moved over to him. "But why? Is everything okay?"

"I'm just taking a few days off to look for an apartment. After what happened the other day, my neighborhood isn't safe anymore. It's getting harder and harder to find a quiet spot in this city, but I'll find something. Don't worry, I knew I'd have to move sooner or later."

"I'm sorry you are going through this. I wish there was something I could do to help."

"But you are doing something. You're here. You've left your home and come 10,000 miles to a country on the other side of the world because you want to make a difference. You are amazing and one of the bravest people I've ever known."

He made me sound like a saint. I couldn't break it to him that I wasn't brave or strong. I wasn't running to save the world. I was simply a coward running away from her past.

Chapter 8

Friday 17 June-Sunday 19 June 2005

On Friday afternoon, Fahdi and I were working on a report together in his office when one of the senior Iraqi analysts stopped by to chitchat. He was Abu Zaid's brother and, like Abu Zaid, he had worked for the former Iraqi intelligence agency under Saddam. Since he was Muslim and had made the trek (the Hajj) to Mecca, everyone called him Hajji Haitham. He very much resembled his brother in stature: about six feet tall, pushing 300 pounds., and had a broad, welcoming smile. He was a little softer spoken than his brother and giggled when he talked about his wife and young children, who were his entire world. He greeted me with a cheery, "Hi, Mandy!" Since that was the extent of his English, Fahdi translated for us as Hajji Haitham continued in Arabic.

"He says he brought you something," Fahdi informed me.

The Hajji then produced a small silver coin and placed it on the desk in front of me. When the Hajji and I first met a couple of weeks earlier, he and I, along with Seth from my team, had discussed the history of Iraq and ancient Babylon. I expressed how interested I was in history and how I loved visiting museums every chance I got.

"He says this coin is a gift to you. It is an old Iraqi silver coin and is nearly two hundred years old. He says he knows how much you'll appreciate the coin's history and is giving it to you as a sign of his appreciation for your service to Iraq."

"This is beautiful," I gasped as I held the old coin up to the light. "*Shukran jazeelan.* Thank you so much. I love it."

After the Hajji left, Fahdi told me he had found an apartment to rent and was planning on moving in the next day.

"That's great!" I exclaimed. "But does this mean you won't be here tomorrow since you'll be moving all your stuff?"

"No, my brother is going to help me. It should only take a few hours in the morning and I'll have plenty of time to make it to work by the afternoon."

Later that evening, the seven gallons of water laced with Crystal Light that I drank had made their way to my bladder. I headed for the sixth floor, where the only operable female restroom in the entire building was located, and made a grim discovery. The bathroom was full of construction workers and was completely torn apart as it was being remodeled. *Great, what am I supposed to do now?* I made my way back upstairs and luckily ran into my boss in the hallway. I informed him of my dilemma and he offered a suggestion.

"The director's office has a private western-style bathroom. Let me make a call down there and I'm sure we can get you in." I felt like I was trying to gain access to a V.I.P. club. It turned out the other females working in the building were using the bathrooms at the hotel across the street, but there was no way I was going to make it that far in the condition I was in.

"Look, just clear out one of the guys' bathrooms for me and I'll be quick," I suggested. Tom just looked at me like I was crazy.

"Trust me," he said with raised eyebrows, "you do *not* want to use one of the men's restrooms here."

"Okay fine, then just get me a water bottle and a closet. I just need to go *now*."

We jumped on the elevator and he escorted me to the office of the director general of the INIS. He flashed his badge to the two armed guards and we entered. The office was huge: about 1,000 square feet, a seating area at one end with comfortable looking leather chairs and a couch, and a conference area at the other end with a large table that seated twenty. Tom pointed to a small door near the conference table and told me to make it quick. The restroom was large and luxurious, complete with full shower, granite countertops, and marble flooring. *Damn, this has got to be the nicest bathroom in Iraq right now.* I did my business and then took my time washing my hands. I knew Tom wasn't waiting for me outside because I saw him turn and leave as I entered the bathroom, so I decided to be nosy. I opened the cabinets and mirror doors and snooped through all the toiletries. There were lotions, colognes, soaps, creams, etc... *This guy's got more skin cream than a chick!* I tested some of the lotions, smelled the colognes, and had a great time primping in the director general's private stash.

Once I had thoroughly inspected everything in the bathroom, I popped the door open and stepped outside. I stopped dead in my tracks. The large conference table was now occupied by the director general himself and fifteen high-ranking Iraqi government officials in suits and ties gathered for what I assumed was going to be an important meeting. They were completely silent and had obviously been waiting for me to finish in the restroom before they began their meeting. I felt the color drain from my face and wondered if they had heard my every move in the bathroom since it was only ten feet from where they were sitting. I was super relieved I'd refrained from belting out the chorus to the song that had been playing in my head all morning–ironically enough, Bonnie Rait's "Let's Give 'Em Something to Talk About." The DG looked at me with a subdued smirk while some of the others smiled and cleared their throats. I eyeballed my escape route, flashed a big smile, and made a beeline for the door. *Note to self: just pee in the bottle next time.*

The next night, Fahdi made his first appearance in my dreams, and like many of my dreams in the months that followed, it was a vivid nightmare. I dreamt that I was waiting to drive through a checkpoint in Baghdad. When the guards opened the trunk of the car in front of me to search it, I saw a dead body covered in blood. I jumped out of my vehicle and ran up to the car and got close enough to see that it was Fahdi. I woke up screaming and jumped up so fast that I slammed my head on the metal bars of the underside of the top bunk. *Son of a...* I went to the bathroom and splashed cold water on my face. I then stared in the mirror and watched the bump on my head slowly transform into an ugly black and blue knot. On Sunday morning, I did my best to cover the injury with makeup and a discreet hair sweep, but Josh made it clear my efforts were fruitless when he picked me up for work the next morning. The first words out of his mouth were, "Damn, did you get in a fight with your roommate?"

That night at work, we were experiencing technical difficulties throughout the building and our equipment was down. Most of the Iraqi workers passed the downtime either playing cards or just smoking and watching TV. We had a ping pong table in one of the larger conference rooms and many took turns participating in tournaments. In my four months in Iraq, I went from being a relative ping pong virgin to being able to hold my own in a match.

I was standing at the window in the break room looking out over the city. The sun had just set and the city was experiencing one of its few hours with electricity. The city lights sprawled out for miles, lighting up palm trees and the rivers and then abruptly ended in a desert of blackness. I was taking in its beauty when I felt hands slip around my waist. I tried to turn but was held tightly and heard Fahdi whisper in my ear, "Let's go get some air." I knew that was code for let's go to the roof, and I simply nodded. When we stepped onto the roof, Fahdi took my hand and led me to the back corner. The area was concealed from the rooftop door and I saw that Fahdi had a small blanket laid out beside a small candle.

"And what exactly is all this?" I asked with a sly smile.

"Well, since we pretty much have the night off, I figured we could come up here and count stars." He sat down on the blanket and gently pulled me down beside him. I laid back and took in the endless night sky. Just as we had arrived on the roof, the city lost power and transformed our rooftop retreat into an amazing planetarium. "Wow," I gasped, "this is so beautiful."

"You're beautiful," Fahdi whispered and then gently brushed my lips with a kiss.

I moved my hands up from his waist gathering his shirt and pulled it off over his head. I slowly brushed my hands back down his back and felt some peculiar ridges along his skin. My curiosity fell to the side as he began removing my clothing and I became completely caught up in the moment. That night, we made love in the moonlight while a soft desert breeze blew hints of sand across our bodies. When we were finished, we lay in each other's arms on the old blanket and gazed at the sky that seemed to be bursting with stars. When Fahdi sat up to put his clothes back on, he had his back to me and I remembered the strange texture of his skin that I had felt earlier. I sat up to get a closer look in the moonlight and noticed faint lines resembling stretch marks running horizontally across the middle and small of his back. I reached out, slowly ran my fingers across the marks, and felt him shiver.

"What is this?" I asked in barely more than a whisper.

"It's nothing," he replied without turning around, and slipped his shirt on.

Chapter 9

Monday, 20 June–Sunday, 26 June 2005

On Monday I awoke in the late morning and jumped on my computer to check my emails. What I discovered in my inbox was a little shocking and gave me an uneasy feeling in the pit of my stomach. I had received an email from Shawn that contained more emotion than I'd seen him express throughout our entire relationship.

I hope you are getting this as you wake up so that you start your day knowing that you changed my life forever-for the good. I also want to let you know that you are so beautiful the way you are right now. I miss those special times that we had waking up next to each other. I never woke up next to one person more times in my life. It was one of the greatest honors of my life. I am so sad right now. You were my world. I know I should have let you know that, but·I am just too stupid. As bad as I feel right now, I know that I was once loved by you and that is the greatest comfort I could have. I want to go back so much and do all the things I never did for you. I want to wake you up while you lay there next to me sleeping and thank you for being in my life and loving me. I want to kiss you on the boardwalk in Atlantic City and let everyone see it. I want to go back, but I know I can't. I miss you. My bed misses you. That is still your place there next to me, I can't see it any other way.

Love, Shawn

I felt nostalgic for about a second and then realized that he didn't really want me, he just didn't want me to not be his. I knew that if I returned to him, things might be better in the beginning, but inevitably he would return to his old ways. I had gotten more in one month with Fahdi than I'd gotten out of the two-and-a-half-year relationship with Shawn. I clicked the reply button below Shawn's email and simply wrote: *I'm sorry. It's too late.*

When I got home from work that night, I checked my emails and found a response from Shawn. After reading it I knew I had made the right decision.

I've been sitting here all day trying to get you off my mind but I can't, so I'll just write to you. Maybe one day you'll tell me the whole truth. I'm sure you're already sleeping with someone else, that's the only way you'd have the balls to end everything between us. You are just another woman that can't admit she's too scared to be alone for five minutes. You're weak. You're everything that I've despised over the years-you use your pussy to get you through life. Have fun screwing your way through every Marine and Army camp you go to over there.

I cringed because I knew on some level he was probably right. I most likely would have gone running back to him after reading his email the night before if I hadn't already fallen for Fahdi. I realized then that the first email was simply a test. Shawn knew he'd be able to analyze my response and figure out what was going on, and I'd swallowed the bait, hook and all. This time, I didn't respond and hit the delete button.

Over the next few days, Fahdi and I were two kids completely infatuated with each other. My war deployment was now officially my summer of love. We nabbed every chance to steal kisses from each other and struggled endlessly to keep from gazing at each other throughout meetings at work. The force drawing us to each other was one of the most powerful things I've ever felt in my life.

While eating lunch together one day, I decided to try and find out a little more about Fahdi's past.

"So tell me about your family?" I asked nonchalantly. Then I recalled that his father had died so I tried to back pedal. "I, uhh, remember you mentioned your father died," I stuttered. "We can talk about something else if you like, I just wanted to get to know a little more about your past."

"No, its fine." He tried to act cool, but I could tell the story of his father was a sore subject. "My father died when I was ten." Fahdi swallowed a bite of hamburger and continued. "He had bad kidneys and needed a transplant. His brother was a match and volunteered to be a donor. The transplant went well, but the medication the doctors were giving him to help his body accept the transplant were too hard on his heart. He ended up having a heart attack and died on the day he was supposed to come home from the hospital. That's why it was such a shock to our family. My mom left the house and told my brother, sister, and me that she was bringing my dad home and then she came back alone."

"I'm so sorry. That's horrible."

"It's been almost 15 years and my mom's still not over it. She swore she'd never remarry and she hasn't."

"Did you all struggle a lot financially after he died?"

"Yeah, it was pretty bad the first couple of years. Our business was functioning, but it was basically just paying its own bills and not turning a profit. A couple of my dad's brothers and some family members on my mom's side helped us out a little, but I had to go to work in a factory when I was twelve so we could buy food. There were many nights we went to bed hungry. My mom spent a lot of time working to manage our business and keep it going so I also had to take care of my brother and sister. But then, after a few years, the business started turning a profit and we were okay."

"So, is there really a big market in Baghdad for veterinary supplies?" I was thinking of small household pet supplies and surprised that a veterinary supply business would be successful in a place I doubted was too concerned with de-worming and vaccinating their dogs and cats.

"Not so much here in Baghdad," Fahdi explained. "We mostly deal with the farmers who live outside the city. Over the past decade or so, they've begun to understand that it is worth it to treat their livestock with vaccines and such as the decreased mortality rates more than make up for the expense."

"So where do you get the supplies from?"

"They're mostly imported from Germany, but from some other countries as well. My grandfather was a farmer in northern Iraq so we also package and sell some of our own original supplies."

"How long did it take for the business to start turning profit?"

"By the time I was fifteen or sixteen, we were doing pretty well. My brother, sister, and I all started going to private schools. I attended a high school where a lot of government officials' kids went. We also added onto our house and completely remodeled it in 1998. We wanted a bigger place to live, but no one wanted to leave the house because it was where we lived with our dad. So, we just decided to make it bigger and nicer."

Since I'd gotten him to open up easily about his family, I decided to bring up the marks I'd seen on his back that night on the roof. "I've been wondering since the other night what those marks on your back are. I know you said it's nothing, but I don't believe you. What happened?"

He shifted in his seat and laid down his hamburger. At first, I thought he was going to stonewall but then he started explaining in a solemn voice. "When I was nine years old, the first gulf war started, Desert Storm. You guys were bombing Baghdad pretty hard for a few days in the beginning and one ended up hitting really close to our house one night. It blew out the windows to my bedroom and caved in part of the roof. I was lying on my stomach when it happened, and the shrapnel and glass from the explosion flew onto me and tore up my back. It's a good thing I was lying face down or I'd probably be dead. I remember my dad running into the room to get me and carrying me out of the house. After that night, we left the city and went north to Mosul to stay on my grandfather's farm to wait out the bombings. I was in a lot of pain for the first couple of weeks, but after that, I was actually kind of happy because we didn't have to go to school." He flashed me his classic smile. "It was the middle of the school year when the war started, and of course, they shut down all the schools in the country when the bombing started and didn't open them again until the war ended."

"Well that's still a horrible thing to go through as a little kid. I'm so sorry. I can understand why you didn't want to talk about it before."

"I didn't want to talk about it because I hated the U.S. for a long time after that. I blamed them for the war and hated them for what happened to me. But, as I got older I understood and slowly let go of my hate. And of course, I'm totally over it now because they brought me you."

All I could do was smile and blush.

On Sunday afternoon, Fahdi came to my office. Kevin was at another office down the hall so Fahdi and I were alone. He leaned down and gave me a kiss and then sat down on the corner of my desk.

"I got you something."

I stopped typing on my computer and spun in my chair to face him. "What is it?" I asked with a smile.

He reached into his pocket a pulled out a small, white box wrapped in red ribbon with a bow. I opened the box and found a beautiful heart necklace in yellow gold. The heart hung at an angle from the chain and there was a small diamond inset on the bottom point of the heart. "Oh my God, it's gorgeous!"

"You like it?"

"I love it. Thank you so much." I put the necklace on but tucked it inside my shirt in order to not arouse suspicions.

"You also need to know something." I saw his facial expression transform from gentle to solemn, and maybe even angry.

"Ok...what?" I asked, bracing for what he was about to say.

"Someone wrote a letter to Abu Zaid that we were having an affair. The tip was obviously intended to start something, but luckily Abu Zaid likes me and he came to me with it."

"Do we know who it was? Was it an American or Iraqi?" I felt my heart rate increase and kicked myself for being so careless.

"It was one of the Iraqi workers. Someone must have seen or heard something. But the letter was written anonymously so I don't know who wrote it. I could dig and find out, but that would only bring more attention." He pulled me into his arms and gently brushed my hair away from my face. "I hate being away from you for a minute, but I think it would be wise if we switched to opposite shifts and laid low for a while."

I knew he was right, but I couldn't hide my disappointment. The thought of not seeing him but for a few minutes at shift change made my stomach turn. "I know you're right but I hate it." I laid my forehead on his chest. "This whole thing sucks," I whined into his shirt.

"I know, Sweetie, but it's just for a little while until the heat lifts a little. Abu Zaid won't cause us any problems, but we can't arouse any more suspicion."

Chapter 10

Monday, 27 June–Monday, 4 July 2005

The final week of June was tumultuous to say the least. I was emotionally deflated since Fahdi and I had switched to opposite shifts and barely saw each other. I tried to focus on my work, but my passion for our missions simply wasn't the same when I wasn't working side-by-side with Fahdi.

The Green Zone had been relatively quiet and peaceful since my arrival, but the war finally caught up with me that final week of June. On my third day of the morning shift, I sat at my computer, half-asleep, with a thermos of coffee that I'd nearly drained since arriving at work just a half hour before. Adjusting my sleep pattern proved more difficult than I'd thought it would be, and I stared at the thermos contemplating just pouring the remainder of coffee over my head to stay awake. While trying to focus my eyes on the blurry computer screen, a massive explosion erupted across the street from the building. I hit the floor as the windows shattered and rained shards of glass onto my desk. After hiding out under my desk for several minutes to be sure another explosion wouldn't follow, I crept out to look through the hole in the wall where the window used to be. I saw black smoke rising from the police station across the street and guessed that the explosion was most likely a car bomb. After a few more experiences with explosions in Iraq, I learned to recognize the distinct difference in the sounds of various explosives. After a couple of months, I could hear even distant explosions and identify if they were car bombs, mortar rounds, or RPGs.

Two days later, I was teaching a class on proper marking and destruction of classified documents and equipment to fifteen Iraqi intelligence officers when a thunderous boom rattled the entire building. Once again, I hit the floor and curled up into a ball with my arms wrapped around my head. When I was sure it was just a single explosion, I slowly brought my arms down and opened my eyes. To my embarrassment, I realized I was the only one on the floor. In fact, I was the only one in the entire classroom who really reacted at all. My fifteen students were calmly seated at their desks, some fighting the urge to laugh at my overreaction as I crawled up off the floor.

"I guess you are not so used to all the booming," Harath, my translator for the class, commented in his heavily-accented English.

I felt my face grow hot. "Ummm...no, not yet," I replied and managed a small smile.

"It was a mortar. The insurgents launch them from the other side of the river. They are firing blind and just hoping to get the mortars into the Green Zone and hit whatever they can. But not to worry, they haven't hit this building in many months now," he said with a proud, toothy smile that I'm sure was meant to comfort me. It didn't.

At the end of the following day of work, I stepped into the eighth floor elevator and slumped against the mirrored wall. I was exhausted from lack of sleep, worn out from another day of nearby bombings that spiked my blood pressure with each blast, and going through withdrawal after several days without Fahdi. After arriving on the main floor, I moped out the back entrance of the building and headed down the stairs. When I made it to the bottom step, I glanced toward the designated smoke break area approximately 100 feet from the building and caught sight of a familiar face. My breath caught in my throat and I felt the rush of butterflies return to the pit of my stomach. Fahdi sat on the top of a rickety picnic table in the smoking gazebo chatting with four or five other Iraqi INIS employees with a plume of cigarette smoke hovering overhead. He hadn't seen me yet. I continued heading for the rear gate of the compound that led to a large parking lot where my armored vehicle was parked, but stopped short. I didn't have the willpower to leave without getting to at least say hello to him and hopefully catch a glimpse of that beautiful smile. I veered off course and circled back to the smoke shack. I walked up behind the picnic table Fahdi was sitting on, and when their conversation paused for everyone to take a drag off their cigarettes I jumped in. "I'm guessing you guys haven't heard of lung cancer."

My comment brought about several confused looks from the other guys, but Fahdi remained with his back to me. "They don't speak English," he said without even turning around. He stubbed his cigarette out on the table and flicked it into the parking lot. Finally, he rose and turned to face me. "Besides, this is Iraq. If you live long enough to die of cancer, then you're doing pretty well." When he didn't flash me his typical smile, I knew I'd made a mistake by coming over. I contemplated just throwing out a quick, "Well, see ya later," and then leaving, but I felt like my boots were nailed to the ground.

"So, are you working tonight?" I asked to break the silence.

"Yep."

One word. One syllable. That's all I got out of him. Two words and two syllables for what this encounter was turning into popped into my head: *train wreck*.

You'd think I'd have figured it out by now and would have just said bye and continued on home, but I kept digging. "So will you be here tomorrow morning when I come back?"

He pulled another cigarette from his pocket, lit it, and then exhaled into the air above him. The afternoon sun reflected off his piercing green eyes as he stared me down. "Most likely," he answered in an expressionless tone.

I finally got the hint and gave a quick wave to Fahdi and the other guys. "Well, I'll see ya then." Then I turned on my heels and headed for the rear gate. I felt Fahdi's gaze burning a hole in my back as I walked away, but I fought the urge to look back.

I had trouble sleeping that night. I lay awake replaying my encounter with Fahdi in the smoke shack over and over. I dissected and analyzed every movement and every word he said. I was pretty sure the ice cold reception I received from him was due to the presence of the other men, none of whom I'd ever seen before. After I finished each replay in my head, I told myself the same thing. *He's just trying to protect us. We have to keep our distance. I shouldn't have gone up to him. He still loves me. He's just trying to keep us out of trouble.* But a nagging voice at the back of my mind kept adding, *or you've been played. He got what he wanted from you and now he's done and doesn't need to risk losing his job over you.*

The next morning, I arrived to work exhausted and with a pounding migraine thanks to my sleepless night. I stepped off the elevator at the eighth floor and literally ran into Fahdi. He'd been camped out by the elevators waiting for me. I felt my face flush in my excitement to see him, but I managed to keep a stone cold face in an attempt to seek revenge for the treatment he gave me the day before. I mumbled a simple greeting and tried to continue on past him to my office. He reached out and grabbed my arm firmly and I spun around to search his face for an explanation.

"Come with me," he said in little more than a whisper.

"I need to get to work." I tried to turn to walk away but he didn't release my arm and only tightened his grip.

"No. You need to come with me." Even though his grip on my arm was just shy of painful, his tone was patient and level, so I relented.

He led the way up the stairs to the ninth floor and up to the rooftop door. We stepped onto the roof and he shut the door behind us. I waited for him to speak but he just stared at me with the same expressionless face. The morning sun was rising behind me and Fahdi squinted as he looked at me.

"Well, you got me here, are we just going to stand here and stare at each other or do you have something to say?" I did my best to sound put out, but I was truly happy to be alone with him again.

"I'm leaving next weekend."

His words blindsided me and left me dumbfounded. "What? What do you mean 'leaving?' Leaving to where? What for?"

"We should only be gone for a month."

"Who are 'we?' What the hell are you talking about?"

"They are sending a small group of us on a mission near the Syrian border. The insurgency is getting pretty strong out there so the Marines asked for our help. Abu Zaid asked if I'd go along as the translator and I said yes. This was all decided before you even got here. I don't want to leave you, but I can't back out now."

I had been hearing horror stories about numerous deadly attacks on U.S. convoys and positions near the Syrian border since my arrival in country. It was a hot area. Fahdi was going to be heading into the middle of a raging shitstorm. I remained speechless as I took in the gravity of what he was telling me. Finally, I was able to begin asking some of the hundreds of questions I had spinning around in my head. "So who all is going? Where will you be staying? Do you *have* to go? It's so dangerous over there right now."

For the first time in a week his look finally softened and he took me in his arms. I felt my knees go weak and I was flooded with joy to have the Fahdi I knew back. "Try not to worry, I've been doing this a long time now. I've been pretty good at staying alive so far."

I felt the sting of tears come to my eyes as I buried my head in his shirt. I felt awful that he was leaving, and I felt ashamed at my selfishness. I was in a war after all. People were dying around me every day. Families were being ripped apart both back home in the U.S. as loved ones deployed to Iraq, and also in Iraq as their country continued to be crippled by war. And here I was in tears because my crush was going to be gone for a few weeks. But I knew Fahdi and I had something that ran deeper than a simple summer fling.

"I've been hearing them discuss this plan for so long now I stopped believing it would ever actually get off the ground," Fahdi continued. "But I talked with Abu Zaid last night and he said it's a sure thing and we are scheduled to fly out on a U.S. Army helicopter next weekend." He kissed me on the top of the head and said, "Come on, you've got to get to work and I need to go get some sleep." Reluctantly, I made my way back down to the eighth floor and trudged through my workday in a fog.

That night, I attended the July 4th pool party at the base, where hundreds of pounds of mid-grade fireworks along with cases of beer and alcohol were on hand. Everyone came to the party to get wasted and celebrate the birth of our country and our efforts to rebuild another. I hung out with the guys from my team and had a couple of drinks while marveling at the attire of the other females in attendance. Many were decked out in full club gear complete with skin tight leather pants, halter tops, and high heels or knee high boots. All I could think was who the hell packs for a deployment to a war in the Middle East and says to themselves, *Well I'll go ahead and throw in the stilettos and leather pants just in case we hit up a nightclub in Baghdad after a long day of fighting the war?*

For the most part, I sat in one spot and just watched the party go on around me because my mind was somewhere else. All I could really think about was Fahdi leaving for the Syrian border and me being left behind. I finally decided to call it a night after hearing the chorus to the *Team America* movie's song "America, Fuck Yeah!" for the fiftieth time. With a nice amount of alcohol in me, I was stumbling across the small, open field toward my room when an idea sprang into my head–a wonderful, awful idea. *If Fahdi's going to the Syrian border, then I'm going too.*

The next morning, I cornered Tom alone in the base office and launched my interrogation. "So who all is going on this forward deployment?" I tried to ask as nonchalantly as possible.

"Well, I was going to call a meeting this afternoon to go over the details with the entire team, but to answer your question, Seth and I are going along with a few of the Iraqi officers."

"So you'll be gone for what, two or three weeks?"

"Something like that. We'd like to run the mission longer, but Seth and I are both due to return to the U.S. before the end of the month and we have no one else available to run the mission. It's strictly volunteer and none of the other guys want to go out there."

Jackpot. "I'll do it!" I tried not to sound too anxious, but to no avail. "I'm here until September. Why don't I fly out with you guys? I'll have you and Seth for a couple of weeks to get me settled in and learn the ropes, and then I can stay on after you guys have to leave."

Tom smiled at me like I was an innocent child and said, "I don't think you want to go on this mission. It won't be easy living like you've got here in Baghdad. We'll be sleeping in tents, eating M.R.E.s, and it's still pretty dangerous in the area where we're going."

"I'm in. I can do this, Tom...*let* me do this."

"I'm not even sure you're authorized to come, even with my approval. The Marine camp at Al Qa'im is a combat infantry camp on the front lines." He lowered his voice as if he was telling me a secret. "There aren't any females out there."

"Oh...I see." I felt my face wash with disappointment. I wasn't a raging feminist, but I sure didn't like being told I couldn't do something simply because I wasn't a man. If a woman couldn't pass the same physical fitness requirements a man had to pass in order to serve on the front lines, then she shouldn't be there. But I wasn't going there to serve in a combat role, so there was really no reason to bar me from the mission.

I could tell by the look on Tom's face that he, too, felt there was no reason why I shouldn't be allowed to go. He placed a hand on my shoulder and said, "But look, if you really want to do this I'll see if I can get authorization for you to go." I nodded and he continued. "You've also got to realize that a U.S. forces female has never headed up a forward deployment with a team exclusively composed of local Iraqis. If Seth and I have to return to Baghdad and leave you out there alone with the Iraqis, it will be an unprecedented move. I trust the guys we've selected for this mission completely and have no fears for your personal safety when it comes to this matter–or I wouldn't even consider allowing you to come–but it is still something the higher-ups will take into serious consideration before granting you permission to attend this deployment."

"I understand."

"Mandy, I want you to seriously think about this whole thing for at least a day. You've only been in Iraq for about a month, and you've been here in the Green Zone that entire time. It's been pretty quiet here lately and folks tend to get a false sense of security being here. You've got to remember there is still a war going on out there. A nasty, bloody war. I just want to make sure you know what you're getting into. Meet me back here at the office tomorrow evening around 5:30. Hopefully, I'll have an answer from above by then on whether or not you can go."

"Roger that. I'll see you then, Sir." I said with a huge smile.

Tom stared back at me with an uneasy expression. "Remember, tents, Mandy. Sleeping on the ground. No running water. Daily mortar attacks and rocket fire. This isn't a camping trip. You really need to think about this carefully."

I simply nodded and smiled as I exited the office and headed off to work at the building.

Once I arrived at the building, I raced up to the eighth floor hoping to catch Fahdi before he left to go home and tell him the good news. I made a beeline for his office and before I even got the door open I blurted out with a huge smile, "Guess what!"

Fahdi jerked his head up from his computer and stared at me in confusion. "What?"

I crossed the room and took my usual seat beside his desk. "I talked to Tom today about the Al-Qa'im mission and asked if I could go, too. He pretty much said I was in as long as he gets authorization from the agency. There might be some issue about me being female. But if they say yes, then I'll probably be coming with you. Isn't that awesome?!"

Fahdi stared blankly back at me with an unreadable expression. Not the reaction I was expecting.

"What? Oh God, you *are* still going aren't you? Did you get out of it?"

He remained silent and reached for his cigarettes. He lit a cigarette as I anxiously awaited his response. Exhaling, he finally spoke in a solemn voice. "Mandy, you shouldn't have done this. This mission, where we are going…it isn't a place for you. It is a hard life and it's too dangerous. Please don't do this."

"But I want to. I don't want to stay here alone worrying about you out there."

"I'm used to it. I know how to stay alive. I can take care of myself. I love you so much, Mandy, and I don't want you in that place. Please don't go. I beg you."

Once again, I was flooded with disappointment. "But they really need me. Tom will have no one to run the mission after he leaves in a couple of weeks. They'll just get things going and then have to pull everything out if I don't go. Please don't ask me not to do this."

"Okay. I'm just going to tell you that I love you and I want you to be happy. But, I think you are making a mistake."

Chapter 11

Wednesday, 6 July–Satuday, 16 July 2005

Even though I hadn't yet received official permission to partake in the forward deployment, for the next week, I shadowed Seth's every move at work to brush up on all the technical aspects of our job while we awaited a solid ship out date. I was well versed in the analysis and reporting requirements of our job, but I wasn't very proficient when it came to setting up and working on the equipment and hardware. I wanted to be prepared to carry out the mission successfully and all on my own if need be.

About a week after dropping the news on Fahdi that I might be accompanying him on the deployment, I was back working the evening shift in order to continue my training with Seth. Fahdi stopped by my office and asked me to step out with him. I was prepared to follow him up the stairs to our usual meeting place on the roof, but he surprised me and led me onto the elevator instead. I was curious as he pushed the button for the first floor, but his silence and serious demeanor prompted me to remain quiet and just go with the flow. When the elevator doors opened to the main lobby, Fahdi exited and made his way to the backdoor of the building with me in tow. As we descended the back stairs of the building, curiosity finally got the better of me. "So, where are we going?"

"For a walk," he replied simply and followed the sidewalk around the building toward the front parking lot.

I figured he was simply going to his car, but then I noticed we were headed straight for the security gate that allowed pedestrian and vehicle traffic access into and out of the parking lot from the main street that passed in front of the building. The building was on the very edge of the Green Zone and anything beyond the front parking lot security gate was technically the Red Zone–forbidden territory for me. Once I realized he intended to exit the parking lot, I stopped in my tracks.

"Wait. Are you crazy? I can't go out there," I said in a forceful whisper.

I'd not seen anything beyond the walls of the Green Zone and imagined the streets of Baghdad were constant scenes of violence and chaos patrolled by hooded insurgents armed with AK-47s, waiting to kidnap westerners who strayed outside the Green Zone. And simply blending in was not an option with my western-style clothing, pasty white skin, and bright red hair. I couldn't fathom what Fahdi was even thinking in trying to take me out there.

He turned around and looked down at me. "I'd never put you in danger, Mandy. You will be safer out there with me than you are in here when I'm not with you. Please come with me, I promise you everything will be fine."

I wanted more than anything to run through the gates with him and into the city, but I stood my ground and hesitated as a million thoughts ran through my head. *What if this is a set up? Do I really trust him? I'm pretty sure he wouldn't do anything to hurt me–at least not on his own. But what if someone is holding his family and they're getting him to bring me in trade for them?*

As if he read all the thoughts on my face as they flashed through my mind he said, "You don't trust me do you?"

"I want to, Fahdi. I really do. But it's not even about trust. If I step outside those gates, I'll be disobeying military orders and even be in violation of certain rules of engagement."

"I understand," he said, but the disappointment in his eyes broke me.

"Okay. Look. Ten minutes and then we have to come back," I declared.

He smiled in triumph then took my hand and led me beyond the gates and into the streets of Baghdad. The wide thoroughfare that ran along the border of the Green Zone was alive with people scurrying about their business, and the street was crammed with honking cars. The sun was setting in the western sky, signifying the close of another day for the citizens of Baghdad who hurried to their nighttime destinations before the dusk curfew went into effect. While weaving our way through the crowd of pedestrians, I noticed some women in burkas and hijabs and others wearing western-style clothing. Some of the men wore the traditional white or tan long robe dresses, but many were dressed in western-style suits or pants. Many had cell phones pressed to their ears and some even had iPods and mp3 players. I received a couple of curious glances but nothing more. Fahdi was one of them, and silent communication between him and the other Iraqis on the street ensured my passage without harassment. Both Arab and English music blared from open car windows sitting in traffic, while shopkeepers swept their stoops and locked up their livelihoods. The city had a palpable heartbeat and soul that you couldn't feel inside the Green Zone. Every sensory receptor on my body was wide open, and I could feel the energy of the city enter my veins and transform into exhilaration and excitement as we moved deeper into the city.

After a short walk, we came to a small outdoor café with a couple of ragged tables lined along the sidewalk. Fahdi quickly ordered some hot tea for the two of us, and we took a seat at one of the tables. "I know we only have a few minutes. I wish I had longer but I don't, so I'm going to make this as quick as I can." He spoke in a serious tone but it was calm and steady, so I remained comfortable and at ease. "This is my city, Mandy," he said with a sweeping gesture of his hand. "My home. This is the *real* Baghdad. I wanted to bring you here to give you at least a glimpse at it. That in there," he gestured toward the Green Zone, "isn't Baghdad. It's like a gray area, a vacuum where all the life has been sucked out. I don't blame you guys, the Americans that is, for doing that. You did what you had to in order to make it secure. I just didn't want you thinking that what you've seen and experienced in there is the true Baghdad. It's far from it." He leaned back in his chair and breathed in the scent of the street. "It's true, this city is often a dangerous and violent place now, but it's also beautiful and I love it." He leaned forward and cupped my hands in his. "And I love you. More than I've ever loved another person on this earth. This is why I wanted to bring you here today. I want to be in the city I love when I ask the woman I love to spend her life with me. I want to marry you, Mandy. I want you to be my wife."

The common reaction would have been for me to cry, or hyperventilate, or squeal with excitement, but I didn't do any of these. Everything felt so natural and comfortable that I remained extremely relaxed and calm. I just smiled and whispered, "Okay."

"But I don't want to do it while we are in this situation. Someday, when we are together, either away from this war or when it's over, we will get married. I loved you from the first minute I saw you and I want you to know that I promise myself to you. You mean everything to me. You are my life now. You are my reason to live and I would die for you in a heartbeat to keep you safe."

"I know you would. I love you too."

*****

Soon after arriving to work the next evening, I headed over to Fahdi's office and surprisingly found the door shut. After a few short knocks I said into the closed door, "Fahdi? Are you in there? It's me, Mandy."

A low voice from the other side of the door simply replied, "Come in."

It didn't even sound like Fahdi but I knew it was him. With my curiosity piqued, I quickly entered the room and saw Fahdi standing on the other side looking out the window with his back to me. The setting sun had almost disappeared beyond the horizon of the city, and Fahdi's eighth-floor office window provided a beautiful view. But as I came up next to him, I quickly realized he wasn't admiring the sunset. His eyes were fixed on the twilight city but his gaze was glossed over indicating his mind was somewhere else. We stood together in silence, both looking out the window.

After a few minutes of silence, I finally asked, "Okay, what's wrong."

He let out a sigh and said, "I had to identify the body of one of my friends this morning."

"Oh God, that's awful. I'm so sorry. Do you want to talk about it?"

He continued to stare out the window. "People die violently in this city every day, Mandy. Soldiers from every corner of the world have come here and died. I've watched U.S. Marines and soldiers hold the bloodied bodies of their friends so many times, trying to be strong as they died in their arms. I don't deserve to feel sad or sorry for myself because I lost one of my friends. I should be thankful that it was just a friend and not one of my family, like my mother or brother or sister." He turned his head and looked me in the eye. "Or you, God forbid. If anything ever happened to you, I don't know what I'd do. I've seen so much death and blood, Mandy. I should be numb to it by now. Or I should at least feel comforted in knowing that so many other people around me have felt the pain I'm feeling right now.

But I don't. All I can see right now is his swollen, bloody face. There were bullet holes in his cheeks caked with dried blood."

"What was his name?" I asked softly, putting a hand on his shoulder.

"Ahmed. He was also a translator for the Americans. He worked at a base near Ramadi."

"Why were you the one called to identify his body?"

"I talked to him on the phone earlier this morning, only a couple of hours before he died. The people at the hospital searched his body for ID after he died. He wasn't carrying any, but they found his cell phone. They just called the last number he dialed."

"Which was you."

"Yep. They told me what time the call took place so I knew who it was before I even got there."

"Do you know what happened to him?"

"It was most likely someone who knew he was working for the U.S. They must have followed him on his way home from the base."

I wanted to console him but I didn't know what to do, so I just told him I loved him and I was there for him.

*****

On the night of July 16th, I was driving back to the base after work when my cell phone rang. I answered and heard Seth's voice. "Hey, Mandy, are you on your way back from the building yet?"

"Yes. I should be there in about five minutes. Why, what's up? You need me to bring something back?"

"No, just come meet us in the pavilion when you get here. We're having a quick team meeting."

"Roger that. See you in a few."

The pavilion was a covered outdoor eating area that had a small bar. It was unusual for us to be having a team meeting so late and we never held them at the pavilion, so I immediately wondered what was up. When I arrived I saw Tom, Seth, and James sitting at one of the tables having drinks.

As I approached, Seth scooted an empty chair out and gestured for me to sit down. "We took the liberty of ordering you a drink," he said as I sat down. "I recall you mentioning that you liked margaritas."

"Thanks." I took a sip of my drink as Tom sat forward in his chair and clasped his hands together with his elbows on the table.

"I just heard back this afternoon from HQ stateside."

Here it comes. I held my breath.

"You've been authorized to attend the forward deployment."

I nearly choked on my margarita. "Seriously!? Oh my God, that's so awesome."

"Here's the plan, Mandy," Tom said as he leaned back in his chair. "We're scheduled to fly out this weekend. Since everything's been delayed so long, you, Seth, and I will all fly out together on this first trip, along with four Iraqis from the building–Abu Zaid, Fahdi, and two operators that Abu Zaid will select. We still don't know for sure what the living conditions will be like, but if it's too difficult for you, you can simply fly back with me in a couple of days. If everything goes as planned, the seven of us will get out there, get everything up and running, and in a few days, I will fly back here to Baghdad because I have to get back stateside by the beginning of August. Seth will stay on a few more days with you, and then he will fly back because he has to be back around mid-August. We will try to get Randall up to speed on everything and get him out there as soon as possible, but you'll most likely be on your own with the Iraqi team for at least a few days. Are you sure you'll be comfortable with this situation?"

I nodded. Randall was the newest addition to our team. He'd been in country only a couple of days, but he seemed like a pretty fast learner and a good asset.

"Okay, here are the preliminary logistics," Seth said, jumping into the conversation. "We are scheduled for an 8 p.m. flight on an Army chopper from here to Al-Asad Airbase, which is about the halfway point between here and Al-Qa'im. We'll spend the night at Al-Asad and then catch a chopper on to AQ sometime the next day."

"We will all carry our 9mms," Tom added. "I also received authorization for Abu Zaid and Fahdi to each carry 9mms as well. We will also take two M-4 rifles with us. One will stay at the site at all times and the other will accompany team members who are in transit. Everyone is required to carry three, fully-loaded clips for their 9mm pistols. These clips and your 9mm must be on your person at all times. Those assigned to carry the M-4 rifles are required to wear a chest pouch with eight magazines. We are also required to wear our body armor and Kevlar helmets at all times while in transit. We will each take one backpack with personal gear, and we will each be assigned mission-related equipment that we are responsible for carrying and keeping track of during the trip. It's going to be a lot of gear to hump practically across the country, Mandy. I'm sure you're in good shape and I know you're a tough cookie, but you are small. In all, it'll be about fifty pounds of gear that you will have to hike with and jump in and out of choppers with. I want you to come to the office tomorrow morning and suit up with everything and see how it feels."

"Also," Seth interjected, "our cell phones won't work outside the city, so leave your phone here at the base. Tom managed to get us a satellite phone to take with us for emergency use and we'll have agency laptops and a portable satellite internet link, so leave your personal laptop behind as well."

"Don't bring any identification other than the badge you were issued when you arrived in country," Tom instructed. "Not even your dog tags."

"Okay," I said with a nod. "Anything else?"

"No, that's about it for now," Tom replied. "We'll see you tomorrow at the office around 7 a.m. Go get some sleep."

I hardly slept that night for thinking about the trip, and I couldn't wait to get to work the next day to share the news with Fahdi. The following afternoon, I practically burst into Fahdi's office and excitedly told him that I would be joining him on the forward deployment.

"That's great," he said with a smile. "Congratulations." But I could tell he was feigning happiness for my sake.

"Look, I know you don't support my decision to go, but at least we'll be together," I said, walking over and putting my arms around his neck. "And this is something I really want to do. It's a huge opportunity for me."

"I know," he said and kissed me on top of my head. "I just worry about you so much, Mandy. But you are wrong." He grasped my shoulders and gently pushed me away from him and looked in my eyes. "I *do* support your decision to go. I'm not sure yet if you're incredibly brave or completely naïve, but I have so much respect for you."

"It's most likely the latter, but thank you anyway," I said with a beaming smile.

Chapter 12

**Sunday, 17 July–Sunday, 31 July
2005**

We received an official notification Saturday morning that
we were scheduled for a flight Monday night at midnight
from the Green Zone to Al-Asad Airbase. Since I usually
spoke with my mother over the phone every few days, I
gave her a call and let her know that I would be out of
touch for the next couple of weeks so she wouldn't freak
out. Monday evening, we loaded all the gear into the White
Elephant, and Randall drove us to the building to pick up
Fahdi, Abu Zaid, and the two Iraqi operators that Abu Zaid
had selected for the mission. When we pulled up to the
back door of the building, I saw Abu Zaid and the two other
guys, but not Fahdi. I hopped out of the truck and asked
Abu Zaid about Fahdi. Using his limited English and hand
gestures, he managed to explain that Fahdi had gone home
to get his pistol and some gear for the trip and still hadn't
made it back.

As I was relaying this information to Tom, I saw
Harith, who worked with us on the eighth floor, emerge
from the building. We caught sight of each other and he
quickly approached and told us that Fahdi was stuck at the
checkpoint gate into the Green Zone. They had searched his
car and found his 9mm that he was bringing in for the
deployment. Since he had no documentation or written
authorization to bring the weapon into the Green Zone, the

gate guards confiscated his pistol and held him for questioning.

Tom let out a frustrated grumble and pulled out his cell phone. He stepped out of earshot and held a quick conversation. After a couple of minutes, he returned to the group and informed us that Fahdi would be arriving in a few minutes. Ten minutes later, a black SUV pulled up next to the White Elephant and Fahdi emerged from the back seat. He had a rucksack slung over his shoulder and was wearing slim-fitting stonewash jeans with a 9mm pistol in a holster strapped to his right leg. He had on a tight black American Eagle Outfitters t-shirt and his green eyes sparkled in the light of the setting sun as he walked over to join the group. Yet again, I found myself breathless at the sight of him.

I recognized the driver as one of the security guys from the base, but there was another man in the front passenger seat whom I'd never seen before. He looked about fifty years old, had silvery white hair, and was wearing a business suit. Tom walked up to the driver side of the SUV and reached through the open window to shake hands with the security guy. He then reached across and also shook hands with the older man in the passenger seat. I was hoping he would roll his window down so I could get a better look at him, but he never did. When the SUV drove away, I asked Tom who the older man was. "He doesn't have a name," he answered with a wink.

We finally arrived at the LZ with all of our gear and people around 10 p.m. Tom went into the air operations trailer to get the status of our flight and to make sure we were on the manifest while the rest of us unloaded everything onto the tarmac. Since someone had to remain with the gear at all times, I took a seat atop one of our equipment boxes while all the guys stepped away to smoke. While sitting there, I noticed half a dozen young army soldiers a few yards away laughing and joking. Judging from their jovial moods and high spirits, they were most likely on their way out of Iraq for their two-week R&R vacation. I felt strange because of what I wasn't feeling. I was on my way to the front lines while they were heading home. I should have been jealous but I wasn't–not one bit. I just smiled at their joy and felt the adrenalin of excitement course through my veins as I awaited our departure.

When the guys returned from their smoke break I was finally introduced to the two Iraqi employees Abu Zaid selected to accompany us as radio operators. Their names were Mohammad and Waleed, and they, too, were dressed in jeans and t-shirts. Waleed was tall and slender while Mohammad was short and stocky. Both were quiet with shy smiles and they seemed like nice guys. Mohammad spoke a little English, but Waleed didn't know any and smiled a lot when he was nervous or uncomfortable.

When Tom returned from the Air Ops shack, he informed us that everything was still on schedule and two Chinook helicopters should be arriving at midnight to fly us to Al-Asad Airbase. I glanced at my watch and saw it was already after 11 p.m. A couple of minutes after midnight, we heard the distinct sound of approaching helicopters and soon watched as two Chinooks landed a couple hundred yards from where we were waiting. Chinook helicopters looked like flying submarines. They had two rotors and a large door in the back that dropped down to load and unload large cargo.

Once the choppers were settled on the tarmac, Tom headed for the one that was lowering its back cargo door. One of the crewmembers stepped out the back to meet him and the two shared a quick conversation full of hand gestures as they struggled to communicate over the loud roar of the helicopters' engines. Tom jogged back over to our location and told us to load everything up into the chopper waiting with the open cargo door. I grabbed the rifles and as many of the small luggage bags as I could carry while the guys teamed up to carry the large metal boxes containing the equipment.

When we reached the chopper, we all stumbled to get everything into the belly of the Chinook because it was pitch dark inside. Typically, there were cargo lights in the back to give a little illumination, but not tonight. Once we had the equipment securely stowed in the middle of the aisle, we all found a place to sit in the web seating that lined both walls. I sat between Fahdi and Tom on one side of the aisle, and the rest of the team settled on the other side. When the back door lifted up and closed, what little light we had inside the chopper was snuffed out. I felt like I was in a pitch black flying closet as the Chinook lifted off the ground. My heart rate increased as I tried to adjust to the disoriented feeling. Fahdi must have sensed my anxiety because he quickly slid his hand into my lap and took my hand in his. Even though crewmembers accidentally knocked into me on their way up and down the aisle, Fahdi's presence enveloped me and calmed my nerves. Once we were in the air, it was as if he and I were the only two aboard the chopper.

After only fifteen minutes in the air, the chopper began to descend and soon, we were back on the ground. The flight was supposed to take about an hour and a half, so I figured we were either at BIAP or Camp Victory to pick up more people needing a ride out to Al-Asad. As the automatic cargo door once again lowered, I leaned forward to get a glimpse of where we might be. I was a little surprised when I saw a group of rather large uniformed soldiers lined up behind our chopper. A few hundred yards beyond the soldiers, bright floodlights, which were posted on a tall chain link fence with razor wire strung across the top, illuminated the LZ. When I took a closer look at the soldiers, I noticed they all wore large armbands with MP printed on them–Military Police. Two of the soldiers also held leashes in their hands with large German Shepherds at the ends. That's when it hit me.

I whispered into the darkness, "Holy crap. Are we at…"

"Abu Graib prison." Fahdi interjected, completing my train of thought.

Suddenly, the chopper's cargo lights flipped on, practically blinding us. The MPs boarded the chopper, making their way past us and our equipment to get to the front of the chopper, where I just then noticed a dozen figures were seated on the floor. Once my eyes adjusted to the light, I realized the figures were local Iraqis who had obviously been picked up in raids earlier that evening. They had black hoods over their heads and their hands were bound behind their backs with plastic ties. I guessed most were probably pulled right out of bed because half of them were in pajama clothing and the others were shirtless and barefoot or wearing simple flip-flop sandals.

"Oh, crap." I said in a whisper that was still a little too loud because it got me a stink eye look from Tom. "I didn't even know they were on here."

"Neither did I," Fahdi said.

The large MPs each grabbed two detainees by the upper arms and began walking (okay, more like dragging) them toward the exit, right past our group. I did my best to make myself as small as possible and plastered my body to the wall of the chopper as they all went by. Our team's gear littered the walkway, making it especially difficult for those with their hands tied behind their backs and hoods over their heads to maneuver in the tight space. I watched as the MPs and their captives made their way toward the looming concrete structure that was the prison.

We arrived at Al-Asad Airbase at approximately 3 a.m. I wanted to prove to Tom that I was a wise addition to the mission, so I jumped up as soon as the chopper touched ground and began loading up with gear to carry off the chopper. I grabbed my weapons, backpack, and two twenty-five to thirty pound duffel bags and headed for the exit as efficiently as possible. The back exit ramp wasn't lowered completely and remained about ten inches off the ground. I attempted to perform a cool boots-on-the-ground-special-forces-war-zone leap off the chopper, but when my feet hit the ground my knees buckled under the weight of the gear. I collapsed in a heap onto the dusty road that we landed on. *Nice.* I scrambled to get to my feet so I wouldn't trip up the guys behind me, but before I was up Fahdi was next to me taking hold of one of the duffel bags.

"Here, I can get it. I just tripped," I said, trying to take the bag back.

"No," he answered curtly. "You're not in Baghdad anymore," he chided. "You need to stop trying to be Rambo and think about where you are. You stay on your feet, you stay light enough to run, and you never *ever* jump out of a chopper, or any vehicle for that matter, first. You wait for the guys to go ahead of you."

"Why? Because I'm a female?" I replied sarcastically.

He turned sharply to face me, but I could see his expression soften in the faint moonlight. "No. Because I don't want to see you shot in the face," he stated simply.

With that, I zipped my lip. I glanced over at Tom and it was apparent he had heard every word of our exchange, but he remained silent. I even noticed a hint of a smile. I'm sure he was going to berate me, too, but he obviously felt Fahdi handled the job well enough.

As a group, we made our way a few hundred yards down the dark road. Once the choppers were gone, I tried to notice as much as I could of my surroundings. The moon was bright and from its hazy gray light, I could tell that we were simply standing on a blacktop road in the middle of nowhere. No cars, no structures, no lights, nothing. The empty desert stretched out in all directions as far as I could see. I felt like I'd just been dumped onto the surface of the moon. I was about to ask what we do next when I noticed Tom had pulled out the satellite phone and was dialing a number. He began talking into the phone, but his voice was low and he was too far away for me to understand what he was saying. When he was done with his conversation, he made his way back to rejoin the group.

"All right, guys, here's the plan. I just talked to one of the company officers of the Marine's 2nd Radio Battalion. We'll be staying with them tonight at their camp, which is about five miles that way," he said pointing into the darkness. "They're sending a couple of pickup trucks to come get us. Keep your eyes and ears open so we can help them find us."

"I thought we were staying at Al-Asad airbase?" I asked, a little confused.

"Al-Asad is only a couple of miles from the Marine camp. The camp is smaller so there will be less confusion and we can keep a lower profile there for tonight," Tom explained for everyone. "We'll get a ride to the airbase tomorrow morning and try to catch a flight out to Al-Qa'im."

We all settled on the side of the road to wait for our ride. Waleed pulled out a cigarette and lit it for a smoke but it didn't last long. Fahdi reached over, pulled the cigarette out of Waleed's mouth, and ground it into the sand with his boot. No one said a word, but Waleed realized the mistake he'd made. Like me, he wasn't familiar with being out in the field. A sheepish look flashed across his face, but Fahdi just gave him a friendly pat on the back and Waleed's cheery expression returned.

Two sets of headlights sliced their way through the darkness.

"You can smoke now," Tom said to Waleed. "The cavalry's here."

We all turned on our flashlights and used them to signal our position. Two Nissan pickup trucks pulled up and one of the drivers emerged from the cab. He was wearing a U.S. Marine uniform and looked to be about twenty-five years old.

"Well, hello, fellas!" He said with a big smile and a southern Georgia accent. "And ladies," he added, noticing me. "Welcome to Al-Asad! I'm Staff Sergeant Rivers with the 2nd Radio Battalion, and I'll be escorting you fine folks to your hotel tonight."

He gave us a wink and offered to help us with our luggage.

The ride to camp, which was a relay station between field Marines and Al-Asad Airbase, only took fifteen minutes. When we arrived, we could barely make out the large tents and few makeshift structures that comprised the camp. We came to a stop in front of one of the small buildings and Sgt. Rivers jumped out.

"You folks just sit tight while I run inside and ask Captain Ramirez where to put you up for the night." When Rivers returned, I could tell his jovial demeanor had reversed a little. "All right, guys, you're gonna head about 300 meters that way," he said, pointing toward the darkness at the rear of the camp. "There will be two large tents. Go into the one on the left. There should be some open bunks for you all towards the back of the tent. Also, I figured you guys might be hungry so I got you a case of M.R.E.s," he said, handing Seth a box. "The chow hall will be open for breakfast in a few hours."

"Thank you guys," Tom told him. "And thanks for putting us up tonight."

"It's no problem, sir. We're more than happy to help you out."

We unloaded our gear from the trucks and headed for the tents. About 100 meters into our walk, the faint shadows and outlines of two large tents appeared ahead of us. We entered the tent on the left and found it occupied by about sixty sleeping men. Both sides of the tent were lined with metal bunk beds, leaving about a six-foot wide aisle down the middle. The only light in the tent came from a single light bulb hanging from the ceiling near the back where Sgt. Rivers said the empty racks should be. Most of the men had their uniforms hanging from the bedposts at the ends of their racks, and by the dim lighting, I could tell that the uniforms weren't the standard U.S. Marine BDUs (camouflage battle dress uniform). I quickly assumed there must be an Army unit assigned to the camp as well, but when I got another look at one of the uniforms, I realized they weren't U.S. Army BDUs either. They were the new Iraqi Army uniforms. I stopped in my tracks and looked at the guys to see if I was the only one who had picked up on this. I could tell by their faces that Tom, Seth, and Fahdi were all way ahead of me.

"Yeah, we know," Fahdi whispered, reading my thoughts.

Tom just put a finger to his lips and shot me a look that clearly said *stay quiet and keep walking*. When we made it to the back of the tent, I could tell Tom and Seth weren't very happy we were rooming with the Iraqi Army, and neither were Fahdi or the other Iraqis for that matter. Many members of the new Iraqi Army were highly questionable individuals, and it was no secret that the Iraqi Army was infiltrated with spies, insurgents, and terrorists– not exactly the caliber of company we wanted to be shacking up with for the night. Fortunately, they weren't armed. They were assigned to the camp to train under U.S. forces and were only allowed to have weapons during their training while monitored by our guys.

Once the gear was placed in the middle of the floor, we all gathered around to discuss our next move. Before Tom said anything, I blurted, "Okay, so why are we roommates with the Iraqi Army?"

Tom explained that we had to stay in the Iraqi Army's tent because we were traveling with locals. I instantly felt defensive, and although I kept my mouth shut, I couldn't hide the look on my face.

"I know. I'm not any happier about it than you are," Tom said in response to my expression. "But that's the policy. We're only here for a few hours anyway, so we'll just have to sleep in shifts and take turns standing watch over the equipment. You all go ahead and get some rest. I'll take the first shift."

A couple of hours later, the Iraqi Army soldiers began waking up and getting ready for their day. Though we tried to keep a low profile, the nearest Iraqis quickly noticed us and spread word of our presence throughout the tent.

"We might as well go get some chow," Tom said to our group once it was clear we were all up and alert. To make sure there were no issues, he didn't want to leave our equipment unaccompanied or for any of our Iraqi team members to walk around the camp without an American, so he broke us out into two groups and we went to breakfast in shifts. Seth took Waleed and Mohammad on the first round and returned with a plate of food for Tom, who wanted to remain with the equipment at all times. Then I escorted Fahdi and Abu Zaid. When we entered, we were given more than a few sideways glances and some of the Marines blatantly stared at us in suspicion. By this point, U.S. troops were accustomed to seeing Iraqi workers in their chow hall. They were not, however, used to seeing *armed* Iraqi civilians accompanied by an American female also in civilian clothing in their chow hall.

In the serving line, I raised an eyebrow at Fahdi when I saw him pile ten pieces of bacon onto his plate.

"Ahhh…bacon. How I've missed you," Fahdi said, noticing my expression. "I haven't been in a U.S. chow hall in months. I was going through bacon withdrawal. I swear if there was just one thing I could convince Muslims to change it would be their refusal to eat pork."

"Oh really? Yeah, I guess the whole Jihad thing is *definitely* second in importance to the no-pork policy."

"Oh, whatever," he said waving me off. "This war isn't about the divine defense of Islam, it's about power, and those who want that power are just using Jihad as a means to manipulate the ignorant masses and convince them to sacrifice themselves."

"Okay, okay–sorry. I didn't mean to get you all heated," I said, putting my hands up in surrender.

"Well, look at Abu Zaid and most of the other Iraqis working with you guys. They're devout Muslims but they're on your side. Why do you think *they* chose to help the Americans?"

"I bet you're going to enlighten me."

"Because they're not backward inbreds, that's why. They know how to think for themselves instead of listening to some douchebag in a mosque who tells them God wants them to build bombs and kill the infidels."

I left the conversation at that and we sat down to enjoy our breakfast. On our way out, we noticed a large stack of cases of bottled water sitting on wooden pallets and grabbed a few to stock up for our upcoming day of travel. When we got to the tent, I had a headache, so I dug a couple of aspirin out of my bag and popped open one of the bottles of water. I took a big swig of the water and promptly spit it out on the ground. The water was nearly boiling hot and tasted like dirty dish water. "Uggh, oh my God that's disgusting!"

"It's probably been sitting in the sun for the past week or so, that's why it tastes funny," Fahdi informed me.

"Don't worry, it won't kill you," Seth added with a chuckle.

Luckily, I brought along my Crystal Light single-serve drink mix packs. I emptied one into the bottle and was able to choke it down after that, but it was still nasty. When I set the bottle down on the ground next to my foot I noticed in all caps on the label, DO NOT STORE IN DIRECT SUNLIGHT. *So much for that.* Tom came and sat beside me on my bunk.

"Hey, Seth and I are going to head over to the Air-Ops shack and see when we can catch a flight out of here. Since you may have to arrange your own flights back to Baghdad, you should come with us and learn the ropes of navigating military travel around the country."

I agreed and hoped we'd be able to get a flight out to Al-Qa'im that day and avoid spending another night with the Iraqi Army. Unfortunately, the Air-Ops guys informed us that a sandstorm was moving in from the west and all flights out of Al-Asad were grounded until the next morning. Al-Asad was about the most depressing place I'd ever been, so being stuck there another night did not at all appeal to me. What depressed me even more was knowing the Al-Qa'im was even less sophisticated than Al-Asad. I imagined the next few weeks would be Hell on Earth, but it was my decision to come and I knew I had to suck it up.

On our way back to our tent, we ran into Captain Ramirez. Tom seized the opportunity to broach the subject of our sleeping arrangements and find out if we could possibly stay somewhere besides the Iraqi Army tent.

"Yeah, I do apologize for your accommodations last night," Ramirez said to us. "It's just that all our boys sleep with their weapons and the Iraqis are unarmed in their sleeping quarters. I just figured it wouldn't be a good idea to have you all stumbling into a tent full of armed Marines in the middle of the night, especially since you're in civilian clothing and traveling with several locals. Some of our guys can be a little jumpy–could have turned into a bad situation for everyone if you know what mean. But I'll make some space for you all in the Marine quarters for the rest of your stay."

We managed to get all of our things moved into our new tent before the sandstorm blew in, which I felt was actually a welcomed relief. The sand blocked the intense sun and reduced the sweltering heat. But, the sand was annoying, too. It got *everywhere,* made us and our things a nasty mess, and made our teeth feel like they were growing hair. I'd much rather be a little dirty than boiling in the desert sun, though. I was a little apprehensive about moving in with the Marines with Fahdi, Abu Zaid, Mohammad, and Waleed in tow, but except a few dirty looks, we weren't discriminated against.

The next day, we packed up and headed to the airbase to catch our ride to Al-Qa'im. We sat at the hanger for several hours and waited for a chopper with enough space to accommodate us and our gear. Luckily, I'd been smart enough to pack a deck of cards to pass the time with. Fahdi and I played marathon rounds of Rummy with the other guys jumping in for a hand here and there. I'd purchased one of the infamous decks of the Iraqi *Most Wanted* playing cards at the PX in Baghdad and got a kick out of Fahdi and the other guys commenting on each of the individuals featured on the cards.

Finally, after five hours of waiting, our names were called over the intercom to prepare to board a chopper. Surprisingly, our names were not the only thing called out. Our military ranks were also announced with our names. Tom, Seth, and I were all active duty military members, but we always wore civilian clothing and kept our military status on the down-low. However, in order to help us get passage on military flights we presented our Military ID cards to the Air-Ops guys. We never informed any of the Iraqis we worked with of our military status and let them all believe what they wanted. Most, including Fahdi, thought we were CIA agents and didn't ask any questions. But since we were active duty military members wearing civilian clothing in combat zones, we were technically in violation of the Geneva Convention–a.k.a. the international rules of engagement. Nobody said a word, but I could tell the wheels were turning in Fahdi's and Abu Zaid's heads when our ranks were announced. I shot a wide-eyed look to Tom, but he just shrugged and didn't seem to be at all fazed by the slip-up, so I didn't give it a second thought.

We once again gathered up our gear and made our way out to the tarmac where two helicopters waited. Tom, Seth, Waleed, and Mohammad went in one chopper while Fahdi, Abu Zaid, and I were assigned to the other. We made it as far as the edge of the runway when we stopped and hovered over a shipment of drinking water that was stacked in cases on large, wooden pallets. The crew of our chopper extended a metal hook and chain through a 3'x3' opening in the floor of the chopper, and someone on the ground hooked us up to one of the pallets. When our chopper ascended and headed out for the open desert, the added weight of the cargo was extremely noticeable. The pilot constantly had to compensate for the unpredictable swinging of the heavy cargo, which made for a hellacious flight. The chopper continuously veered from side to side, abruptly slowed and sped up, and ascended and descended in an effort to steady the pallet. A mere ten minutes into our hour-long flight I was green with motion sickness from the rough ride, excessive heat, and smell of fuel fumes. I fought back my urge to vomit for as long as I could, but then I simply couldn't hold it down any longer. I instinctively dropped to my hands and knees and proceeded to projectile vomit out the opening in the floorboard. Luckily, a crewmember grabbed the back of my shirt and kept me from falling out the bottom of the helicopter. When I was finished, I felt a little better and Fahdi and the crewmember helped me back to my seat (which was atop an ice chest shoved against one wall). He handed me a plastic bag and Fahdi asked me if I was okay.

When I told him I thought I was going to be okay until we landed, he flashed me a sarcastic grin and said, "You do know you just puked all over the entire next months' worth of drinking water for the Marine camp we're going to."

"That's just effing perfect."

"Don't worry. Your secret is safe with me."

"What about with him?" I asked, gesturing toward Abu Zaid.

"Lucky for you, he doesn't speak English."

When we finally landed in Al-Qa'im (which we simply referred to as AQ), we met up with the rest of our team. Tom and Seth set off to find someone who could tell us where to stay while the rest of us waited in the small wooden shack that served as AQ's flight terminal. About an hour later, Tom and Seth returned with a vehicle, a British Range Rover with right-sided driver's seat.

"Wow, they even gave us a car?" I asked in amazement.

"It belongs to the battalion commander who's off on business in Baghdad right now," Tom explained.

"It's pretty safe to say we'll no longer have use of the vehicle when he returns. Enjoy it while it lasts," Seth added.

We loaded up our gear and headed to the far side of the camp. The Range Rover had a manual transmission and it was obvious Seth was having issues since the gearshift and clutch were on the wrong side. Tom made fun of him when we stalled for the third time, but I didn't say a word. I can't drive a standard in an American car much less with everything on the opposite side. Finally, we pulled up in front of a rundown train depot with the words *DIXIE NORMOUS* stenciled on the front of the building.

"Well, it's obvious this is a Marine camp," Seth commented with a smile.

The camp was roughly two miles long and a mile wide, with a set of train tracks that ran straight through the center. There was a large factory a few miles north of the camp. The site the Marines now occupied was obviously a storage, shipment, and receiving compound for the factory, which was now abandoned.

"Is this whole building ours to use?" I asked, surveying the depot that appeared to be several thousand square feet in size.

"Half of it is ours," Tom answered. "We're sharing it with one of the Marine QRF (Quick Reactionary Force) teams. But it's divided down the middle so we each have our own space. We'll have enough room to run the mission and set up sleeping quarters. At least we won't be sleeping in tents. The building has power but no running water or bathroom facilities. There is a large conex trailer with showers and latrines over there," he said and pointed to a singlewide trailer about 200 yards from the depot. "The bad thing is we'll have to drive to the chow hall because it's on the other side of the camp."

Once again, we unloaded our gear and dragged everything into our new home. I was relieved we wouldn't have to haul it around again for at least the next couple of weeks. An inch of dirt and sand covered the concrete floor and it smelled awful. There were a couple of large tables, some chairs, and a large chest freezer in our room. The air conditioning unit on the far wall was a welcome sight. Mohammad went to the AC unit, pushed a few buttons, and flashed us the thumbs-up to let us know the unit was actually functional. Fahdi and I were interested in the large storage freezer, which seemed to be an awkward object in the room. We opened the lid and immediately discovered the source of the foul smell in the room.

"Oh my God...damn!" I sputtered and smacked both hands over my mouth and nose as I jumped away from the freezer. "Were they keeping dead bodies in there?"

"It sure smells like it," Fahdi answered as he peered inside.

The freezer was empty, but it was filthy and literally smelled like rotting flesh. We assumed the freezer probably had meat in it at one point that rotted while inside. The funny thing was that the freezer was turned on and working when we got there, but the odor was so strong that whatever had been rotting in it couldn't have been removed too long before we arrived. The rank odor of the freezer remained a debated mystery amongst our group for the duration of our stay in Al-Qa'im.

The Marines loaned us each a cot to sleep on, and we arranged the room so that one side was set up to conduct the mission and the other side was designated the living area. Once we unpacked and set up all the equipment, we went back outside to look for a good place to set up our antenna. Tom and Seth decided it wasn't a good idea to just slap a huge antenna on the roof of our building because that would just be asking for trouble. We might as well stick a bull's-eye on our new house. The base already had existing tall power/telephone poles, so Seth volunteered to climb one and blend our antenna into one as close to the top as he could get. It wasn't the perfect scenario for our needs, but it worked. Once we had all the equipment set up, Seth and I drove up to the headquarters building and met with Captain Sigler, the Marine intelligence commander we would liaison with daily and pass our gathered information to. Captain Sigler was excited to have our help because he currently had no real intel support for his mission.

"Man, you guys are definitely a sight for sore eyes. We have no real actionable intelligence coming in, which means we're pretty much driving around blind out there in the desert. Let me know any way I can help you guys out while you're out there because I know you'll be helping us out immensely."

"We have a couple of Iraqi native operators and a native translator on our team, but none of them are familiar with this specific area of Iraq," Seth explained. "If you have any topographic or street maps of the neighboring villages or cities that we could copy or borrow to use for reference material, that would be a huge help."

"No problem!" Captain Sigler said and immediately opened a file cabinet. "Maps I can do–we've got maps and charts out the ass here."

He handed us each a stack of maps of the entire surrounding area, including the Iraqi/Syrian border towns of Haditha, Karabalah, Ubaydi, Hussaiba, Rawah, and Al Qa'im. The Marines were having rough run-ins with the insurgency in those towns over the past few months, and the situation in the area was quickly transitioning from aggravating to serious.

When we left HQ, we took a walking tour since we were in the heart of the camp. Although the camp was technically just a small outpost, it still had a small PX with the essentials (and by essentials, I mean bootlegged DVDs and porn magazines), a post office, a medical tent, a laundry trailer, and of course, a chow hall. We made a quick stop at the chow hall and filled our pockets with cans of soda and snacks to take back to the depot. Since we were so far from the chow hall, we figured we better stock our place up with snacks and drinks to hold us over between meals. We managed to find some bleach to clean out the rank freezer and turned the temp up to make it a large refrigerator to keep our drinks and snacks in.

Waleed and Tom were doing their best to clean the place up a little while Mohammad and Abu Zaid were already working the mission. Fahdi, I noticed, was missing. Tom told me he'd walked outside a few minutes ago, so I went out to look for him. I walked all around the building, but there was no sign of him. Then something told me to look up. I backed away from the building and saw Fahdi on the roof, staring out across the desert. He didn't seem to notice me as I went around to the ladder and climbed up to the roof. I stood beside him and waited for him to break the silence while I watched the setting sun slowly sink into the distant sands.

"I don't like the layout of this base," he finally said without taking his eyes off the desert. I didn't answer and just waited for him to continue. "There aren't even any T-walls, just sand bags. It's also way too big and spread out for the amount of Marines they have here. If there's ever even a half-assed attack against this place, we're screwed. This camp is a sitting duck. We're literally in the middle of nowhere. I'm guessing the nearest U.S. reinforcements are Al-Asad, and we know how far away that is."

"So what are you thinking?" I asked.

"I'm thinking we need a contingency plan," he answered with a serious note in his voice.

"I'm guessing you've probably already got one worked out."

He nodded and turned to face me. "If anything does go down, we stick with the Marines as long as possible. It sucks that we're so far from the center of the camp. When shit happens, it happens fast, and I don't even know if we'd have time to make it to the center of the base. The good thing is that the QRF team is out here with us. They're the guys you want to be with anyway if stuff starts blowing up, but they're still a relatively small QRF team. If the place starts sinking, we, and I mean just you and me, head west on foot. The Syrian border is about a two-hour walk from here. We take no weapons, just water. Keep your digital camera handy because we'll need to grab that if possible." A look of confusion crossed my face when he mentioned us needing the camera, so he elaborated. "We will pose as journalists. You're a freelance writer and I'm your translator. Tom once mentioned that you speak Russian. How well can you get by with it?"

"I'm far from fluent, but I could probably do well enough to convince a non-Russian that I'm a native."

"That'll be good enough. Let's review. Drop all weapons, grab water and camera, we head west to the border, you're a Russian freelance journalist, and I'm your translator you hired in Baghdad. You got it?"

I nodded.

"Good."

Chapter 13

Monday, 1 August–Saturday, 13 August 2005

The primary thought on my mind when I woke up my first morning in Camp Al-Qa'im was a shower. It'd been several days since my last real shower and I was feeling less than fresh. The baby wipes just weren't cutting it anymore. I grabbed my backpack and stepped outside to head for the shower trailer. The desert was beautiful at sunrise and sunset. The sand sparkled like diamonds and gold, and the temperature was bearable so you could actually stand outside and enjoy the scenery. The sun had just broken the horizon, but the breathtaking view of the morning desert was nothing compared to the scenery I was exposed to on my way to the shower trailer. I was treated to a view of a dozen butt-ass naked Marines also making their way to the showers.

The QRF team had just finished their morning PT. They didn't bother hauling any clothing the 100 yards back and forth between the showers and the depot, they just casually strolled to and from the showers wearing nothing but their flip-flops, dog tags, and M-16s slung across their backs. *Good God, it must be nice to be so confident with your body.* I did my best to stare at the ground and made a beeline for the showers at a brisk walk, but I caught myself sneaking a peek here and there. After all, I am but a mortal woman.

After breakfast, Seth spent the rest of the morning trying to teach me how to drive the Range Rover in the empty lot beside the train depot. I couldn't drive a stick-shift to begin with, and everything being on the opposite side of the vehicle made things even more challenging. I was screaming and cussing after just ten minutes of repeated stall outs. My driving lesson must have provided great entertainment for the Marines because with every stall out and subsequent stream of profanities, more and more of the QRF guys appeared on the front porch to watch my efforts. Whenever I managed to get the vehicle to move, they cheered, and every time I stalled, they shouted encouragements. I even think they were placing bets with each other on whether or not I'd figure it out.

We spent the rest of the day organizing our workspace and focusing on operations in the depot. That evening, Tom and I met with Captain Sigler before dinner to conduct the first of our nightly debriefings. When we arrived at HQ, it was obvious something was going down. We passed several red-faced and puffy-eyed Marines who'd obviously been crying, and there was a somber chill in the air. Captain Sigler informed us that the camp had lost six Marines that morning in a single attack–one of the most significant losses that camp had ever sustained. Two, three-man sniper teams were ambushed while they were on foot patrol outside Haditha. Insurgents from the Ansar al-Sunna group quickly overran and slaughtered them.

"Son of a bitch," Tom muttered and shook his head.

I knew he was thinking what I was: *if only we'd have arrived a few days earlier.* We may have been able to intercept some communications regarding the attack and perhaps prevented it.

"We'll be gearing up for a retaliation strike and probably be heading out in a couple of days," Sigler explained. "This attack was a hard hit for this camp. Every Marine here is taking it personally. Practically the entire camp will be going out on this one, and only a small

contingent will be remaining behind to relay
communications and conduct logistics here. So you guys
will pretty much have the place to yourselves for the next
couple of weeks."

"Well, we'll conduct round-the-clock operations
and do everything we can to support you guys while you're
out there," Tom promised. "Will anyone be remaining
behind for us to pass information to?"

"Yes, my second in command, Lt. Gabe, will be
running operations from here. You can pass any intel to
him, and he'll get it to us out in the field. Thank you guys
again for being out here. We appreciate anything you can
do to give us a better advantage out here."

"No problem. We're just so sorry for your loss. We
wish we could have gotten out here earlier."

"It's the reality of the situation out here, but we're
going to do our damndest over the next few weeks to
change that," Sigler said. "Enjoy the quiet while we're
gone."

Having the camp clear out was good and bad. It was
good because we'd have the place to ourselves–no waiting
in line at the chow hall, showers, or laundry facilities, etc.
It was bad because if the camp was attacked, we'd be up a
creek with no paddle. The main body of the Marine unit
leaving drew unwanted attention away from the camp, but
if someone really had their heart set on attacking the camp,
this would be a perfect opportunity. Tom was scheduled to
fly back to Baghdad with Abu Zaid the next day, and Seth
would be leaving just a few days later, so the news that the
Marines would be away while I was left alone with the
Iraqi team made Tom even more nervous.

"This changes the game a bit," Tom said on our way
back to the depot. "Obviously, I didn't plan on this when I
decided to let you stay behind alone with the team."

I was a little leery of being stuck on a deserted base
in such a hot area, but I didn't want to let Captain Sigler
down since we'd just promised him we'd stay and support

the upcoming mission. Tom was conflicted, but in the end, he decided to let me stay.

When we got back to the depot, we filled the others in on what had happened. Fahdi immediately jumped on the Internet and began searching the common websites terrorist organizations used to post videos and photos of attacks to see if he could find any information about that morning's ambush on the snipers. Sadly, there was a video and it was already viral–prominently posted on at least three different sites. Fahdi called us all over and we watched the video. It showed the Marines being ambushed by more than a dozen insurgents in white Nissan pick-up trucks. The end of the video showed an insurgent ripping the dog tags from around the neck of a fallen Marine. It was gruesome.

"Scumbags didn't waste any time getting this one up, did they?" Seth commented as he watched the video from Fahdi's shoulder.

"Yeah it was *too* fast. If you look at the time it was posted and the time stamp on the video, you can see they had it online in only three hours," Fahdi pointed out.

"What do you mean *too* fast?" I asked.

"This isn't the U.S., the equipment needed to edit and post this online isn't commonplace way out here. Usually, these videos are sent to Baghdad or Mosul to be edited and posted online. There's no way they got this recording back to Baghdad and up online in less than three hours," Fahdi explained.

"Which means it had to have been edited locally," Tom chimed in.

"Exactly," Fahdi said. "It was most likely done at a computer shop or internet cafe in one of the main towns around here, maybe Haditha. There are probably only a couple of such shops in this entire valley. I'm willing to bet there's a computer in one of them that still has the raw footage of this video on its hard drive. Find the shop…"

"Find the assholes that did this," Tom added, once again completing Fahdi's train of thought.

Tom grabbed the satellite phone and called Captain Sigler. He relayed our discovery, and the captain said he'd have the patrols keep a lookout for computer shops and internet cafes during the mission.

Tom flew back to Baghdad the next day. After his departure, Seth spent the next two days doing his best to prepare me to be on my own. We went over security measures, safety procedures, equipment maintenance, technical troubleshooting, etc. The afternoon Seth flew out, I drove him up to the LZ.

"You know you can still head back with me," he said before getting out of the truck. "You've still got time to change your mind. We can pack it all up right now and all fly back to Baghdad together."

I didn't even give it a second thought and just shook my head. "I'll be fine," I said with a smile. "I made a promise."

"Tom and I will make sure another team is out to relieve you guys in a couple of weeks. Good luck, it was nice working with you."

"You too. Have a good trip back to the States."

As I drove through the camp on my way back to the depot, it was obvious the Marines were getting ready to head out soon. There were piles of gear, weapons, ammunition, and personal items scattered outside the tents and stacked in front of the warehouses. The guys were inventorying, cataloging, and packing everything up for the mission. There was also a long line of Humvees and other armored military vehicles lined up on the shoulder of the main road. They were about to head out and rock someone's world. When I pulled up in front of the depot, Fahdi was sitting on the porch smoking a cigarette and watching the QRF guys get ready.

"Everyone's packing," I said somberly as I walked up the concrete steps to the porch.

"Yep," he said tersely, squinting his green eyes as he stared at the Marines working in the blazing afternoon sun.

"Is everything okay?" I asked as I sat down beside him on the small bench next to our front door.

"I didn't think the QRF guys would be leaving, too. They usually stay behind and only go out later if they are needed."

"I think everyone's going–this is personal. You should see the center of camp. Everything is lying outside on the ground to be packed up. It's like they're evacuating."

"It's definitely big." He took another drag on his cigarette and then stubbed it out on the concrete porch floor. "This whole area is about to blow up around us."

"Are you worried?"

"Well, this is the exact reason why I didn't want you out here. I knew this place was a ticking bomb. But I'm glad I don't have to go with them this time," he said with a smile and half laugh. "I can't even count how many times I had to pack up for missions just like this. They're not fun. You're crammed into the back of a hot Humvee for days at a time in full battle gear. You don't get any sleep. You have to piss in water bottles because it's too dangerous to leave the vehicles. You never know when you're going to get shot at or if you're going to run over an IED or get hit by an RPG. It's literally days of hell on Earth."

"You think we'll be okay here with all of them away?"

"We should be fine. With all of them gone, there's really nothing here worth coming after. Unless someone on the other side finds out about us. What we're doing here wouldn't make them happy."

"So what about them," I asked gesturing toward two Marines packing their rucksacks in the open parking lot. "You think they'll be okay?"

"From what I've heard, there's a lot of activity in this area. A lot of bad stuff has been coming in from Syria–

weapons, fighters, and God only knows what else. The job these guys are heading out to do isn't an easy one. It's good they're sending everyone they've got because it could be another Fallujah."

The convoy drove out of the camp at sunset and Operation Quick Strike was underway. Fahdi, Waleed, Mohammad, and I all climbed up on the roof of the depot and watched the massive convoy of vehicles exit the main gate of the camp and slowly make their way out across the desert in a large cloud of dust and sand. When they were out of sight, an uneasy silence fell over the camp. It was quiet–too quiet.

Two nights later, there was an unexpected knock at our door. I'd just returned from taking a shower so I was dressed in sweatpants, a tank top, and flip-flops. When I heard the knock, I immediately looked to Fahdi with my eyebrows arched in confusion. He quickly put his finger to his lips, signaling for everyone to keep quiet. He pulled his 9mm out of the holster and walked over to the door, waving for me to follow him. He stood against the wall behind the door and I put my hand on the doorknob. There was another knock. Before I turned the knob to open the door Fahdi mouthed the words, "Ask who it is."

"Who is it?" I called out through the closed door.

A deep raspy voice that was distinctly American answered, "This is Sergeant Rice of Regimental Combat Team-2, Camp Al-Qa'im, Ma'am."

Fahdi nodded for me to go ahead, so I pulled it open. Standing before me was a 6-foot-tall Marine in full battle gear–body armor, night vision, and armed with a SAW (a huge-ass machine gun). The base was blacked out at night for security purposes, so it was pitch dark outside and the only illumination was what filtered out the open doorway from inside the depot. After registering the massive size of the Marine standing on our doorstep, I noticed his right arm was extended out from his side and his forearm and hand were hidden behind the wall. He was standing so close to me that I couldn't lean forward to see what was in his hand.

"Sorry to bother you, Ma'am, but is there any way I can borrow your satellite phone? I'm trying to get back to HQ, but my Humvee broke down just on the other side of the railroad tracks over there. I'm having trouble reaching my guys on the radio, but I remembered you folks had a SAT phone over here. I was with the QRF team next door and I thought I saw you with one. I need to contact Captain Sigler."

"Yeah, sure, no problem," I said, and Fahdi went and retrieved our satellite phone. I stayed at the door with Sgt. Rice and noticed that his arm moved while we waited for Fahdi to return with the phone.

He turned his head and said with clenched teeth, "I said, 'Don't move.'"

I leaned out just enough to peek around the corner of the doorframe and saw that Sgt. Rice was holding a small man by the neck and had him up against the wall. The man was obviously a local Iraqi and looked to be in his mid-twenties. He was wearing gym shorts, a white t-shirt, and flip-flop sandals. He'd probably been pulled right out of bed during a raid. Fahdi came with the phone and handed it to me. I turned it over to the Marine, and he backed away from the door and into the shadows still holding the man by the back of the neck. I took a step outside the door to keep my eye on the pair and Fahdi was right behind me. Sergeant Rice dialed a number and a few seconds later was talking to someone. He told the person on the other end where he was and that he needed a ride to HQ.

When he hung up, he shoved the satellite phone into the Iraqi man's chest and said, "Call your family."

The man took the phone but didn't quite understand what the Marine wanted him to do with it.

"Call your family and tell them everything is fine," he demanded again.

It was obvious the guy didn't understand English, so I took a step to approach the Marine to see if Fahdi could help translate, but Fahdi grabbed me by the shoulders and yanked me back.

"Stay behind me," Fahdi said to me in the same tone the Marine was using on the Iraqi man. Fahdi stepped in front of me but didn't get any closer to the pair. He said something in Arabic and the man began dialing a number on the satellite phone.

"I told him what you said," Fahdi told the Marine.

"Thanks, man," the Marine said.

The Iraqi man connected with someone on the other end and began speaking into the phone in a low voice.

"What's he saying?" I whispered into Fahdi's back.

Fahdi relayed what the detainee said: "I'm in the American camp...everything is fine...I'll be leaving soon...don't worry...I'll be home soon...everything is fine." Then he clicked off the phone and handed it back to the Marine Sergeant.

"Thanks again, guys," Sergeant Rice said as he handed Fahdi the phone.

"Yeah sure, no problem," Fahdi answered without taking his eyes off the detainee. "Is there anything else we can do for you? Are they coming to pick you up?"

"Yeah, they should be here in about fifteen minutes."

"What happened to your Humvee?" I asked from behind Fahdi.

"It's the crap diesel fuel they have out here. It's not refined properly for these vehicles and it keeps corroding the gaskets. They break down all the time. It's a real pain in the ass." Sergeant Rice escorted the detainee down the steps of the porch. "Well, I'm going to head back to my Humvee with this guy and wait for some others from my unit to come pick us up. Thanks again for letting us use your phone."

"Yeah, anytime," I called out as he led the detainee away by the neck.

When we got back inside I noticed Fahdi had an unhappy look on his face. I figured he wasn't happy seeing a U.S. Marine drag a fellow Iraqi around by the neck.

"I think he was being a little rough with that guy, too," I said trying to break the ice.

"Forget that guy," Fahdi practically spat back. "The Marines don't just pick up guys for no reason. I used to help them do it. That guy either did something or knew about something, and you were just going to walk right up to them like they were your buddies on the street. Wearing your friggin' PJs!" he added in an even harsher tone. "You're not in the U.S. anymore, Mandy. This is Iraq! There is a *war* going on! People are dying. You've *got* to be more careful than that." He shook his head and exhaled audibly. "He could have killed you," he said bringing his voice back to normal volume.

"A six-foot-tall, fully-armed Marine had him by the *neck*," I responded in defense.

"These people aren't afraid to die, Mandy," Fahdi replied with a steely glare. "They're not afraid of anything."

I knew he was scolding me out of love, the way a father would a child, but it still upset me.

"Look, I'm sorry I snapped at you," he said, softening his tone and putting his arms around me. "You're just too trusting and naive, and these traits will get you killed out here."

The next morning, a loud banging on our door woke us up at sunrise. Waleed was on duty manning our comms station, but he had his headphones on and obviously didn't hear the banging because he didn't budge.

"I wonder who needs to borrow our phone now," Fahdi mumbled as he rolled off his cot and shuffled to the door.

As Fahdi fumbled with the lock, I slipped on my flip-flops and made my way to the door as well. We saw two American guys in civilian clothes standing on our doorstep. One had dirty blond hair covered with a backward baseball hat. He was wearing cargo shorts and tennis shoes. The other was taller with darker hair and a full beard.

"Oh man, we're sorry," the short one said, obviously noticing we had just woken up. "We didn't mean to wake you guys up."

"It's no problem," I quickly replied while trying to rub sleep gunk out of my eye. "We were just up until 3 a.m. covering our…"

Suddenly I remembered what Fahdi had said the night before about being too trusting, so I cut myself off midsentence. "I'm sorry, who are you guys?" I asked starting over.

The men looked at each other and then back at us.

"My name is Gary," the taller one with dark hair answered. "And this is Chuck," he said gesturing to his friend. "We're with Task Force 121, and we were told by the Camp Commandant that this building would be ours to use for our base of operations for the duration of our stay here in AQ."

"What?" I practically screeched. "But the Marines assigned this building to us."

"You're welcome to go talk to him yourself, <a'am," Chuck replied. "Just make it quick because the birds will be arriving soon with our gear and we need to get set up."

I was standing there speechless with my mouth open so Fahdi spoke up. "Give us half an hour to get up to HQ and talk to our people."

He pulled me back inside and closed the door.

"Crap," Fahdi muttered half to himself.

"No kidding, we're being evicted!" I complained.

"Not oh crap we have to move," Fahdi said, putting his boots on. "Crap because Task Force 121 is here–at this camp. Wherever these guys show up, Hell always follows. I was in Fallujah when Task Force 121 arrived. This area just became the frontlines of this war, and this camp is going to be ground zero. We're smack in the middle of it now."

I later learned that Task Force 121 (or TF-121) is a unit of approximately fifty men from the special forces of all four U.S. armed services, along with members of various government intelligence agencies. Several foreign governments, including the U.K., Canada, and Ireland, have also had intelligence individuals working with TF-121. Those were the guys who carrid out the infamous Black Ops and covert missions most movies were based on. TF-121's primary job was to apprehend "High Value Targets"–key figures in organizations involved in the War on Terror.

"Alright," I said coolly. "Let's just go up to HQ and see what the hell is going on."

"If these guys want this place, they're going to take it," Fahdi persisted. "Getting the commandant's blessing was just a formality. These guys do whatever they want, whenever they want, however they want. No one knows who they even answer to, but it sure as hell isn't any military commander."

When we finally got in to see the commandant in person, we got the bad news straight from the source. "Yeah, folks, sorry about this whole thing," the commandant said after we told him about the two guys showing up at our door earlier that morning. "I'm not real happy about this situation either, but it's out of my hands. I've arranged to have the QRF team's things next door moved out so you can relocate into their space. It's smaller than where you are now, but it should be enough for what you all need. I'll also send you back with a dozen Marines to help you move all of your equipment. If there's anything else I can do to make this as painless on you as possible just let me know."

It was no use complaining to him–he had no more weight with these guys than we did. "That'll be great, Sir, thank you for all your help," I said and Fahdi and I turned to go.

"Please don't hesitate to let me know if there is anything else we can do to help you folks out there, Ma'am," he called after us as we opened the door to leave his office.

I had to smile to myself. I was simply an E5 enlisted member of the Navy and this Marine Corp Colonel and Camp Commandant was calling me Ma'am and asking what he could do for me. I felt like I was in the Twilight Zone.

As promised, a group of large Marines arrived at the depot to help us move everything within an hour of our meeting with the commandant. In less than another hour, all of our equipment and personal items were relocated into the old QRF quarters next door. We were lucky to be staying so close to our original position considering we only had a limited amount of cable, and if we'd moved any further away, we'd have had to climb up the tower and relocate our radio antenna. Our new office/home was about a quarter of the size as our previous place, but it was big enough.

Waleed and Mohammad worked the day shift, which ran from 7 a.m. to 7 p.m., while Fahdi and I worked the graveyard shift from 7 p.m. to 7 a.m. Unfortunately for Fahdi and me, our new neighbors decided to do a full renovation on our old place next door when they moved in, and every morning at 7 a.m., banging hammers and buzzing table saws began and didn't cease until late into the afternoon. By day three, Fahdi and I were exhausted from working twelve hours and then lying awake for the next twelve hours.

"What the hell are they doing over there?" I asked no one in particular while lying in my cot. "It sounds like they're filming an episode of *Flip This House*."

"They're building holding cells," Fahdi answered from his cot where he was laying with his back to me. "They'll need a couple different interrogation rooms, a few holding cells, an office space, and of course a special room set up with equipment designed to encourage those detainees who are less willing to talk."

"How do you know all this?"

He rolled over and faced me. "I used to help with interrogations."

"You worked with these guys?" I asked excitedly pointing to the wall that separated us from our neighbors.

"No, not with them. I worked with the Army intel guys, but I'm sure the set up and logistics are pretty much all the same."

"You seriously think they're going to be torturing people right next door to us?"

"I'd be willing to bet on it."

"Lovely."

That afternoon, having given up on getting any sleep, Fahdi and I lounged on the front porch. We watched the task force guys run in and out of the door down from us with equipment, building materials, and large black boxes. A few of them erected a large radio antenna in the lot in front of the depot. Their antenna closely resembled our own, but it was about twice the height–of course. Once they had it all together, four of them toted the antenna to the stairs that led to the roof of the depot. I noticed Fahdi slightly shake his head as he lit up another cigarette, but he remained silent.

At sunset, Fahdi and I were walking back to the depot from the shower trailer when I came face to face with the reality of what was now going on around us. I heard a low hum in the air that quickly turned into a loud whistling sound and then a loud boom! I looked to my right and saw a large cloud of dust, sand, and smoke just beyond the wire of the camp. A few seconds later, another whistle came across the sky and ended in another loud boom a couple hundred feet closer to the camp. Once I realized what was happening and that it was a mortar attack, instinct kicked in and I started running toward the depot to take cover. I got about twenty-five yards when I was tackled from behind. I stumbled down onto my hands and knees, and before I could continue my scramble for the depot I was yanked back.

"What are you doing?!" I screamed as Fahdi half dragged and half carried me back the opposite direction.

"Not that way!" he yelled back.

I squirmed like a panicked animal, but he put his strong arm over my shoulder and chest and held me close to him as he clambered for one of the empty train cars sitting on the tracks. He practically threw me inside one of the open boxcars and then jumped in behind me. Another whistling mortar exploded so close I knew it had to have landed inside the camp.

"The depot was closer!" I shrieked. "Why did you drag us all the way over here?!"

"Shut up and keep your head down!"

After a couple more explosions, the camp fell silent. We waited a few more minutes to make sure the attack was over and then peeked our heads out the door of the boxcar.

"They were aiming for that," Fahdi said pointing to the tall antenna the task force had erected earlier. "I had a feeling it was a bad idea and the dicks didn't waste any time using it for target practice."

"Son of a bitch, it's right on our roof. You think they'll take it down or move it?"

"Probably not," Fahdi answered seeming not too worried. "I'm sure in less than 24 hours the assholes that just launched on us are going to be hurting."

The next day, we had our first morning of relative peace and quiet. I'd just dozed off after finishing our shift when Fahdi gently shook me awake.

"Hey, wake up. There are two Marines at the door that want to talk to you. I told them you were sleeping but they said it was important."

"Bitches," I moaned as I rolled off my cot. "Is decent sleep illegal now?"

It was lucky I fell asleep fully dressed and even wearing my boots because the Marines needed me to accompany them up to HQ.

"Sorry to have to get you out of your rack, Ma'am," one of the staff sergeants said when we loaded up into the Humvee. "But there is a big conference going down this morning at HQ and Captain Sigler said your presence was specifically requested. He said something about the general's people wanting you to give the general a brief regarding your mission status."

"What?!" I exclaimed. "Give a brief to *which* general?"

I freaked out, realizing that my hair was probably sticking up everywhere, my clothes were wrinkled from sleeping in them, and I definitely hadn't brushed my teeth.

"*The* general, Ma'am. General George Casey," the other Marine chimed in.

Oh crap. General George Casey was the current Commanding General, Multi-National Forces Iraq: the top military leader in the entire country.

"We do apologize for such short notice, but this guy doesn't exactly announce when and where he's going to be. He and his entourage landed this morning at sunrise. Guess they're here to check out the party we started."

They dropped me off at the main headquarters building and pointed to the door to the large conference center. "You just go right in through that door, Ma'am. The conference has already started, so just duck in and take a right towards the back of the room."

I did as the Marine sergeant instructed and was relieved that my late entrance didn't cause too much disruption. A speaker was at the podium addressing the room, so I quickly sat in a folding chair against the back wall and remained as still and silent as possible. I surveyed the room and saw several high-ranking Marine officers and numerous individuals in civilian clothing (including the two guys from Task Force 121 who moved in next door with their team). General George Casey was seated at a large table near the front of the room, surrounded by his posse. When the current speaker at the podium stepped down, Gary, the tall, dark-haired TF-121 guy with the beard, took the microphone and began describing to the general and the rest of the room the new interrogation and detention facility they'd recently established at the old train depot on the far side of the camp. Fahdi was dead on in his assessment of what they were doing over there.

While Gary was still talking, a woman with long, dark hair and wearing civilian clothes made her way to the back of the room and sat in the chair beside me.

"Hi, I'm Jenna," she whispered to me with a smile. "I'm a CIA representative traveling with the general." She extended her hand and I shook it. "We heard about *your team*. The general is looking forward to meeting you folks and seeing your set up, if that's okay."

Was she serious? She was asking *me* if this was okay? Like I was going to tell General George Casey, "No, I really need to get some sleep, you'll have to swing by another time."

"Of course," I said probably a little too enthusiastically. "Whatever you folks want to see come on by. We'd be honored to have the general tour our facility."

"The general is really pushing hard to get the Iraqis more involved in their own defense and intelligence monitoring activities. It's a really great thing you folks are doing in teaching them these operations. We also heard you had a pretty big breakthrough this past week with some of the intel you gathered. Congratulations," she added with a big smile.

I just smiled back, not quite sure what exactly she was talking about.

She must have noticed my confusion and said, "That information you passed to the Marines regarding the computer shop that may have the original copy of the video of the ambush on the Marine snipers turned out to be right on target. The Marines raided an internet café in Haditha yesterday and found the computer used to edit the video."

"Really?" I said with a huge smile. "That's awesome!"

"They took the shop owner into custody, and he gave them some useful information regarding the men who brought the film in."

"The flow of information here has been pretty unilateral," I explained. "We just collect and pass everything of value on to them, but we don't get much feedback, which is fine. We didn't expect to be briefed regularly on what the Marines are doing with the information. But this is really great to hear. I can't wait to tell my team. They'll be really excited that their reports are being read."

When the conference adjourned, I accompanied Jenna to a line of dark SUVs waiting outside the building. We climbed into the backseat of the first SUV and waited for the others. When Jenna asked if the general could stop by, I thought she meant just the two of them and maybe a couple other people; but as our SUV pulled away for the depot, four other vehicles loaded with people trailed us. I suddenly became nervous and thought about what kind of shape our place was in when I left. Since we were now in such a tight space it was pretty messy most of the time. When I left, clothes were strung out across messy cots, gear was piled in all corners, and Fahdi was in the process of cleaning all of our weapons so they were all disassembled and spread out on a sheet on the floor. When we pulled up to the depot, I practically flew out of the vehicle. "Let me just run inside real quick to make sure everyone is decent," I spurted out to Jenna with a nervous smile. I burst through our front door and slammed it shut.

"Are we under attack?" Fahdi asked nonchalantly as he cleaned the barrel of his 9 mm.

"Worse," I panted. "We've got *serious* company. General George Casey and his entire entourage are outside right now getting ready to come in here to tour our facility and meet you guys."

"You're kidding me?" Fahdi said, his jaw practically hitting the floor.

"Oh how I wish I was."

Waleed and Mohammad were staring at us with confused looks, so Fahdi translated for them and their eyes opened to the size of dinner plates.

"So look alive people, but most importantly, look busy," I added and spun around to go back outside.

The general and his people were all climbing out of the SUVs when I came back out on the porch. Jenna came up the steps first and asked if it was okay for them to come in now. I nodded and the group filed into our room.

"So give us a brief description of what it is you and your team are doing out here?" Jenna asked loudly enough for the group to hear.

I felt my face flush but managed to speak. I gave the general a quick overview of what our mission was and what our team was doing.

"Outstanding," General Casey said when I concluded my spiel.

I beamed with pride. The general then went around the room and shook all of our hands and thanked us for our service in Operation Iraqi Freedom and our dedication to the building of a new democratic Iraq. He then presented each of us with a gold coin that could be handed out only by the Commanding General Multi-National Forces Iraq.

That evening, Fahdi and I lounged in the shade of the front porch as the sun set, something we'd started doing every evening before starting our shift. We put a cot against the wall of the depot, and Fahdi sat with his back against the wall while I lay with my head in his lap. I gazed up into the crystal clear desert sky that was transforming from day to night, and we just talked. We discussed everything: our childhoods, our past, our families, what we want for the future, etc. In those few weeks in Al-Qa'im, we grew closer, and our relationship strengthened immensely on an emotional level.

Chapter 14

**Sunday, 14 August–Wednesday, 17 August
2005**

At the beginning of our third week in AQ, I received an email from Tom. He told me he was leaving Baghdad to head back to the U.S. and our new boss had arrived in country. His name was Sam and, unlike Tom, he wasn't military but an agency civilian. Tom said as soon as Sam learned the ropes in Baghdad he'd focus on putting together another team to fly out to AQ and relieve us within the next week or so. After reading that, I began making preparations for our departure back to Baghdad. Since we were the first team to forward deploy from the INIS, Sam and Tom began writing an SOP (Standard Operating Procedure) for teams following us to use as reference. It was basically a logistics guide that included topics such as how and where to set up the equipment, troubleshooting tips, destruction methods, important points of contact, and a crude map of the camp highlighting the locations of the chow hall, shower trailer, latrines, post office, HQ, PX, etc. Neither of them had a chance to complete the SOP, so Tom asked me to finish it as best I could. When it was finished, he wanted Fahdi to translate it into Arabic. He also wanted a hard copy printed and kept at the depot, as well as a soft copy saved to a thumb drive and brought back to Baghdad so teams could study it prior to deployment. I'd put off completing the SOP because it was one of the most boring types of documents to write, but since I now had a deadline, I needed to finish it.

I was working on the SOP while Fahdi was translating some transcriptions from the previous shift when we heard muffled shouting from next door. We both looked at each other for a minute and listened. We heard more shouting, so we both got up and walked to the thin part of the wall that separated us from TF-121. Our ears to the wall, we heard people talking but couldn't make out what they were saying. Then we heard what sounded like a scuffle and more shouting.

"What the hell is going on over there?" I whispered to Fahdi.

"Sounds like they're trying to get someone to talk, and I'm guessing he's not cooperating real well."

"Oh my God, Fahdi. You think they're actually torturing people right next door?"

He pushed himself away from the wall. "Look, it's just the way things are done here–the way it *has* to be done," he said, returning to his translations.

"But what if the people are innocent?" I persisted. "If you torture someone, they're going to tell you what you want to hear even if they're innocent."

"Like I said before, these guys don't just randomly select detainees. If these guys are captured, they're most likely up to something bad. Yes, an innocent guy gets mixed up now and then, but that's just, as you guys say, 'how the cookie crumbles.'" He could tell I wasn't convinced. "It's not like they're chopping off their fingers or ripping their ears off like Saddam would do. They're just smacking them around a little. And trust me, it works. When you guys first got here, you were capturing detainees and basically checking them into the damn Holiday Inn. They got three meals a day and a shower every morning. They don't have damn air conditioners in their houses. They complained the military cots they had to sleep on were uncomfortable so your guys gave them pillows and blankets, hell, *fuzzy* blankets!" he said, almost rolling with laughter. "They were like, 'Shit, go arrest the rest of my family!' You've got to remember this is a war, not summer camp. The point is to get it over with, not make it as pleasant as possible while conducting it."

At 4 a.m. the next morning, another loud banging on our door startled Fahdi and me. Waleed and Mohammad were both sleeping, so I jumped up to answer the door before whoever was outside banged on it again. A portly white-haired man wearing jeans and an Australian outback-type hat stood at our door.

"You must be Mandy," he said in an exhausted tone. "I'm Sam, your new boss," he added, extending his hand for me to shake. "I took over for Tom. I'm here with your relief crew," he announced triumphantly.

He turned to the Humvee parked in front of our building and waved for the guys to get out and come inside. Randall exited the Humvee followed by four Iraqis and the British guy on our team, Paul. Technically, it was supposed to be an American who stayed with the team, but since we were kind of short on people, Paul offered to stay with the next team in AQ and the Marines were cool with it.

Once everyone was out and had their gear in hand, we all crammed into our small quarters. I was familiar with one of the new Iraqi team members and knew his name was Harith because he and Fahdi were friends, but although I recognized the other three as employees at the INIS, I couldn't remember their names.

"Well, hi, guys," I said once everyone was inside. "It's great to see you. We didn't even know you all were on your way. We were beginning to think we were going to get to spend the rest of the war out here," I said to Sam with a smile.

"We found out at the last minute there was a direct cargo flight heading out here from the Green Zone, so Abu Zaid and I threw a team together and we pretty much just jumped on," Randall said.

"Damn, you guys were lucky. But you did miss out on the pleasure of staying over at a beautiful little resort town just east of here by the name of Al-Asad Airbase," I said in a cynical tone.

The new team was worn out from their journey, so we offered up our cots for them to catch a couple hours of shuteye. Our space was comfortable enough for our four-man team, but eleven people made for a fairly cramped situation. Sam told us we'd be free to head back to Baghdad later that day. So while they were resting, Fahdi, Mohammad, Waleed, and I began packing for our trip home. After our relief team's power nap, we all went to breakfast together. Over breakfast, we filled them in on what was going on regarding the mission and went over everything they'd need to know to make their way around the camp.

Afterward, I took Sam and Paul to meet Captain Sigler, who was in from the field for a few days. Sam was a civilian and it was obvious he didn't think too highly of military personnel, because he spoke quite condescendingly to the Captain. He acted as if the Marines should be thanking their lucky stars we showed up to assist them with our "renowned intelligence expertise," which was "largely responsible" for the success the Marines had experienced on their recent operation. I'd grown quite fond of Captain Sigler and respected him greatly, so I was not only embarrassed, but also extremely disenchanted with my new boss when he treated the captain with what I felt was blatant disrespect. The captain remained true to his gracious nature and expressed his gratitude to Sam for all of his support and thanked our team for our sacrifice. Sam then turned on his heels and strutted out of the captain's office like a puffed-up rooster. I gave the captain an apologetic look and told him that I hoped he and his men would stay safe until their return back to the States, which was now less than a month away.

A few hours later, the new guys were settled in at the depot and the rest of us headed to the flight line to try and catch a ride back to Baghdad. Waleed and Mohammad were excited to return home, while Fahdi and I did our best to hide our gloominess. We knew once we were back in Baghdad, we'd no longer be able to be with each other 24/7.

When we got to the flight line, Sam informed the Air-Ops Chief that we all needed to be placed on a flight to the Green Zone. There was nothing going to Baghdad but a couple of choppers which would be leaving for Al-Asad in about an hour, but the chief thought we'd probably be able to catch a flight to the Green Zone from there.

"Well that's just ridiculous," Sam said in an exasperated tone. "We were able to get a direct flight out here last night with no problem."

"Only because we got lucky," I heard Randall mutter under his breath. It was obvious he wasn't too impressed with our new boss either.

"I do apologize, Sir, but there is nothing scheduled," the chief said to Sam. "Did you place an ASR for your team, Sir?"

"A what?" Sam asked with a confused look.

I thought to myself, *Even if we do make it to Al-Asad, without an ASR, it'll be a four-day wait to get back to Baghdad.* The chief went on to try and explain to Sam what an ASR was, but Sam didn't even let him finish.

"Look, Chief," Sam interrupted, putting his hands in the air, "I am a senior *Intelligence Officer*," he said with an emphasis on his title. "I am needed back in Baghdad and I need to be there today."

"I'm sorry, Sir," the chief reiterated, "I'll do my best to get you all squeezed onto the flight to Al-Asad, but getting you a ride to Baghdad is out of my hands. Even getting you to Al-Asad may be an issue since you don't have an ASR."

About an hour later, the two choppers landed. The chief informed us they had room for four of us so we'd have to decide who would stay and who would go. Considering my team and I had been out there for several weeks, I figured Sam would let the four of us have the seats and he'd stay behind with Randall, but I'd underestimated his self-centeredness. He decided he'd be the one to return to Baghdad triumphantly with the Iraqi team while I remained behind to wait for another ride.

"You've already been stuck out here several weeks with these guys," Sam said with feigned thoughtfulness. "I'm sure you're ready to get away from them. Besides, these guys have a lot of people interested in hearing about what a grand success this mission has been, so they need to get back pronto," he added, flashing an arrogant smile at the guys.

"Sir, if I may request," Fahdi interjected doing his best to remain respectful, "we'd rather remain behind as a team and all leave out together when possible. You and Richard can both leave now if you like, and we'll catch up when there is enough room on a flight for *all* of us."

Even though Fahdi was as respectful as possible, it was clear defying Sam's decision was a bad move. Sam's grin hardened.

"No, it's best if I take you three back with me," he declared. "You gentlemen have debriefings you need to complete and reports to write. I'm sorry to have to split the team up, but it is necessary."

And with that, he turned and headed for the choppers, indicating that the issue was no longer open for discussion. Fahdi dropped his head and then looked at me and mouthed the words, "I'm sorry." I did my best to smile and act as if I really wasn't bothered by the situation. Mohammad, Waleed, and Fahdi all came up and hugged me, and I cheerily told them I'd see them in a couple of days.

"I'm so proud of you guys," I told them after we hugged. "Now get back to Baghdad and tell everyone what an awesome job you guys did out here."

"I don't like leaving you out here alone," Fahdi said after the other guys walked away. "Stick close to Captain Sigler if shit hits the fan."

"Don't worry, I'm going to be right behind you," I said trying to reassure him.

"I love you."

"I love you, too," I said and then watched Fahdi jog to catch up with the others who were already climbing into one of the choppers. I stood on the tarmac and watched as the guys got settled in. After a few minutes, Sam stuck his head out the open door of the chopper and gave Richard and me a pompous wave.

"Have a great trip, you pompous jerk," I said with a smile and a wave back. Luckily, the choppers' engines drowned out my voice. As Randall and I walked back to the Air-Ops shack to call for a ride back to the depot, we crossed paths with the pilot of the second chopper. Without a second thought I stopped the pilot and blurted out, "Excuse me, Sir, is there any chance you'd have room for a couple of stowaways on your chopper?"

He eyed Randall and me hesitantly and most likely did a quick calculation of our weight in his head. "How much luggage you got?"

"Just our backpacks," I answered quickly. "Less than ten pounds. each."

He looked at his chopper and silently contemplated for a few seconds. "Yeah, we can squeeze you on," he finally answered, obviously seeing the desperation in my face.

Randall and I thanked him and boarded the chopper.

Since the other guys were already settled in the chopper in front of us, they didn't see us make it onto the other chopper. After we landed at Al-Asad, Randall and I spotted our group making their way to the terminal. I practically leaped out of the chopper and jogged up behind Fahdi. I tapped him on the shoulder and when he turned and saw me his face lit up with that beautiful wide grin.

"Hey, how'd you guys get here?" Sam asked.

"My cunning personality, I guess," I replied, glaring at Sam.

Sam was completely clueless when it came to navigating the inter-country air travel system, so it was up to me to organize our flight and lodging. I filled out an ASR for us, and then got in touch with the Radio Battalion Marines we stayed with on our way out to see if they could put us up again for a couple of days until we could get a flight out. When I hung up with the Marines, I asked the Air Boss if there happened to be any open seats on flights to Baghdad leaving that evening. I knew it was a long shot, but it couldn't hurt to try. However, before I could get over to talk to the Air Boss, Sam stopped me.

"Look, Mandy, we really need to find a chow hall," he said with a desperate look on his face. "These guys told me they're starving," he said, gesturing to Waleed and Mohammad who in turn wrinkled their foreheads in confusion. "We've got to get them some food and then we'll figure all of this out."

I knew Sam was full of crap because I'd just spent every minute with "those guys" for the past several weeks and knew the last thing they would whine about is being hungry, especially considering we'd had a large breakfast back in AQ and our team had gone more than a day without hitting a chow hall on several occasions. Sam was just a lazy, fat reject who couldn't go more than four hours without thinking about stuffing his face. I did my best to suppress my disgust and asked Fahdi to take Sam and the guys to the chow hall while I stayed behind to check on any available seats with the Air Boss. To my surprise, there were actually a couple of open seats on a midnight flight to the Green Zone. I went ahead and booked them for our team and just told the Boss we'd decide later which two of us would be going. I tracked the guys down at the chow hall and informed Sam of the situation.

"Well, I know you all understand that I have to get back," Sam announced to the group. "Do the rest of you want to decide on who comes with me or would you like to draw straws?"

"I'd rather stay," Mohammad immediately stated without lifting his eyes from his plate of food.

"I'll wait, too," Waleed said in heavily accented English.

"Oh wow, I didn't know you boys could speak any English," Sam said with a surprised look.

"We can speak only a little, but understand a lot," Mohammad answered with a straight face in an attempt to send Sam a message.

"I go with Mohammad and Waleed," Fahdi added when Sam looked at him for an answer.

"Mandy, you can go ahead and fly with Sam," Randall offered. "You've been stuck out here long enough. I don't mind hanging out."

"Thanks, Randall, but I'd rather stay with my team," I answered, glaring at Sam. (Not that he noticed since he was now completely preoccupied with stripping every speck of meat from a chicken wing with his teeth while making repulsive slurping sounds.)

"All right, it's settled then," Sam said finally, tossing the chicken wing into a growing pile of freshly cleaned bones.

After lunch, Sam and Randall returned to the terminal to await their evening flight, and the rest of us caught a ride out to the 3rd Radio Battalion camp to see if they would put us up again for a couple of days. When we arrived, I went to the HQ tent and asked for the captain who had assisted us on our way out to Al-Qa'im, but his platoon had returned to the U.S just a few days before. His replacement was a female captain who returned from lunch a few minutes later and greeted us with a warm smile.

"Hello, I'm Captain Carter," she said, extending her hand to me. I shook it and introduced myself along with the rest of the team. "I hear you guys are having some air transport issues and are probably going to be stuck here a few days."

"Yes, Ma'am. We didn't put in an ASR," I explained simply. "I'm sorry for dropping in on you all like this, but we'd appreciate it greatly if we could just have a place to stay for a couple of nights. We don't require much, just four cots along with head and chow hall privileges would be great."

"No need to apologize," she said with a wave of her hand. "We're more than happy to help you folks out. I heard about your work out west."

"Really?" I asked with genuine surprise.

"Yes, the intel support your team's been providing has been a huge help to operations along the Syrian border."

"Wow, well that's really nice to hear," I said smiling at the guys.

"C'mon, let me show you to your hotel rooms," she said jokingly and led us out of the HQ tent. "The guys can bunk in our main residential tent. It's right across from the chow hall and close to the heads."

She escorted us to a large tent that was crammed with small green cots and was home to approximately eighty Marines. Captain Carter had a couple of the Marines hanging out there clear off three cots and line them against one of the side walls close to the entrance of the tent. When everything was situated, Fahdi, Waleed, and Mohammad piled their gear against the wall and practically collapsed on their respective cots.

"This tent is strictly male-only so you're going to be staying in one of the conex trailers," she informed me once the guys were settled in. "The room belongs to one of our female officers who is currently away on R&R. It's pretty tight, but it's got AC and a decent bed with a *real* mattress," she said, flashing me another warm smile and tossing me the door key to the trailer.

"Thank you so much, Captain. We really appreciate this," I said, doing my best to express my gratitude.

"No problem, it's the least I can do. They'll be serving chow for another forty-five minutes if you and your boys want to get some food. And if you don't make it, we've got MREs on hand at all the resident tents. If you guys need anything, please don't hesitate to ask. If I'm not at the HQ tent, someone there will know where to find me. Have a good stay and just drop the key to the room off at the HQ tent when you get a flight out."

When the captain left, I surveyed my temporary home. It was about 6'x12' and the AC worked great. In fact, it was freezing in the room, so I immediately turned down the blast of frigid air that was pumping in from the back wall. I pulled my small pillow and blanket from my bag and put them on the bed. The room had a wall locker with a key sticking out of the lock, so I happily locked my M-4 rifle and 9mm in the closet. The rule when it came to weapons was it either had to be on your person or securely locked up at all times. Since a lockable storage unit wasn't always available, you got stuck sleeping with your weapons a lot of the time. We wouldn't be leaving the security of the Marine camp for a few days, so I gladly locked my guns away and looked forward to being free of them for even a couple of days.

All I wanted to do was curl up on the bed and sleep, but I figured I'd check on the guys first. I was also starving because I didn't eat earlier with the guys, so I planned to grab an MRE while I was out, too. When I got to the guys' tent I found them lounging on their cots, dozing.

"Well, this is better than bunking with the Iraqi Army," I announced, standing at the foot of their cots. "I know my place is a pretty damn good upgrade."

"Where are you staying?" Fahdi asked from his cot where he was lying on his back with his hands clasped behind his head. He was wearing a tight, army green Under Armor shirt tucked into stonewash jeans, and he was still wearing his desert military boots. I told him the captain had given me use of one of the conex trailers and I even had AC.

"Well, you little spoiled brat," Fahdi replied with a twinkle in his eye.

I knew he was thinking exactly what I was thinking: this three-day layover in Al-Asad wasn't going to be so bad after all.

"I'm in trailer number 676," I informed the guys as I turned to leave, and I connected eyes with Fahdi to make sure he got the message. "You guys just come get me if you need anything."

About an hour after sunset, there was a soft rap on my door. My heart fluttered because I knew it was Fahdi and I knew he was alone. I feigned my best surprised expression when I opened the door. "Hey, you guys need something?" I asked as nonchalantly as possible.

"Yes," he answered curtly and then kissed me on the lips. He pushed me backward into the room and slammed the door shut behind him with his foot. For the next three hours, we were able to completely focus on each other without having to worry about someone catching us. It was the first truly private time we'd had together, and I'm sure it was the most magical experience anyone's ever had in a 6'x12' tin can in the middle of the desert.

We were lying in each other's arms when there was a knock at the door. Fahdi and I both sprang out of the small bed and put our clothes on as quickly as possible. I just hoped it wasn't the captain coming to check on how I was settling in because I know co-ed habitation is strictly against base rules.

"Should I hide?" Fahdi whispered as I reached for the door.

"No, just sit there like we're talking," I instructed. When I opened the door, I saw Mohammad leaning on the wall next to the door and Waleed sitting on the wooden deck that lined the front of the conex trailers.

"Hey, guys, what's up," I asked, wondering what they were doing up and out so late.

Mohammad simply asked if Fahdi was there, but I could tell something was wrong. Fahdi stepped out on the porch with the guys and they began speaking in Arabic. Fahdi's expression remained neutral but he was nodding his head, and then he put his hand on Mohammad's shoulder in a comforting way.

"What's going on?" I finally asked, unable to stand the suspense anymore.

"They're having issues with some of the Marines in the tent."

"What do you mean 'issues?'"

"They're not happy about a couple of Iraqi locals rooming with them."

I felt my face instantly go red. "*What*!? Are you serious? Don't worry, I'll fix this."

I was ready to march down and have a little conversation with the captain, but Fahdi grabbed my arm to stop me.

"No, we will just go stay in the Iraqi army tent," Mohammad said. "We just wanted to let you guys know where we're going to be."

"I'm going to go over there with them," Fahdi added. "I don't want them there alone."

"No," I declared shaking my head. "Go get all your stuff and come back. You all are staying in here with me. Bring a couple of cots and we'll squeeze them in. We stay together."

"No, we don't want you to get into any trouble," Fahdi argued. "It's not a big deal."

"We stay together," I insisted. "Either you all bunk here with me or I'm going to the Iraqi Army tent with you."

Fahdi grunted but gave in. "Alright, we'll all stay here."

We snatched a couple of cots from the Marines' tent and stuffed them into the little room. Between the two cots and the twin bed, there was barely enough room to stand up. But, we had four walls, a roof, peace and quiet, and, most importantly, an air-conditioner, so we were happy.

That night, I was jolted from a deep sleep. The room was pitch black, so I sat up and struggled to discern the strange sound that had woken me up. I heard the sound again and realized it was coming from the floor next to my bed. Fahdi was lying with me when I fell asleep but now I was alone, so I assumed it was him down there. I leaned over the side of the bed and caught the faint outline of his figure. He was lying on his back, squirming and moaning with his head jerking from side to side. I reached down and placed my hand on his chest. His t-shirt was soaking wet with sweat and he was breathing heavily. He didn't respond to my touch so I knew he was still asleep. My stepfather is a Vietnam War veteran who, after thirty years, still suffered from slight Post-Traumatic Stress Disorder. He periodically had horrible nightmares while I was growing up, so I was familiar with the symptoms and knew what a PTSD dream looked like. I also knew it wasn't a good idea to abruptly wake a person having a bad nightmare, so I slowly got off the bed and kneeled on the floor next to Fahdi.

I firmly grasped both of his shoulders and leaned down to whisper close to his ear. "Fahdi, wake up," I said in a calm tone.

No response.

"Fahdi, wake up," I said a little louder and gently shook his shoulders.

I felt him jerk, and then he stopped moving and opened his eyes. I draped my body over his and held him tightly.

"Are you okay?"

He didn't answer, but his breathing returned to normal and his heart rate slowed so I just lay there with him in silence. I don't know if either of the other guys woke up during this incident, but if they did, they remained motionless and silent.

Finally, Fahdi raised his hand to my head and gently stroked my hair. "Get back in bed," he whispered. "I'm sorry for waking you."

"Are you going to get back in the bed?"

"No, I want to stay on the floor."

"Then I'll stay down here with you," I told him and tightened my embrace around his chest.

Although I was curious, I didn't ask him about his dream. He didn't offer to discuss it and I knew it would be touchy to push the subject. It was a serious reality check that made me realize this man and his life were very different from mine and what I was familiar with. He'd been surviving a war for the past two years and it wasn't the first war he'd had to cope with in his life.

I later learned there were numerous nights he'd been violently rocked out of his bed as a ten-year-old boy when the U.S. conducted aerial bombing raids on Baghdad during the first Gulf War. He also had memories of the bloody Iraq-Iran war that ate at his country like a cancer for the better part of a decade in the 1980s. He'd spent the past two years hanging out with the U.S. forces, bouncing from hellhole to hellhole around Iraq and helping to root out the terrorist insurgency and resistance forces. He went shoulder-to-shoulder with Marines in Fallujah and Ramadii, kicking in doors, dragging people from their beds in the middle of the night, and then assisting with interrogations of detainees. Finally, after being shot and breaking his arm, he now had somewhat of a desk job. But, he still lived in Baghdad where there was no such thing as a normal life for anyone. I didn't have a clue about all the horrible things he'd seen and done. So I just lay there next to him, only imagining what that dream could have been about and wishing there was something I could do to comfort him.

When I opened my eyes the next morning, I realized I was no longer lying on the floor and was back in the small bed. I did a quick scan and noticed I was alone in the room. Lying on the pillow next to my head was a folded up piece of paper and a picking of beautiful small white flowers. I propped myself up on one elbow and reached for the paper. I recognized Fahdi's handwriting. *Happy Birthday. I'm sorry you have to spend it here, but I'm happy to get to be with you. I promise to do everything in my power to make your next birthday a lot better.* Fahdi signed the bottom, and below his name Waleed and Mohammad both wrote *Happy Birthday* and signed their names. I put the flowers to my nose; they had a refreshing light, sweet smell. With the flowers still in my hand, I rolled out of bed, slipped on my shoes, and opened the door. The guys were all sitting on the wooden deck right outside the room just hanging out and smoking cigarettes.

"Hey, hey, happy birthday," Fahdi said with a broad smile when I poked my head out the door.

Mohammad and Waleed both smiled and wished me happy birthday as well.

"I see you got our present," Fahdi added noticing the flowers in my hand.

"They're beautiful, and they smell a hell of a lot better than I do right now." I said smelling the flowers again. "But where in the world did you find flowers out here in the middle of the desert?"

"Ahh, that is a secret," Fahdi said cryptically.

"Oh, okay," I said with a smile, nodding my head. "So what are you guys doing out here? Did you go eat breakfast yet?"

"No, we were waiting for you," Fahdi answered. "We didn't want to wake you so we went and grabbed showers and then came back here until you got up."

"Well let's go, I'm starving," I said and jumped to my feet.

After breakfast, I checked in with the Air Ops guys to see if on the off chance they would be able to squeeze us onto a flight a little early. Much to my surprise, they said several seats had just opened on a flight to Baghdad later that afternoon. I was happy to be getting out of Al-Asad, but I dreaded having to go back and work under Sam. I only had a few more weeks left of my tour, but this only depressed me further since it meant I'd be leaving Fahdi with no idea of when we'd see each other again.

The four of us sat huddled together playing rummy with our luggage in the familiar makeshift terminal at the Al-Asad LZ later that afternoon. While playing cards, I got a good chuckle out of a conversation I overheard from three jovial Marines sitting nearby waiting to head out on their two weeks of R&R. The exchange went something like this:

Marine #1: Man, I can't wait to see my girlfriend. She's meeting me in Germany and we're going to hang out there for a few days. It's gonna be so great.

Marine #2: Are you still with that hot Latin chick, or is this a different girl that's meeting you in Germany?

Marine #1: No, it's the same girl, Carmen. She's from Costa Rica and I'm going to marry her someday.

Marine #2: Yeah, a lot of Central American girls are fucking gorgeous, but a lot of them don't keep their pits and pubes shaved the way they should. It's just gross.

Marine #3: (With a confused expression on his face) Now, that's not true. My girl is from Indiana and she keeps everything nice and trimmed.

(Several seconds of stone silence.)

Marine #1: Donnie, you retard. You're about as bright as a bag of smashed puppies.

Marine #2: No wonder Gunny makes you wear your helmet in camp.

Marine #3: What?

Marine #1: Somebody please take his gun away from him.

*****

We boarded our chopper right at sunset and began the final leg of our journey back to Baghdad. Unfortunately, we had to stop at almost every U.S.-operated camp, base, and hot dog stand between Al-Asad and the Green Zone, so we didn't arrive at our LZ until after midnight. Since our departure was pretty sudden, I didn't have a chance to arrange for us to have a ride from the LZ to the building, but it wasn't a very long walk from the LZ to the base. I planned to just leave the guys at the LZ while I hiked to the base and pick up the White Elephant. When we finally landed in the Green Zone, I emerged from the chopper and was pleasantly surprised to see the White Elephant parked right outside the LZ fence. When we got closer, I saw Randall leaning up against the hood.

"Hey, you sure are a sight for sore eyes," I hollered to Randall as we approached. "How did you even know we were landing tonight?"

"Abu Zaid told me he heard from Fahdi earlier this afternoon and said you guys might be coming in tonight. I figured you'd need a ride."

Unbeknownst to me, Fahdi had managed to convince the Marines to let him use their internet room back at Al-Asad after we found out we'd be flying back to Baghdad that evening. He got a hold of Abu-Zaid on instant messenger and informed him of our approximate arrival time in Baghdad. Abu Zaid said he'd try to get someone to pick us up but he couldn't promise anything, especially with the "new asshole American" that was now in charge.

"I told Sam you guys would be in sometime tonight, but since we didn't have a solid window for your arrival, he decided it wasn't worth an evening of waiting around and you'd be fine just walking to the base when you landed," Randall explained with a touch of bitterness in his tone. "But since you guys have been practically on the front line for the last three weeks, I figured the *least* we could do was make sure you had a ride home."

"Thank you, Randall, we really appreciate it," I told him. "You're a really good guy."

Randall first drove us to the INIS building to drop the guys off. Although I was dead tired and in desperate need of a shower, I went inside with the guys. Abu Zaid was upstairs awaiting our return and I wanted to at least say hello to him and thank him for his help. When the four of us emerged from the elevator on the eighth floor, we were enthusiastically greeted by a large group of employees from our department. We received handshakes, pats on the back, and hugs congratulating us on our safe return. Our entourage followed us through the double doors into our department announcing in loud shouts, *"The warriors have returned!"* to the rest of the crew. Fahdi and I made our way to his office so he could drop his gear. When we entered, Abu Zaid was already inside waiting to greet us with a grin from ear-to-ear.

"My friends, you have returned triumphantly," Abu Zaid announced in a heavily accented voice.

While he and Fahdi exchanged greetings in Arabic, I noticed there was a young, slender Iraqi man standing just behind Abu Zaid. I remembered him vaguely as one of the night shift crew members, but I didn't know his name and had only seen him a couple of times before. When Fahdi and Abu Zaid finished their exchange, the young man pushed past Abu Zaid and embraced Fahdi. He also had a huge smile and a look of relief on his face.

Noticing my surprised expression at the way this young man greeted Fahdi, Abu Zaid leaned in and whispered, "Fahdi's brother."

I gasped in surprise and blurted, "Your brother works here!? How come you never told me this was your brother?"

"We don't want everyone to know we are brothers," Fahdi explained. "It's safer that way, considering all the people after me. I don't want anyone to know I have a family."

"Has he been working here since I got here?"

"Yes," Fahdi replied with a sheepish grin.

"Well it's very nice to meet you," I said shaking his brother's hand. He just smiled and nodded and then returned to his office.

"He's shy and doesn't speak English," Fahdi explained. "His name is Fa'iz."

Abu Zaid invited us to have a seat in his office and drink hot tea with him. I didn't want to leave Randall waiting downstairs too long, but figured I'd have a quick drink to not be rude. Abu Zaid was excited to hear all the details of the mission and bombarded us with questions. Before we even had a chance to answer the first question, he'd already asked five more. We did our best to give him as much detail and information as we could in our exhausted state, and he filled us in on how things had been going there for the past couple of weeks. He made it clear that he, too, was not very fond of our new boss and expressed his desire for Tom to return soon. When we drained the last of our tea, Abu Zaid could tell we were ready to head out and apologized for inundating us with questions. As a sly reminder of the homework we were assigned, he said he'd wait to read about further details of the missions in our report. Before he left Al Qa'im, Tom told Fahdi and me we were to write a report detailing every aspect of our mission and trip when we returned to Baghdad. He told Fahdi to make an Arabic translation of the report as well because copies of the report were to be passed to both the American and Iraqi leaderships. Fahdi promised Abu Zaid we'd start on the reports first thing in the morning, and Abu Zaid released us to get some much-needed sleep.

Chapter 15

Thursday, 18 August–Wednesday, 22 August 2005

Sam gave me the morning off following my return to Baghdad. When I woke up I called my mom to let her know I made it back to Baghdad in one piece; I hadn't been able to contact her since Al-Qa'im. When she answered the phone and heard my voice she became hysterical.

"Mandy? Oh my God, are you okay?" Her voice was shaky and audibly strained so I knew she was nearly in tears.

"Mom, what's wrong? I'm fine."

"Shawn called me and...told...me that...you were missing!" she managed to squeak out between sobs.

"What? What are you talking about?" I screeched completely flabbergasted. "I emailed you and told you I'd be traveling the past few weeks and probably wouldn't be able to call or email you."

"I know, but he said he heard from some of his contacts at NSA that your chopper may have gone missing."

"I don't believe this," I said more to myself. "He's full of crap. He doesn't have any contacts that would know a damn thing about my movements out here."

I didn't even recall including Shawn on any correspondences I sent regarding my return to Baghdad, but I didn't have time to think about that at the moment. I was too busy trying to calm my mom down. I simply figured he'd heard it from one of my friends at work whom I was emailing.

"So you're okay?" my mom asked again in a relatively calmer tone. "You promise?"

"Yes, Mom, I promise. I'm fine. Everything is fine. I'm lying in my bed right now."

"Okay. I'm okay now," she said, taking several deep breaths. "Why the hell would he tell me that?"

"Probably to get closer to you," I answered. It was obvious Shawn wasn't going to give up easily and was going to fight dirty. "He's not handling our breakup very well."

Shawn had only met my mother once, and briefly at that, during our two-and-a-half year relationship and had never spoken to her on the phone. That's how interested he was. But now that he knew I was pulling away from him, he was going to use every trick in the book to stay connected to me.

"Just ignore him," I told her.

"Do you have any idea what that asshole put me through for the past forty-eight hours?" she said angrily. "I could kill him right now."

"I'm so sorry, Mom. I'll handle it."

"You better be careful with this one, Mandy," she warned. "I have a feeling he can be a nasty son-of-a-bitch."

Fahdi called me soon after I hung up with my mom. He told me he'd be returning to work that evening for the night shift and was wondering if I'd be there so we could start working on our report. I didn't know what Sam's plan for my work schedule was, but I told Fahdi I'd see if I could come up to the building that evening at least for a couple of hours. I noticed Fahdi's tone on the phone was a little somber and assumed he was just still worn out from the trip. At 2 p.m. I headed to the office at the base to meet with Sam. He said I could have the next two days off to rest up and relax, but I told him I'd rather return to work. I volunteered to go ahead and take the evening shift up at the building that night because Fahdi and I wanted to get our report written and out of the way. Sam said that was fine, and Randall and I headed out for the 3 p.m. shift. When I got up to the eighth floor, things were back to normal. I went to Fahdi's office and found him at his desk already working on the report.

"Hi, did you get some sleep?" I asked as I sat in the desk chair beside him.

"Hey, I missed you," he said and leaned over and gave me a quick kiss on the cheek–a brazen display of affection considering his office door was wide open. "I slept enough," he answered.

I heard the same strange edge in his voice he had on the phone earlier that afternoon and wondered what was up.

"Are you okay?" I asked.

"No." He answered curtly. "My family received a death threat while we were in Al-Qa'im."

"No wonder your brother was so relieved when you came back."

"Yep. It was sent to their house last week. It said if I don't stop working for the Americans they will kill all of us and this is their final warning."

"Did you keep the letter? Are you going to show it to our security forces?"

"I already turned it in," he said brusquely. "People turn in letters like this every day. A lot of us working here in the building are threatened all the time. We tell the Americans and they do nothing but say they're sorry. It's a waste of time."

I felt guilty and so helpless. "So what are you going to do?"

"I'm trying to arrange for my family to go to Jordan. I have an uncle who lives in Amman with his family. Hopefully, they can stay with them for a little while and give this thing some time to blow over."

"Well that sounds like a good plan," I said hopefully.

"Yeah, but I have to convince my mom to leave Iraq. She doesn't want to go to Jordan without me."

"I agree with her. You're the one in the most danger here. I wish you would go," I pleaded.

"I can't just leave, Mandy," he said returning to his report. "What am I going to do in Jordan? How would I make a living? There's nothing there for me. I'd rather stay here and risk my life doing this than go there and be nothing. But I can't put my entire family in danger. This is the work and the life *I've* chosen, not them. It's not fair to drag them into this with me. My brother made his own decision to work here, too, but my mom and little sister are a different story."

We spent the rest of the evening trying to focus on writing our report, but we were both preoccupied with the issues facing his family. With every passing minute, Fahdi became more stressed and slipped deeper into depression. The next morning, I woke up and immediately thought about Fahdi and the horrible circumstance he was facing. I wanted to help him, but more than anything, I wanted to comfort him. I wanted to be there for him and show him how much I cared. He decided to take the next couple of days off from work to stay with his family and work on a solution to their issue.

I tried calling Fahdi several times over the next two days, but he didn't answer his phone. While checking my emails one night, an ad for online greeting cards popped up. I browsed through the cards and decided to send one to Fahdi's email just to show him I was thinking about him and his family. I searched for a few minutes, but Yahoo! Greetings didn't exactly have an *I'm sorry the Iraqi insurgency is trying to murder you and your family* category. I finally settled on a simple *hang in there* e-card and wrote a short message telling him how much I loved him and would always be there for him to help in any way I could. A few minutes after sending the e-card, my computer chimed alerting me that I had received a new email. I excitedly clicked on my email icon thinking it was probably Fahdi replying to the e-card.

I was sadly surprised to discover it was actually an email from the agency with my itinerary and information regarding my return trip to the U.S. in two weeks. I couldn't believe my deployment was already almost over–I felt like I'd just gotten here. A lot of the guys talked about taking leave on their way back to the U.S. and spending a week or two hanging out in Amman and touring Jordan. I was definitely interested in seeing the historic sites there and I wondered if perhaps Fahdi would be able to come with me. At least we'd have a few more days together and we'd be able to relax and spend some normal time together. I went ahead and re-booked my flight to give myself a five-day layover in Amman and extended my hotel stay. I just hoped Fahdi would be able to make it.

When I saw Fahdi at work two days later, I told him about my idea of us taking a small vacation together in Amman. He was all for the idea and said he'd arrange to take a week off from work. I asked him if he'd have any issues getting into Jordan, but he said he'd work it out and promised he'd be there. Later that afternoon, I received a call from Sam. I went to my office where we had a direct line to the base office to take the call. Sam informed me that the "higher-ups were anxiously anticipating the completion of Fahdi's and my report on our deployment. He told me in no uncertain terms that the report better be completed by the end of my shift. He also told me the station chief wanted to ask about the trip. When I hung up with Sam I went back over to Fahdi's office and told him we'd better finish our report so I wouldn't have to put up with any more harassment from Sam–the less time I had to spend talking to Sam, the happier I was.

A couple of hours into the report, we went out for a smoke break. When we passed Abu Zaid's office on our way back in, we noticed he was sitting at his desk with his head in his hands.

"Hey, what's up with Abu Zaid?" I asked Fahdi, stopping in front of Abu Zaid's office. "Is he just tired?"

"I don't know," he answered with a shrug. "I'll go check on him."

Fahdi went in and started talking to Abu Zaid, but since the exchange was in Arabic, I didn't know exactly what was said. I observed from the hallway, but when I saw Fahdi's expression go from concerned to serious I headed in to see what was going on.

"What is it? What's wrong?" I asked as I entered the office.

"My brother," Abu Zaid simply replied.

I turned to Fahdi for an explanation.

"Hajji Haitham went missing a few days ago," Fahdi explained. "Abu Zaid just found out that he was arrested by the Interior Ministry police force."

I recalled the day Hajji Haitham gave me the antique Iraqi coin. I pictured his wide childlike smile sunken into his round almost cherub face and his eyes that twinkled as he told me stories of his country's history. I sunk down on the couch across from Abu Zaid's desk and imagined what Hajji Haitham was probably going through. The Iraqi Interior Ministry (IM) and the INIS were rival forces. The INIS was funded and run by U.S. agencies and employed mainly Sunni Iraqis, many of which had former government experience acquired under Saddam's regime. Whereas the Interior Ministry officials and high-ranking officers were being covertly funded with Iranian money, managed by members of the Iranian Secret Service, and publicly staffed by Iraqi Shi'ites loyal to Iran. You can see where a conflict of interest might arise.

The IM was in charge of the country's internal security and controlled the Iraqi Police but also spawned their own illegal force called the Badr Brigade, which they utilized as a commando unit but had evolved into a killing squad. The Badr Brigade was a significant spark that contributed to the sectarian violence in Iraq following the fall of Saddam. The militia hunted down Sunnis, mainly those who had held government positions under Saddam, and tortured and murdered them. Mutilated bodies of former Iraqi government agents and prominent Sunnis were found dumped in Baghdad alleys on a daily basis. Many of the bodies were riddled with holes from power drills, showed signs of electrical shock, and exhibited evidence of other torture techniques.

Many employees wanted the INIS to start its own militia to counter the Interior Ministry's and protect INIS employees, but like U.S. intelligence agencies, the INIS was not constitutionally allowed to create and control an armed force of its own. The only protection the INIS employees were offered was the relative safety of the building and its Green Zone location, which was why a majority of the employees lived in the building and only ventured out into Baghdad proper when necessary. A lot of the immediate families of the employees were sent to live in Jordan and Syria for their protection.

U.S. officials, at least those on the ground in Baghdad, knew this underground war was starting. I remember Tom talking about Iranian spies inside the INIS building and the ever-growing issue of the Badr Brigade soon after I arrived in Iraq, but it was such a delicate situation no one knew exactly how to handle the issue. It was a classic case of two powerful nations battling it out on the soil of a third country—much like the way the U.S. and Soviet Union faced each other in Cuba. Iraq was still such a fragile house of cards, and the U.S. didn't want to cause the entire country to collapse while trying to root out the corruption within the government.

In November 2005, a handful of U.S. military leaders and government intelligence officials in Baghdad finally convinced the U.S. to take some action against the Interior Ministry's illegal activities. The atrocities of the Badr Brigade were exposed to the world when U.S. forces raided one of the IM's large detention centers in Baghdad and discovered nearly 200 undocumented prisoners. A journalist on the scene during the liberation described the inmates as resembling concentration camp survivors– emaciated and showing visible signs of torture and mistreatment. But this was only a small victory, and the war was far from over. The Iraqi Interior Ministry received merely a slap on the wrist, and the Badr Brigade continued their operations, establishing more secret prisons along the way.

Needless to say, Abu Zaid's brother's fate was bleak. He was most likely being held in one of the IM's secret prisons, and finding him would be like searching for a needle in a haystack. Fahdi and I told Abu Zaid how sorry we were and reluctantly returned to our report. We were both preoccupied with worries for Abu Zaid and his poor brother, but we managed to finish the report before the end of my shift. I saved the report to a thumb drive and stuck it in my backpack to take back to the base for Sam.

When it was time for me to leave for the night, Fahdi, as usual, accompanied me out to the parking lot to make sure I got safely into the White Elephant. When we stepped off the elevator, we noticed a group of men in suits gathered in the lobby. The group appeared to be mostly Americans with a couple of Iraqis sprinkled in. Fahdi and I just continued to the back door of the building, but we were intercepted by one of the men from the group. He was a tall and slender American and looked to be in his late forties. He quickly excused himself from the group and rushed over to us.

"Hi, are you Mandy and Fahdi?" He asked with a broad smile.

Fahdi and I shot each other *who-the-hell-is-this* looks. I nodded and he thrust out his hand and introduced himself.

"I'm Charles, the new chief of station here in Baghdad."

This was the big boss in charge of the CIA in this location. I put on my nice face, and Fahdi and I both shook his hand.

"I arrived while you two were still out on your forward deployment, but I've heard all about you and your mission. You guys did some great work out there and I've been hoping to meet you."

He asked me to meet him at 9 a.m. the next morning at his office in the embassy for a one-on-one to discuss our mission in AQ.

I headed over to the embassy a little early because the place is humungous and I wasn't quite sure where Charles's office was located. The compound was always crawling with U.S. government officials in suits and ties, so I avoided it like the plague. I loved my job but hated all the bureaucratic B.S. that went along with it. Once inside the main building, I climbed a large, winding marble staircase to the second floor and began searching door-by-door for Charles's office number. When I found the door with his name on it I knocked, but there was no answer. I tried the knob, but the door was locked. There was a chair outside his office, so I sat down and waited. Within minutes, I saw Charles briskly walking down the hallway toward me with a smile.

"Hey, Mandy," he greeted me enthusiastically. "Sorry I'm late. I hope I didn't keep you waiting too long," he said as he dug in his pocket for his office keys.

"I don't think you *are* late," I said glancing at my watch. It was 9 a.m. on the dot. "I just got here myself. It's a good thing I left a few minutes early because it took me a little while to find your office," I explained as we entered his office. "I've only been over here a couple of times and I just followed Tom around."

"Only a couple of times?" He asked with surprise. I worried for a second that I'd said something wrong, but his jovial tone returned. "You don't come over here to use the pool? Everyone comes for the pool."

I wanted to tell him I have no desire to partake in the unofficial hot-body contest that went on daily at the embassy pool, but I just said I preferred the small pool at our base because it was closer. The embassy pool was constantly packed with American girls in string bikinis and guys who obviously spent more hours working out in the gym than rebuilding a country.

Charles's office was surprisingly small and simple considering he was the head of the CIA in central Baghdad. It held a desk with a computer, a couple of chairs, and a large filing cabinet with pictures of his two daughters stuck to the side with a magnet. We sat down and spent the next hour talking about my time so far in Iraq and the deployment to AQ. He asked me what I thought of Tom and Sam and I told him the truth. I told him I felt Tom was a far superior leader who knew the mission much better and was personally easier to get along with. I explained what occurred on our way back from AL-Qa'im and how it was a bad first impression of Sam that left me with a bad taste in my mouth. Like a good diplomat, Charles neither positively nor negatively endorsed either of my bosses. He simply listened to what I told him and nodded.

"I'm also really interested in knowing how you're getting along with the Iraqi employees out at the INIS building," he said moving on. "You're working side-by-side with some pretty intense fellows that used to work in Saddam's intelligence agency. How have they accepted working with a female, if I may ask?"

"Actually, the experience has been positive all around," I answered. "I've learned a lot from them and I think they've learned from me, too. I never felt like I was being discriminated against at all and I've had a really enjoyable time out there," I finished with a smile to myself.

"Well, that is really great to hear," he said, leaning back in his chair with a genuine smile. "Some were a little skeptical of sending a young woman out there, but I'm glad everything worked out. You guys did an outstanding job and that's really what I wanted to tell you this morning."

After the meeting, I returned to my room and began getting ready for my night shift at the building. About an hour before my departure, Sam contacted me on the radio and asked me to come to the base office before I left for the building.

"Hey, I read your report," Sam said when I walked in the office. "It'll suffice for the higher-ups, but you need to classify it properly before I disseminate it to the agencies."

"Well, it's the same report Fahdi translated for the Iraqis, so it can't really be classified since none of the Iraqis technically have security clearances. You want me to just mark everything unclassified?"

"No, go ahead and classify the whole thing as secret. It's just a formality to cover our butts."

"Okay, no problem," I relented just to shut him up. "But considering it's already been passed on to the Iraqis, it's kind of useless."

Chapter 16

Thursday, 23 August–Friday, 2 September 2005

I anxiously counted down the days until Fahdi's and my mini-vacation in Jordan. It was bittersweet because I knew we would have the most amazing time together, but when it was over, I had no idea when we'd see each other again. I'd done some research online and even if we were married, it could take eighteen months to three years to get a foreign spouse a visa to come to the United States–and possibly longer if the foreign spouse was Middle-Eastern. I wanted us to have a civil marriage performed in Jordan so that I could apply for his visa as soon as I returned to the U.S., but Fahdi was skeptical. He wanted to try and get to the U.S. on his own because he was afraid of people thinking he used me just to get a green card. But I didn't care what anyone thought. I just wanted him out of Iraq as soon as possible. God only knew how much longer he'd survive.

Work became more demanding following my return from Al-Qa'im. Since I was now the most senior member of the team and Sam wasn't worth the oxygen he consumed, I had to take up his slack as well. His performance was so poor that Abu Zaid considered lodging a formal complaint with the chief of station to have Sam replaced, but we didn't know who would replace him. It was a total crapshoot, and we had the chance of ending up with someone even worse. We heard through the grapevine that Tom was in the process of preparing to return to Iraq in the next few months, so we decided it would be best just to hold out until then and hopefully, Tom would be able to clean up after Sam. In the meantime, I was the go-to-girl. My shifts up at the building went from eight hours to fifteen hours, and I was constantly on call when I wasn't at the building. I was awoken numerous times in the middle of the night to resolve issues over the phone or make my way to the base office in my pajamas where I could get on to a computer linked with the building.

Sam was just a figurehead. He spent most of his time at the base (in the cafeteria) or brushing shoulders with important officials at the embassy swimming pool cabana. He made it to the building only two or three times a week and, on those visits, he just walked through and shook hands with some of the employees and reveled in the attention showered upon him. I was the one they called when the equipment malfunctioned or there were mission-related questions. I felt alone and out of my league. I missed Seth and Tom and wished I'd paid more attention while they were there.

Toward the end of another exhausting day, I went over to Fahdi's office to get the latest reports. To my surprise, Fahdi's office was packed with employees from throughout the department, carrying on a tense discussion in Arabic. I knew something was wrong by the grave looks on their faces.

"Hey, what's going on?" I asked as I pushed through the crowd to Fahdi's desk.

"Another one of the INIS employees was kidnapped yesterday," Fahdi informed me.

I immediately thought of Abu Zaid's brother who was still missing. "Oh God, another one?"

"A new guy. He's only twenty-two and just started working here a few weeks ago," Fahdi said.

"Was it Badr forces again?"

"Most likely," Fahdi said with a nod.

Before I could say anything else, a few of the guys in the room began throwing questions at me in both Arabic and broken English. I looked to Fahdi for help with translating.

"They want you to report this to your bosses and get the American forces to organize some kind of protection for employees here and go after the Badr forces."

With Fahdi translating, the group kept pressing me with questions and closing in on me.

"Why haven't you found Abu Zaid's brother yet?" one asked in my right ear.

"We help the Americans but they no protect us!" I heard from the left.

"Our families are being attacked because we work with you!"

I shot Fahdi a wide-eyed look as the hostility of the group increased. He read my plea for help and sprung up from his desk. He shouted angrily at the crowd in Arabic. The crowd quieted down but stood their ground.

"I said get out!" Fahdi practically screamed in English and he pulled my 9mm out of the holster on my hip. He did not point it at anyone, but they got the message and left the office. He slammed the door and locked it. I sank into a chair and put my head in my hands.

"Are you okay?" He asked putting a hand on my shoulder. I just nodded. "They didn't mean any harm. They're just scared."

"I know, this whole situation just sucks," I said into my hands. "I'm just as frustrated as they are. I don't know why the U.S. isn't doing more. They say it's not our place to get involved, but how can it not be? We came here and dismantled the entire country and people are now getting kidnapped every day and being slaughtered, and supposedly it's not our business? This whole war is going to be a huge waste of our time if we don't finish what we started. We had the balls to roll in here and take down a regime, but we won't stand up to the thugs now running wild–it makes no sense at all." I looked up at Fahdi. "I'm truly sorry we did this to your country. We started out well, but I know we're going to screw it all up."

*****

That night, my ringing cell phone woke me from a sound sleep. I glanced at my watch and saw it was just after 2 a.m. I figured it was work calling about something, so I moaned and reached for the phone. I looked at the screen and was surprised to see it was actually Shawn. *Why the hell is he calling me in the middle of the damn night?*

"Hello," I answered groggily.

"What the hell, Mandy? You love him?" Shawn spat in a disgusted tone.

"Excuse me?" I said coming out of my daze.

"I just read the little e-card you sent your translator, Fahdi, I believe his name is. You told him you *love* him and will *always* be there for him? Are you kidding me! I knew you were screwing someone else! I *knew* it!"

"You hacked into my email?!"

"Yes, as a matter of fact, I did," he replied haughtily. "Big deal–I think that's minimal compared to what you've been doing the past few months. You *whore*! No, whore is too good of a title for you–you're sleeping with a sand nigger! I can't believe this! You know he's using you. He's probably a Jihad terrorist. How can you be so stupid? You can kiss your career goodbye–that's for sure. God, I can't believe this. You disgust me."

As he berated me, I had a million thoughts running through my mind. He must have been monitoring my emails for at least the past month. I'd sent several emails to my mother and sister telling them about Fahdi, but never completely detailed how intimate our relationship was. That was also how he knew about my return to Baghdad from Al-Qa'im and was able to scare the hell out of my mother.

"Well it's none of your damn business," I finally said. "We broke up. Or don't you remember?"

"This isn't about us. You're committing a security violation, and I have no choice but to report it to the agency," he shot back in a spiteful tone and hung up on me.

Son of a... I was already more than willing to give up my security clearance, and ultimately my career, for Fahdi, it just pissed me off that Shawn was going to be the one spearheading the operation.

Wednesday, August 31, I went to work at the building around 10 a.m., as usual. But an hour after my arrival, I received a phone call from Sam. He told me I needed to come back to the base for our weekly team meeting at noon. I hated our meetings not only because they were boring, but because I had to look at Sam for an hour or more as he conducted the meeting as if he was giving the State of the Union address to the nation. Before I left for the base, I stopped by Fahdi's office to let him know I was leaving for a meeting and I'd be back later that afternoon. I didn't feel like lugging my backpack back and forth with me, so I left it in Fahdi's office and asked him to keep an eye on it until I returned.

When I got back to the base, I found Sam alone in the office. "Where is everyone for the meeting?" I asked confused.

"Oh, just hang out here for a minute, I'll be right back," Sam answered and then flew out the door.

I could tell he was acting weird, but I just shrugged it off and took a seat in one of the desk chairs. I was starting to get a little restless when the office door finally opened again nearly twenty minutes later. Sam came back in followed by a man and a woman I didn't know. I vaguely recognized the woman because I'd seen her a couple of times in the guard shack at the main gate, so I was pretty sure she was a member of the security detail. *This can't be good.*

The three of them all sat down around me, and Sam broke the tense silence. "Mandy, these folks are here to discuss your relationship with Fahdi."

Uh-oh.

Although I half expected something like this, the fact that it happened so quickly caught me off guard. The man I didn't recognize spoke next and politely introduced himself.

"Hi, Mandy, my name is Greg Larkin and I'm head of the Special Security Office here at the base. It was reported to us that you are possibly having a personal relationship with one of the local nationals."

Local national? It was the first slice I received from the dagger of double standards that would be held over my head for many months to follow. Fahdi had been a voluntary participant assisting the U.S. mission for the past three years. He'd helped the Marines kick in doors during night raids in Ramadi. He'd been shot in a firefight. He'd suffered broken bones while patrolling with the Army. He'd put his life and his family's lives at risk to help the coalition forces in Iraq, and, most recently, he'd been the translator for a successful U.S.-mandated intelligence mission. But now that we were having an affair, he was nothing more than a *local national*.

Although I was seething at the double standard, I knew it was in my best interest to remain silent. So I quietly sat there as Larkin told me I was to be ejected from the country and sent back to the U.S. where there would be an investigation into my relationship.

"The arrangements have already been made," Sam added when Mr. Larkin finished. "You'll fly out on a chopper to Baghdad International tonight at 7 p.m. You'll spend the night there and then continue on to Amman tomorrow afternoon, and then your flight to the States will leave the following morning. You'll be met at the airport by security officials on the U.S. end."

"Brenda here will accompany you for the remainder of your time in country," Mr. Larkin said, pointing to the woman who was now my guard.

She was tall, in her mid-thirties, and rather butch-looking with short blond hair. She regarded me with a look of disgust, so I quickly averted my gaze and stared at Sam.

"Before we send you off to pack, we're going to need you to hand over all your weapons as well as all cellular telephones and any other communication devices you have on your person or in your possession," Mr. Larkin instructed. "You can keep your laptop computer with you, but it must remain closed and powered off until you are out of the country. Once you are on the plane to Jordan, you'll be on your own. You'll be free to contact your family in Jordan, but I highly recommend you refrain from contacting any foreign nationals."

"You mean Fahdi," I said harshly.

"Especially him," Mr. Larkin said in a stressed tone.

"I don't believe this," I muttered to myself as I handed Mr. Larkin my 9mm pistol, cell phones, and radio. "I left my backpack at the building. Can you have someone get it for me?" I asked Sam.

"Not a problem, you'll have it before you leave," Sam said with a tone of compassion in his voice that surprised me. I felt the lump in my throat grow bigger.

I didn't want these people to see me cry, so I clenched my teeth and said with a set jaw, "Okay, let's go."

"The chopper for BIAP leaves at 1900, so that gives you…" Mr. Larkin's voice trailed off because I was already out the door and down the office steps before he finished.

The tears were already burning my eyes and I couldn't handle listening to any more. All of Fahdi's and my plans were blowing up in my head. Our week together in Jordan was now gone. I wouldn't even be able to say goodbye to him before leaving Iraq. I didn't know when I'd be able to speak to him again and God only knew when or if I'd ever see him again. I also knew my career was in serious jeopardy, but that didn't matter to me at all. I already knew I'd have to choose between Fahdi and my career and the choice was simple. Brenda was a shadow on my heels as I made my way to my room, but I was thankful that she at least remained quiet as the fire burned in my mind. We arrived at my room and I began the daunting task of packing up four months' worth of living in a couple of hours. I'd acquired a lot of additional belongings since arriving in Iraq: gifts from the U.S., souvenirs from Iraq, presents from Fahdi, etc. I had planned to ship them back home prior to my departure because I knew I wouldn't have room for everything in my luggage. I was forced to pick through everything and choose what I'd take and what I'd have to leave behind, which was nearly half of my belongings. Brenda sat silently at my desk with her arms folded across her chest watching my every move as I scurried around my room, packing. The disgusted look that let me know she felt I was subhuman never left her face.

"Alright, I think I'm done," I announced as I closed the zipper on my last bag.

"We'll go to my trailer and wait there until it's time to catch the chopper," Brenda informed me.

No one had shown up yet from the building with my backpack so I was worried I'd be gone before they got back with it. I asked Brenda to call Sam and see if they were on their way with it and let them know where we'd be until the chopper left. After two hours of sitting in silence in Brenda's trailer, there was a knock at the door. She answered the door and I caught a glimpse of Richard standing on the steps with my backpack. I got up to retrieve my backpack from Richard, but Brenda snatched the bag out of his hands and practically slammed the door in his face before we could even say a word to each other. But before the door closed between us, Richard gave me a quick little nod. I felt like a rat trapped in a shoebox. I knew by now Fahdi was going crazy, wondering where I was and I desperately wanted to just talk to him for two minutes. Although everyone was told to keep quiet about the whole situation, Richard's nod gave me hope that he would get some kind of word back to Fahdi about what was going on.

A quarter to seven, Brenda and I gathered up my luggage and headed to the convoy staging area. I loaded my luggage into the back of one of the dark SUVs and climbed into the back seat. Six elated individuals obviously on their way home, too, joined us in the SUV. We were heading home, away from the sand, sun, and blood of Iraq, but I was the only one not smiling. When we got to the LZ, everyone hopped out and started unloading their luggage, but since I was forbidden to speak to anyone, Brenda told me to remain in the vehicle until the choppers arrived. I leaned over and rested my forehead on the seat in front of me and prayed to God to protect Fahdi and keep him safe until we could get this whole situation straightened out.

The choppers were nearly two hours late when I finally I noticed the wind whip up the layer of dust that covered the LZ and helicopters descended from the pitch-black desert sky. Once the other passengers were settled onto the choppers, Brenda jogged toward the vehicle and motioned for me to board the lead chopper with her. Two gentlemen offered to give up their seats so that Brenda and I didn't have to sit on the floor. I ended up with a seat directly in front of one of the few open window portholes. This wasn't a safe place to be, but I was happy to be near the open window. Being able to look out and feel the breeze on my face helped ease the knot in my stomach and kept me from getting motion sickness. As we flew over Baghdad, the city below was unusually bright and peaceful. It was the last day of August, and although I was in a foreign land, I immediately noticed the change in the air as it blew across my cheeks. Summer was coming to an end. As I gazed into the sea of lights, thoughts of Fahdi never escaped my mind. I knew he was somewhere out there doing his best to survive, and I knew he was thinking of me, too. I just hoped that somehow, someday I would see him again.

After landing at B.I.A.P. we were all driven to the same transit house I stayed at when I arrived in country nearly four months prior. It felt so strange. The first time I was there I was so scared and nervous, but I kept telling myself that in just a few months I would come back through and be happily on my way home. I never imagined my trip home would be more depressing than my arrival. The cargo plane that would take me to Jordan was scheduled for 1300 the next afternoon, so we would be spending the night and much of the next day at the transit house. Since the transit house was equipped with telephones and an internet room, communication devices I was strictly prohibited from being near, Brenda holed us up in one of the rooms and only let me leave to cross the hall to use the restroom and eat meals in the dining room, to which she accompanied me.

My stomach was in so many knots I picked at my dinner and breakfast the next morning. The mere thought of food made me nauseated. My nerves were shot and my mind was reeling from thoughts of Fahdi and the distress he must be going through over my sudden disappearance. Brenda told me I was allowed to read a book to help pass the time, but I couldn't get my eyes to focus on the words on the page. The minutes dragged by like days, and I couldn't stop the tornado raging inside my skull. I felt like my head would explode, so I finally did the one thing that has always been able to bring me back to center. I pulled a pen from my backpack, flipped to a blank page in the back of the book I was trying to read, and began to write. My father had given me a diary before I left for Iraq. I'd written in it nearly every day of my deployment documenting my adventure. I addressed my composition to Fahdi. It was an immediate relief to feel as if I was talking to him. I explained how sorry I was for the way I had to leave, but told him not to worry because we would be reunited someday. I promised to love him forever and swore I would never forget the beautiful memories we made together, no matter what the future held.

When it was finally time to board the plane for Jordan, Brenda escorted me on board ahead of all the other passengers.

"Well, this is the end of the line for me," Brenda stated matter-of-factly. "The shuttle will take you to your hotel in Amman and then another shuttle will take you to the international airport tomorrow morning to catch your civilian flight home. You'll be on your own in Amman, but I *highly* recommend you don't make contact with any *foreign nationals*."

She said the words "foreign nationals" like people say "child molesters." I wanted to tell her she was a bigoted bitch, but I bit my tongue. I was just happy to be rid of her. I laid my head back against the cold metal wall of the aircraft and slipped into a Dramamine-induced sleep shortly after takeoff and didn't wake until we touched down in Jordan.

When I checked in at my Hotel in Amman, my plane tickets for my flight back to the U.S. were waiting for me at the front desk. As soon as I entered my room, I ripped my laptop computer out of its case and jumped online. I logged into my instant messenger account and saw that Fahdi was online. He must have been camped out by the computer and waiting for me to sign on because he sent me a message before I could get my fingers on the keyboard.

> **Fahdi**: What happened? Why did you never come back yesterday? And why didn't you come to work today? What's going on?
>
> **Mandy**: I am in Jordan. I am so sorry.
>
> **Fahdi**: You're where?!? Oh my God. I knew something like this happened. Give me a few minutes. I'm calling you.

I gave him the name of my hotel and room number; four minutes later, my phone was ringing. I explained to Fahdi the details of what had transpired over the past twenty-eight hours.

He just kept repeating, "I can't believe they took you away from me."

I felt worse for him than I did for myself. He was trapped in a living hell, he didn't understand what was happening to me, and his heart was breaking. I did my best to reassure him, but even I didn't fully believe the words coming out of my mouth.

"I'm coming there, I'll leave right now," Fahdi said trying to fight back his emotion.

"It's no use," I said solemnly. "I'll be gone before you get here. My flight back to the U.S. leaves at 4 a.m., that's less than ten hours. I wouldn't let you come anyway, the drive from Baghdad to Amman is a suicide route, you know that."

"I don't care how dangerous it is," he pushed out through sobs.

I tried my best to hold it together, but I broke down and we cried together for several minutes. Finally, he calmed down enough to speak.

"I haven't cried like this since I was ten years old and my mother came to tell me my father was dead. I've been through a lot of crap in my life. I've seen childhood friends killed in front of me, but nothing I've ever known before can compare to the hurt I feel in my soul right now."

"This isn't the end," I said with a determined tone. "I'm going to fight for this with everything I have in me. I promise you that."

I heard a series of three short beeps on the line indicating the phone card Fahdi was using only had a couple of minutes remaining.

"Please don't forget me, Mandy. Just always remember that there is someone in Iraq who loves you more than his own life."

"I won't forget. I swear."

We said our goodbyes, and as soon as I hung up the phone, I collapsed on the giant hotel bed in a pile of tears. When I heard the chime of the instant messenger window I peeled myself off the bed and returned to the computer to continue talking to Fahdi online.

I stepped away from the computer for a few minutes to use the restroom and wash my face. When I flipped on the bathroom light I caught my reflection in the mirror and was taken aback. My eyes were completely bloodshot from crying, sunken into my skull, and ringed with dark circles. My face looked haggard and pale from lack of sleep, and although it hadn't even been a full two days, it was evident that I hadn't eaten or drunk much in the past forty-eight hours. I looked at the matching terrycloth bathrobes hanging on the wall and mourned for the romantic vacation Fahdi and I had planned but would now be greatly postponed or perhaps never occur at all. We were supposed to be sharing that big beautiful bed together. We were supposed to shower together in that spa-like bathroom. We were supposed to finally relax together without having to worry about work, someone catching us, or hearing mortars and car bombs exploding all around us. Everything was all wrong.

When I returned to the computer to resume my chat with Fahdi, I noticed my laptop's battery was running low. I was digging through my backpack to find my power supply when I came across my thumb drive from work. We weren't supposed to leave the country with the thumb drives because, although they were not technically classified, they could still contain sensitive documents or information that shouldn't be traveling internationally. I quickly popped the thumb drive in to see what all was on it. Much to my relief, the only work-related material saved on it was my Al-Qa'im trip report and the standard operating procedures manual for the forward deployment that I finished writing for Seth. Aside from these two documents, the rest of the stuff I had on the thumb drive was benign. I had some pictures saved on it and some emails and instant messenger chats between Fahdi and me. I saved these things for sentimental reasons as well as for future reference. I had researched fiancé visas and found out that if we ever wanted to apply for one I would have to provide evidence that Fahdi and I have a genuine relationship– phone records, emails, letters, instant messenger chats, etc. I saved my personal documents back onto my computer and considered destroying the thumb drive, but since I was already in deep shit, I figured that might look suspicious so I just kept it on me and planned to turn it in to the NSA security office when I got back.

Fahdi and I chatted online until the last possible minute before I had to grab my luggage and rush downstairs to catch my shuttle to the airport. I had another several-hour layover in Amsterdam, so I told Fahdi I'd try to get back online when I landed there. I made it out the main entrance of the hotel just as my airport shuttle was pulling up. I took a seat by a window and laid my head against the cool glass. During the thirty-minute drive to the airport, I stared out at the passing city. It was brightly lit but with a dusty haze common to desert cities. I vowed to return to Amman someday to stamp out the painful memories I was leaving with and replace them with happier ones.

When I made it through customs, I sat in a depressed daze and watched as the other people who would be on my flight gathered at our gate. Although the flight was bound for Amsterdam, 80% of the passengers were Americans obviously on their way home from Iraq. Most were muscular guys in their mid-thirties with military haircuts and wearing Levi jeans. They were probably government contractors for companies like Blackwater and other private security companies who had contracts in Iraq. When I arrived in Amsterdam, I once again pulled out my laptop and jumped online. I logged in and sent an instant message to Fahdi. I checked my email while I waited for a reply and found one from him.

My Love,

I want you to know that I will never let go of you and that I'm ready to do anything just to be with you. I will go anywhere, to the ends of the earth if I have to, just as long as I'm with you. I LOVE YOU SO MUCH Mandy and I want you to be my wife. I'll do anything to make this happen. Please be strong and don't be sad. I want you to be happy all the time. We will make it through this and one day we will sit together and laugh about what happened. I just want you to wait and I promise that I will make it up to you. I love you. I love you so much and I will love you until my last breath. Dying to kiss you and hold you.

Love,

Fahdi

Before I even finished reading the email, Fahdi had answered me on the instant messenger. I told him I'd made it to Amsterdam without incident and had about four hours before my next flight. Since I had no idea what they were going to do with me when I landed in the U.S., I told Fahdi not to worry if he didn't hear from me for a few days. I didn't know if they'd put me on restriction in the barracks on base, let me go home to my apartment, or, God forbid, send me to the brig. I gave him my mother's phone number and email address, figuring she would be updated on my situation and be able to pass the information along to Fahdi in case I was unable to get word out. When I mentioned restriction and the brig, Fahdi became even more frantic.

"I can't believe they're doing this to you," he typed. "I am so sorry. I don't know what to do. I feel like my heart has been ripped out of my chest. I've never felt so powerless in my life. I'm going to talk to everyone with any kind of pull here at the INIS–Abu Zaid, his boss, I'll go to the director general himself and beg for help if that's what it takes. I swear, Mandy, if they hurt you Al-Qe'da will be the least of their problems here in Iraq. I'll blow this whole place up, I swear to God I will."

"You know better than to say stuff like that on here," I warned. "They're probably already monitoring our conversations. We can't give them anything they can use as leverage against us. And don't worry, they're not going to tie me to a pole and flog me or anything like that," I joked. "My enlistment is up next August so the worst case scenario here is we will be apart for a year. We'll just have to hang on that long. You have to hang on that long. Don't worry about me. You just worry about staying alive until we can get you out of there. No matter what, just stay alive. We can overcome everything else."

It killed me inside to think that I may not see him for a year, but I thought about the thousands of military families who have put up with being separated for a year or more because of deployments and knew that Fahdi and I would survive the separation. He just had to survive physically.

Chapter 17

Friday 2, September–Tuesday, 6 September 2005

The flight from Amsterdam to Washington D.C. was the most nerve wracking seven hours of my life. I had no idea who or what awaited me at the airport. I just hoped there wasn't an embarrassing scene. Horror images of dark-suited, FBI-like agents slapping cuffs on me as soon as I emerged from customs flashed through my mind over and over again. I just kept thinking, *How did I end up like this?* As the plane closed in on the U.S., my nervousness escalated. My stomach was in complete knots, I felt nauseated, I broke out into a cold sweat, and I was covered in blotchy red hives. Who'd have thought I'd be in worse shape landing back in the U.S. than I was touching down in Baghdad. The U.S. felt like it had become the land foreign to me. I'd left a respected hero volunteering to serve her country at war and was now returning in shame.

I slowly made my way toward customs while the butterflies in my stomach swirled in full force. I kept scanning the walkways, waiting for agents to dart out and apprehend me, but no one gave me a second glance. The customs official stamped me through with no problem, and I proceeded to baggage claim. I stood by the baggage carousel waiting for my luggage when I finally caught sight of a man in a kaki Naval uniform heading my direction. I immediately recognized him; it was Senior Chief Crismond, the senior enlisted head of my unit. I didn't know him extremely well, but he was a soft-spoken pleasant guy. Much to my relief, he greeted me with a smile and welcomed me home. But he was not alone. Another Navy chief and a first class petty officer were with Crismond, and I didn't recognize either of them. A member of the Dulles airport security was also in tow. Unlike Crismond, the other three eyed me with stern expressions. They helped me retrieve my luggage. Then, in my cargo pants and t-shirt, I was escorted from the airport through the security exit surrounded by four large men in uniforms.

When we reached the government van, the airport security guard returned to the terminal and the other Navy chief introduced himself and his sidekick.

"Petty Officer McEwen," the chief started in an official tone, "My name is Chief Viraez and this is Petty Officer Simmons. I am the Chief Master-at-Arms and Simmons is the acting Master-at-Arms for Naval Security Group Activity Fort Meade."

The Master-at-Arms is responsible for law enforcement on Navy bases. They would basically be my babysitters until it was decided what would ultimately be done with me. We all climbed in the van, and once we were on the road, Chief Viraez turned from the passenger seat and addressed me again.

"Do you understand what's going on and why you were sent back?" Viraez asked.

I nodded and said yes.

He continued, "Okay, good. It has been decided that you are not a flight risk and will be released to your home for the weekend to rest up and recover from your trip. You are to report to my office in the headquarters building at 0900 on Tuesday morning, and at 0930, you have an interview with the NSA security agents to debrief you and discuss your situation. Also, I am to pass a direct order to you from the Commanding Officer that you are not to have contact with any foreign nationals, at least until after your interview on Tuesday. Do you understand this?"

Again, I nodded and gave him a simple yes answer. I knew Fahdi and I would go crazy without being able to talk to each other for four days, but since I also knew our emails and phone lines were probably already tapped, it would land me in even hotter water if I disobeyed a direct order from my CO. I just prayed that after Tuesday, we'd be permitted to communicate again. I would be able to talk to my mother and I just hoped Fahdi would get in touch with her.

When we pulled up in front of my townhouse, I noticed Shawn's truck parked next to my Ford Ranger. *Nice.* While Viraez and Crismond were helping me unload my luggage from the van, Shawn emerged from his vehicle and walked over to us. He gave me a quick welcome back from Iraq hug, but I remained limp. I was seething inside, but I didn't want to make a scene and he knew it. I gave him a simple hi and he turned his attention to senior Chief Crismond. He and Crismond knew each other from work and got along well so they shook hands and said hello to each other. While Shawn and Crismond chatted, Viraez reminded me what time I was to report to his office on Tuesday and reiterated the instructions of the no-contact order. I told him I understood and then they got back in the van and drove away, leaving me alone with Shawn.

Without saying a word to Shawn I began dragging my bags into my house. I wasn't able to carry them all in one trip, so Shawn followed behind with the one I wasn't able to get. I dropped my bags in the living room and when I went to retrieve the last bag he was standing in my foyer with it.

"You can go now," I said venomously as I picked up the bag.

"Come on, Mandy," he said, half pleading and half demanding. "You can't blame me for what I did. I *had* to do it, you know that."

"You have *no* idea what you have set in motion," I spat back. I fought hard to hide my pain, but tears stung my eyes and I felt their heat as they began to run down my cheeks. "You didn't *have* to hack into my email and completely invade my privacy. You know you did what you did out of jealousy and nothing more."

"Hey, I'll be totally honest and admit that my pride was hurt when I found out about you and this...guy." He said the word "guy" with a twist of disgust, obviously not sure if Fahdi was even worth being referred to as such. "But once I found out about your relationship, I had a moral obligation to report it. And I got you out of there for your own good. I didn't want you to get yourself into serious trouble or, God forbid, even killed as a result of your emotions."

"Ah yes, my knight in shining armor," I announced mockingly. "You don't have the right to be 'hurt' by anything I do. You're the one who torched our relationship. I spent two and a half years kissing your ass in hopes that someday you'd treat me as well as you treat your friends. You had that long, Shawn, and you barely treated me better than a one-night stand. This man treated me better from minute one than you did after two years."

"You're so naive," he said as if he was talking to a child. "You know that things will never work out between you two. They are never going to allow him into this country. He is an Iraqi male in his early twenties. It will take an act of God."

"Why are you still here? I don't even have anything of yours here that you need to take back because even after two and a half years, you weren't comfortable enough to ever stay at my place. It was always your place. Everything was your way. I was such a doormat," I said half to myself shaking my head. "You're right. I was naïve, and maybe I still am, but I sure as hell see you for what you really are now. My eyes are wide open. I do believe this is the longest span of time you've physically been in my house. Now get the hell out."

"Mandy, I still care about you and I don't want to see you throw your life away. Have you even considered that this guy could be using you? Hell, he could be a really *bad* person. Especially the way they yanked you out of the country so fast and sent you home. Maybe they did that for a reason. You're like a wide-eyed little girl lost in fairyland. You have no idea what this guy's true intentions could be."

"Look, all I know is that I've received more love, compassion, and affection from him in three months than you gave me in nearly three years, so that's enough for me to give it a shot."

"You're making a huge mistake. I just don't want to see you regret it in the end."

"Shawn, the only thing I regret is wasting two and a half years of my life on you," and with that I turned and went upstairs. I guess he got the message, because I heard my front door slam shut followed by the roar of his truck's engine as he peeled out of my parking lot.

I spent the next three days trying to get over my jet lag and wondering what the Tuesday meeting would entail. I also had fun readjusting to U.S. milk. Switching back brought on a whole new bout of cramps and diarrhea–good times. My stomach was also in knots wondering how much trouble I was actually in and wondering how Fahdi was doing. I just prayed all I'd have to do is surrender my security clearance and they'd let me quietly step away from the Navy. It took everything in me not to break the no-contact order, but I figured I'd better not dig myself any deeper of a hole than I was already in.

When Tuesday morning finally arrived, I drove myself to Fort Meade. About a mile from the exit, I saw the familiar sight of the massive, dark-glassed NSA headquarters building looming in the distance. It was the same sight I'd encountered every day I'd driven to work for the past three years. I'd only been away for four months, but the feelings that now flooded me when that building came into view were completely different. Everything had changed. I'd changed. I was so excited to be working at the National Security Agency when I started, and though many aspects of my job aggravated me, I was always proud to be working in one of the main bellies of our government's intelligence conglomerate.

I pulled up to the vehicle checkpoint at the gate and flashed my badge to the armed security guard to enter the NSA compound.

"Hey! You're back!" the guard called out, taking me by surprise.

I took a second look and realized it was Darrell, the security guard who usually worked the graveyard shift. We'd become friendly acquaintances because he was the one I usually saw when arriving to work my night shifts. I'd mentioned to him that I'd be deploying to Iraq for a few months the last time I saw him, but didn't think he'd even notice my absence considering he saw hundreds of people passing through those gates every day. At that precise moment, I was feeling like a definite nobody so it made me feel really good to be noticed and greeted by a friendly face.

"Darrell!" I called back with a smile. "What are you doing up so early? Did they switch you to the day shift?"

"Yeah, my fiancé had the baby last month, so I requested to come off the graveyard shift so I could be home with them in the evenings and at night."

"Well, congratulations. I'm so happy for you."

"How was the sandbox? I'm glad you made it back safely."

"Eh, it was war," I replied with a cynical shrug.

I glanced in my rearview mirror and noticed a line several cars deep now waiting behind me to pass through the checkpoint.

"Well, I better not hold up the flow," I said, gesturing to the waiting vehicles.

"You take care and welcome home," he said and gave the side of my car a friendly tap.

"You, too. Take care of that new baby."

The building that houses the Navy's administration offices, including the Master-at-Arms office, sat across the parking lot behind the main NSA building. When I parked my truck, I sat and stared through my windshield at the massive NSA building that I would probably never be allowed to step foot in again. I was now an outsider–kicked out of the club. I was no longer worthy of breathing the same air as those still truly dedicated to upholding our nation's security. I was a traitor who people like Darrell would never be able to look in the eye again. But it wasn't too late. I could repent. I could admit my sins, apologize for my temporary lapse in judgment, and probably be able to return to my old life. With a polygraph and a promise to never have contact with Fahdi again, they'd probably welcome me back. I could get back in.

I closed my eyes to picture it, but I didn't see a vision of a smiling me in uniform walking in to work at the NSA. I saw his face. I saw Fahdi and the look of fear in his eyes when the mortars started falling in Al-Qa'im. He was afraid for my life, not his own. I saw the look of complete love in his eyes when he kissed my lips on the roof of the INIS building beneath the desert night sky. I heard the passion in his voice when he told me I was the only person in his life not just worth dying for, but worth living for. I opened my eyes and stared at the NSA building. My eyes traveled to the top of the building and I saw Fahdi. The sun was beginning to set in Baghdad and I knew he was sitting on the roof of the INIS building smoking a cigarette while watching the sunset and thinking of me. I saw him as if he was right in front of me. I could smell the desert on his skin. I could see the cigarette smoke swirling above his head. I could even feel the fine grits of sand on my face. I knew what I had to do. I knew which path I was choosing. I had to fight. I had to fight for him, for us, and I knew it was going to be a long, difficult battle.

I got out of my truck, took one last look at the NSA building, and then turned my back on it and headed for the Navy building. I made my way down the long corridor, reading the titles on the office doors as I passed until I came to the Master-at-Arms's office. I closed my eyes and took a deep breath, and then opened the door. I told the female petty officer at the desk who I was and that I was told by Chief Viraez to report to him at 0900. She told me to have a seat and gestured to a blue doctor's office looking couch sitting against the wall across from her desk. When she got up and went over to an adjoining office, I noticed several other Navy personnel seated on other chairs in the office with grim looks on their faces. The Master-at-Arms's office was basically the equivalent to the principal's office, and I figured the others were there for minor violations such as showing up late for work, underage drinking, failing a drug urinalysis test, etc.

A few minutes later, Chief Viraez was standing in front of me. "Good morning, Petty Officer McEwen. Are you ready to head out?"

I nodded.

We took a government vehicle to one of the NSA satellite offices on the other side of the base. We sat in the lobby for nearly an hour until a tall slender guy approached us in his early thirties, with sandy brown hair and blue eyes. He was wearing a business suit and held a soft-shelled briefcase. He had a frat-boy look to him.

"Good morning, Amanda, I'm Special Agent Argyle," he introduced himself with a kind smile, but I sensed a used-car-salesman tone in his voice. "Before we head up to the office, I am going to need your NSA badge."

And so it begins. I removed my NSA badge from around my neck and handed it over to Argyle, who slipped it into his pants pocket. That badge had been a part of my daily work attire for three years. It was physical proof that I held a Top Secret clearance and I used it to gain access to almost every building on the NSA compound. In its place,

Argyle handed me a bright red tag that read "VISITOR," a scarlet letter that let everyone know I was no longer in the club. Chief Viraez remained in the lobby while Agent Argyle led me upstairs to a small, sterile-looking windowless room furnished with nothing but a metal table and three metal folding chairs. *Oh boy.*

"Just so you're aware, there is also going to be an agent from the Naval Criminal Investigative Service present while we talk. This is simply protocol due to the fact that you are active duty Navy," Argyle informed me as we entered the room. I took a seat in one of the chairs while Argyle laid his briefcase on the table, opened it and began rummaging through it. As he was pulling things out, there was a light knock on the door.

"Come on in," Argyle called out while he continued to pull things out of his case.

The door opened and a slender dark-haired woman, who also looked to be in her mid-thirties, walked in.

"Sorry I'm running late," she said and extended her hand to Agent Argyle. "I'm Special Agent Andrea Foster with NCIS."

She and Argyle shook hands and then she turned to me. I stood and shook her hand.

"Hello, Petty Officer McEwen, allow me to present my credentials," she added and pulled out her badge and NCIS identification. "We just need to ask you a few questions. Hopefully, we won't take up too much of your time," she said with a fake smile.

This can't *be happening. I'm hallucinating or dreaming. I just know it. Is this seriously happening?*

"Just to let you know, we are going to record this conversation. Are you comfortable with that?" Argyle asked me.

"Yeah sure, no problem," I answered, and he flipped a switch on the wall.

Agent Foster then pulled some papers from her briefcase and laid them on the table in front of me.

"Okay, before we start we have to ask you to sign these," she said.

They were the legal waive-your-rights-to-an-attorney documents and the military version of the Miranda Rights. The top of the first sheet was already conveniently filled out for me and read, "I, CTI2 Amanda McEwen, understand that I am suspected of having unauthorized foreign contact with an Iraqi National." I thought to myself, *Damn, that just sounds so bad.* But, I shrugged it off as simply more protocol. I had nothing to hide and I feared requesting a lawyer would make me look guilty, so I signed the papers.

"Great, let's get started," Argyle announced clasping his hands. "So, we simply want to hear about what happened over there between you and this, uhhh…" He shuffled through some of his notes, searching for the name. "This Fad-ee individual," he finally got out. He completely butchered Fahdi's name, but I let it go.

I proceeded to relay a synopsis of our relationship from the day we met until the day I was sent home. I left out a lot of the juicy details, but hit on all of the major points in order to paint a clear picture. I made it evident that our relationship was indeed much deeper than a friendship and told them of our plans to probably get married someday. When I was finished with my speech, the two agents glanced at each other, and I could see the apparent dissatisfaction written on their faces. They knew I wasn't telling them every detail, and that's what they needed to hear, no matter how explicit. Good thing I'm not a modest person.

"So, do you remember the exact date that your relationship say, crossed the line from friendship to intimate?" Argyle asked as apathetically as possible.

I felt my face flush and memories of Fahdi's and my first kiss on the roof flooded my head. I knew at that moment this investigation was going to be a no-holds-barred invasion of my life. I reasoned with myself that I would tell them anything I had to in order to get this situation resolved as quickly as possible. I'd paint them pictures and act out sex scenes if that was what it took. I swallowed, took a deep breath, and then told them the story of our first kiss on the roof and recounted other intimate moments Fahdi and I had shared together. I still held back some details, but they seemed to be satisfied with what I gave them.

Once they had me spilling details of our sex life out for the record, they moved on with the questioning. They asked me if I'd ever visited Fahdi's home in Baghdad or if I'd ever met his family. I told them I knew his brother because he also worked in the INIS building in our department. They also asked if we spoke outside of work and I told them we chatted on instant messenger online and spoke regularly over the phone. I told them I made him call me every day when he got home to make sure he made it back safely. Finally, they asked me if Fahdi had plans to come to the United States. I told them he wanted to apply for a tourist visa and had an appointment the following week with the U.S. embassy in Jordan to get more information about obtaining a U.S. visa. Both agents perked up at this information.

"Do you know the exact date of his appointment?" Argyle asked me.

"September 15," I answered. "Next Thursday."

They both scribbled in their notebooks and then looked at each other.

"Well, all of this seems pretty cut and dry," Argyle commented, closing his notebook. "The agency, and probably NCIS as well, might ask you to take a polygraph just to rule out any forms of espionage or improper disclosure of classified material. Also, since your security clearance has been temporarily suspended, a polygraph will be required if you wish to appeal to have it reinstated." Argyle then looked at Foster and said, "Well, that's about all I have. Did you have anything else you wanted to add?"

"Umm, no. I think that's it for me, too," she said reaching for her briefcase.

Both agents began packing up their briefcases and then Argyle snapped his fingers, remembering something.

"Oh yes, there is one more thing. Would it be possible for us to have a look at your laptop computer and any kind of information storage devices you brought back with you from Iraq?"

I immediately remembered the thumb drive I'd inadvertently returned home with, and I knew from the look in Argyle's eyes that this thumb drive was exactly what he was talking about. *How the hell did they already know about it?* The only person I had even mentioned the thumb drive to was my mother. I told her about it when I called her the day I got back. When I remembered this, bells and whistles went off in my head. I realized my cell phone was already tapped and being monitored. I was in some deep doo-doo.

My jaw clenched as I tried to mask my sudden anxiety at this realization.

In a calm, steady voice that I hoped conveyed my willingness to cooperate and prove I had nothing to hide I simply said, "Yeah sure, no problem. When they ejected me from the country I came across my thumb drive from work in my backpack. Luckily there was really nothing on it, but you are more than welcome to have it. I meant to bring it today to give to the Security Office but I forgot it on my dresser."

"Do you live far from here?" Foster asked. "Would it be possible for us to drive you out to your house to pick these items up?"

"It's no problem at all," I said shaking my head. "I live only about fifteen minutes from here."

On the way out to the parking lot, Argyle and I stopped by the visitor's center lobby to let Chief Viraez know what was going on. "I'm going to have to follow you all in our van, if that's ok," Viraez told Argyle. "The

Commanding Officer wants me to stay with her at all times."

Great, this just keeps getting better.

When the four of us arrived at my house, I ran upstairs to collect my laptop and the thumb drive and then handed them over to the agents. They filled out a confiscation receipt for me denoting the description and serial number of each item. Epic waste of time; I never saw my $1,600 laptop again.

The agents departed in their shared vehicle, and I climbed in the van with Chief Viraez so I could return to Fort Mead and retrieve my truck.

On our way back to Fort Meade, I asked the chief, "So, what happens now?"

He merely shrugged his shoulders and replied, "We just wait to hear from them."

I hate waiting, but I would soon become extremely good at it. This marked the beginning of the longest, most painful, and mind-numbing waiting game I have ever played in my life.

Chapter 18

Tuesday, 6 September–Friday, 16 September 2005

For the next week, I reported to the Master-at-Arms' office every morning at 0730 and hung out there in the office or around the Navy building doing odd jobs like pulling weeds and cleaning bathrooms. It sucked, but I guess I was lucky I hadn't been restricted to the base and was free to return home every evening. I realize now they gave me that freedom because they were monitoring me and were giving me enough rope to potentially hang myself. Both my phone and Internet communications were being monitored in an attempt to gather more evidence against me and discern what information Fahdi and I were sharing.

Since the no-contact order was only in effect until after the interview, I jumped back into contact with Fahdi the very evening following my meeting with the agents. Needless to say, he was ecstatic to finally hear from me and he wanted to know every detail regarding what was going on with the investigation against us. I told him all about the interview with the agents and about them taking my computer. I stopped by the PX and dropped a few hundred dollars on a replacement laptop so Fahdi and I could remain in touch. I also told him that I'd informed the agents of his plans to go to the U.S. embassy in Amman to inquire about receiving a visa to the U.S. He told me he was still planning to head out that Tuesday, two days before his appointment because it was a good twelve-hour drive from Baghdad to Amman.

I begged him to take a commercial flight because the road between Baghdad and Amman had been dubbed the most dangerous drive on the planet. The route was riddled with terrorists, criminals, insurgents, thieves, freedom fighters, and just plain pissed off individuals that attacked vehicles going between Baghdad and the Jordanian border at every point. The road cut directly through the heart of the Sunni Triangle and passed through some of the roughest towns in Iraq, including Fallujah, which still had not calmed down since the showdown between U.S. Marines and terrorists following the bloody massacre of the Blackwater contractors. He told me to try not to worry and that he'd be okay.

"I've made it this far and have survived a lot of crazy stuff," he said. "I don't think I'm destined to die on a road-trip."

During my first week of working for the Master-at-Arms' office, I got to know the other individuals who were also stuck there, going through their own issues. I got along well with the others and found them quite interesting, even though they were the bad apples of our unit.

After a week of waiting, Chief Viraez informed me that the NCIS and NSA agents wanted to meet with me again. We went back to the same building and met again in the same little windowless room. Before starting, I was once again asked to sign away my rights to an attorney. Once I signed the waiver, Andrea, the NCIS agent, pulled a document from her briefcase, laid it on the table in front of me, and began reading it aloud to me.

"I, Amanda McEwen, hereby acknowledge that I violated the Uniform Code of Military Justice (UCMJ) Articles #192 and #34 for failing to disclose an unauthorized foreign contact and improper transfer of classified information. Due to these violations, I understand that I am suspected of illicit disclosure of classified information and espionage."

I stopped her at the word "espionage."

"Whoa," I said putting my hands up to stop her cadence. "Excuse me, but what? Espionage? Are you serious?"

"Amanda," Agent Argyle cut in with a sigh, "we have some questions to ask you about what we discovered on your laptop and the thumb drive you provided us with."

He pulled out two documents from his briefcase and laid them in front of me. They were my trip report that I wrote about Al-Qa'im and the Al-Qa'im Standard Operating Procedures manual that I finished up for Seth.

"This first document," he said, gesturing to the trip report, "is clearly marked with the classification identifier Secret at the top of the page. Can you explain *why* you had this in your personal possession when you returned from Iraq?"

"I already told you," I blurted out defensively, "that thumb drive was used for my work out in Iraq. Everyone on our team carried one around with them. It was in my backpack when they threw me out of the country. I didn't even realize I still had it until I discovered it in my hotel in Jordan. If I was trying to hide anything, I had ample opportunity to pitch it or destroy it while en route back to the U.S. I wouldn't voluntarily hand it over to you the way I did."

"Yes, but we also discovered that the document was written on your personal laptop computer? As you well know, classified documents are not to be drafted or saved on unclassified mediums, including personal laptops or storage media," Andrea added.

"Yes, I understand this. When I wrote the report, I was under the impression that it was not to be classified because it had to be distributed to our Iraqi counterparts, who hold no U.S.-sanctioned security clearances via their unclassified computer system. However, when I submitted the report to the U.S. side, my bosses told me to give it a 'secret' classification heading for the official copy submitted to the agency. I questioned this and brought up the issue of how everything contained in the report was common knowledge amongst many of our uncleared Iraqi counterparts and was told that it was simply protocol."

"So you are admitting that you plugged the same thumb drive into a classified computer system that you also used with your personal laptop computer as well as the unclassified Iraqi computer system at their agency?" Argyle asked in a threatening tone.

"Look, I am not *admitting* to *anything*," I retorted. "These thumb drives are used to transfer data between their agency and ours. It is a common procedure that might not be 100% kosher by agency regulation here in the U.S., but in Iraq, it's what we had to do to get the job done." I hated pulling the I-was-simply-following-orders card, but I was in self-preservation mode by now. "I was merely doing what I was told and following the examples set by my more experienced coworkers and bosses. I refuse to be the scapegoat for this foul up. And I have no idea how I can be suspected of espionage and sharing classified information with individuals who had just as much knowledge and access to this information as I did. We all worked together on the same missions. There were no separate U.S rooms, and the intelligence was not even gathered by U.S. individuals. It was all collected by the Iraqis. We were simply assisting them with the finance of their equipment and training of their personnel. In return, they allowed us to disseminate the intelligence they gathered to U.S. and coalition forces. So this whole thing is ridiculous!" I felt my face flush with anger and despair for the unexpected turn of events.

"We are simply trying to find out what went on over there between you and this guy," Argyle stated calmly. "I do not personally believe you intentionally committed espionage. I am sure that you are no spy. But I am afraid that this guy might have been trying to use you. Do you understand now why we had to pull you out of the country so fast?"

I gave him a stony stare and shook my head in disbelief.

Argyle continued, "Regardless, it is not our decision to make. These things get forwarded way above agent Foster and myself and the evidence is stacking up against you."

"Over the next week, we are going to draft up a statement that we would like you to sign and swear to," Agent Foster interjected.

"Okay, whatever," I said curtly.

As the agents escorted me out the front of the building, I glanced at my watch and saw that we had spent six hours in that tiny room–the most strenuous six hours of my life. I made a call to the Master-at-Arms's office, and Simmons came to pick me up.

When Simmons pulled up in the government van, he must have noticed the anguish on my face.

"The accusations were flying weren't they," he stated in a knowing tone.

I was unable to speak around the giant lump in my throat, so I just nodded as I stared out the window.

"You need to get to a lawyer," he suggested. "And don't sign *anything*. That's all the advice I can give you."

When I arrived to work the next morning, Chief Viraez called me into his office. "Petty Officer McEwen," he addressed me in an official tone. "I've got to issue you a written no-contact order per the Commanding Officer of Naval Security Group Activity Fort Meade."

He pulled out a piece of paper that said that I was to cease all forms of communication with Fahdi or face disciplinary action under several articles of the UCMJ.

I was pissed. "Are you serious?!" I exploded. "This just gets better every day. This guy took bullets for this country and we both dodged bombs and this is how we're treated? I feel like I'm living a really *bad* Tom Clancy novel."

Viraez gave me an understanding look, but he had a job to do.

"Just sign it," he said in a calm tone. "Let them do whatever investigating they want to do and just be patient. You'll get through this."

I shook my head and scribbled my signature across the bottom of the order. "And what happens if I don't obey this order?"

"As the Chief Master-at-Arms I strongly suggest you follow this order or risk facing severe penalties under the UCMJ," he said sternly, but then his expression softened. "But sailor to sailor, I'm sure you can handle a slap on the wrist, which is most likely all it would be."

I nodded, "Thanks, Chief."

Taking Simmons's advice, I made the forty-five-minute drive to Washington D.C. after work that afternoon to meet with a JAG attorney at Naval District Washington. When I got in to meet with a JAG, I gave him a brief synopsis of my case and he gave me some basic advice.

"Do not meet with the agents again," he advised. "Nothing good can ever come from talking to them. Their job is to find guilt, not innocence."

"So I can just refuse to meet with them?" I asked uneasily since I was so used to just doing and going where I was told.

"Absolutely."

"Do I need to get a lawyer now?" I asked.

"Since you haven't been officially charged with anything, you don't need one just yet. The Navy will assign you a JAG team if or when you are charged, but until then, I would do exactly what you're doing–research. Learn your rights and I recommend looking into civilian lawyers. If you end up in really hot water, you don't want a lawyer who works for the Navy defending you against the Navy.

Get an outside lawyer and your chances of getting off will be much higher."

"Thank you so much for your advice, Sir."

I got up and went to the door, but before I could open it to leave, the JAG stopped me.

"You most likely won't have to refuse another meeting with the agents," he said with a cryptic tone in his voice.

I shot him a confused look.

"They already know you're here talking to a lawyer," he added with a wink. "And that's usually their cue that their suspect is no longer an easy target and is ready to fight back."

I nodded and gave him an appreciative smile.

Chapter 19

Saturday, 17 September–Friday, 30 September 2005

Although I begged and pleaded with him to take a flight to Jordan, Fahdi drove the twelve hours to Amman and luckily, made it through safely. He arrived at the U.S. embassy for his scheduled appointment to gather information on coming to the U.S. and thought he'd gotten really lucky when they called him in ahead of everyone else in the waiting room. Unfortunately, he wouldn't be the one getting information, but the one giving it.

Two government agents shuttled him into a room and interrogated him for five hours about our case. They asked him all of the same questions they asked me regarding our relationship and also asked about his past. They were polite and courteous, but they laughed when he asked before leaving if he could still have some information about obtaining a visa to the States.

"Look, Fahdi, do you have any idea what kind of hell you are going to put Mandy through by trying to pursue this relationship?" one of the agents asked him. "If you really care about her you will walk away and never speak to her again."

"I can't do that," Fahdi answered shaking his head. "The only way I will let this go is if she called me up herself and said she doesn't want anything to do with me anymore. Then I will walk away. But not until that happens."

"Things will never work out between you two," the other agent added. "It's impossible. The sooner you realize this, the easier this will be for everyone involved."

"Are we done here?" Fahdi asked with an icy look at the agents.

The agents exchanged exasperated glances, but relented and told Fahdi he was free to leave. But they told him to expect more people to get in touch with him back in Baghdad regarding the case.

"I'll talk to anyone I have to in order to get us through this," Fahdi told them as he stood to leave. "I'm sure you all know where to find me, I'll be waiting."

When Fahdi returned to work at the building, a couple of high-ranking agents from my former base in Baghdad met with him. They informed him in no uncertain terms that he was not to leave the country again, or Baghdad for that matter. They also asked him to sign a no-contact order of his own and a sworn affidavit that he would not travel outside of Baghdad. He refused to sign either, which didn't sit well with the agents. They told him that not cooperating would only cause more problems for us, and of course, they pulled the if-you-truly-love-this-girl-you-will-sign line, but Fahdi stood his ground.

"I'm not signing anything that says I can't talk to her," Fahdi informed them. "You have my word that I won't leave the city. You know where I work, gentlemen. I'll meet with you whenever and wherever you like and I'll tell you anything you want to know, so don't try to say you don't have my cooperation."

While at work the following week, I received a phone call from JAG lawyer Lieutenant Angela Marons, who informed me that she was recently assigned to be my attorney. I stopped breathing because I remembered what the JAG in D.C. told me: I probably wouldn't be given an attorney until I was actually brought up on charges. Since they assigned me a lawyer, I figured it meant NCIS was probably on their way to officially charging me with a crime and hauling my ass to the brig.

In a shaky voice, I asked her if this was what her being assigned to me meant, but she said there was nothing to indicate that I was being charged with anything yet. She explained the only reason the Navy decided to go ahead and assign me a lawyer is due to the severity of the *possible* charges I faced and the fact that I would require a lawyer with a Top Secret security clearance if anything went to trial.

Once I realized her call didn't mean I would be taking a trip to jail that evening, my heart started beating again and she and I discussed plans to meet. She was based out of Norfolk, Virginia, a four-hour drive south of me, so it was difficult to work out meetings since I wasn't allowed to leave the area. I thought to myself, *I'm thirty minutes from D.C. and the closest lawyer they could find me is four hours away?* Lieutenant Marons said she would be able to come up in a few days for a few hours, so we scheduled our first meeting for a Thursday morning.

On Thursday morning, I went to the JAG office on Ft. Meade and met Lt. Marons. I was relieved to finally be meeting with someone who was going to be on *my* side instead of another person I'd have to defend myself to. But the simple fact that I now had a lawyer made me feel like a criminal. Unfortunately, Lt. Marons and I didn't hit it off. When I arrived at the JAG office, she and Lt. Klitch, our resident JAG lawyer in charge of the Navy's legal office at Ft. Meade, were laughing in his office and sharing law school stories. Lt. Klitch already thought I was a dirty slut who slept with the enemy and should be locked up, so seeing my new attorney so chummy with him made my heart sink. When they noticed me standing in the waiting room outside his office, he rolled his eyes and rose from his desk.

"You can just have a seat right there, Petty Officer. Lt. Marons and I will call you in when we're ready for you," he said to me in an insolent tone and then slammed his office door in my face.

The two of them went back to their jovial conversation while I sat out in the waiting room and received disparaging glances from his secretary as she typed on her computer. A few minutes later, Lt. Klitch's office door reopened and I was called in. He informed us that we could meet privately in his office for the next hour because he had to go out anyway. I was desperate to have a confidante and someone to stand by me as I fought my way through this case, so I was anxious to get to know Lt. Marons and get her expert advice. But I knew from the judgmental look in her eye that she was not going to be that person. She saw me as an assignment and not one she was proud to have. To her, I was simply an ignorant, love-struck, lowly enlisted sailor who wasn't even worthy of her time. I saw her as a stuck-up, spoiled college brat who thought she was better than me because daddy paid for her to attend college before she joined the Navy, allowing her to join the officer ranks and bypass serving with us galley slaves on the enlisted side.

"Hello, Petty Officer, nice to meet you," she said, shaking my hand and flashing me a fake smile.

We sat down across from each other at Lt. Klitch's desk.

"Okay, so all I know is that you had an intimate affair with an Iraqi man serving in the Iraqi Army while you were on TDY in Baghdad."

Dear God, it was beautiful how everything could get so twisted and transformed as it was filtered through the channels and minds of numerous individuals. I promptly informed her that Fahdi was *not* a member of the Iraqi Army, he never was a member of the Iraqi Army, and would *never* be a member of the Iraqi Army. I also, as politely and delicately as possible, defended that he was not some guy I bumped into on the streets of Baghdad and decided to spread my legs for, but was, in fact, my coworker and translator assigned to work with me on my agency mission.

Of course, she just pursed her lips at my defense of our relationship and said, "Well it really doesn't matter. Our job is to keep you from being court martialed and found guilty of the charges they are investigating you for. My advice to you as your lawyer is to forget about this guy. He may not be using you to gain classified information, but I'd say he is most likely using you as at least a ticket into the U.S. Don't be stupid and let a crush on a boy ruin your entire career and possibly your life."

I was terribly frustrated and disheartened by her words, but I remained silent. I was so tired of fighting and defending myself to everyone that I just let it go and simply stared at her blankly–so much for having someone in my corner. I was at least hoping she'd be able to tell me something new regarding the status of my case, but it turned out she knew less than I did. All she was able to tell me was what I possibly faced if charged and convicted. Anything from a simple non-judicial punishment (NJP) to a full-scale court martial followed by prison time. She told me to cut Fahdi out of my life right now or risk getting deeper into the hole I was already in. I just shook my head and told her I was not about to let the Navy or anyone else tell me who I could and could not be in love with. I was willing to risk a court martial, but I hoped and prayed it would all end in an NJP, which was basically just an official ass-chewing by my commanding officer followed by a reduction in military rank, loss of pay, extra duty (military community service), and restriction to the base for 45-60 days. The great thing about an NJP was it didn't appear on any permanent records outside of the military, but a court martial would carry over to civilian records and could follow me around the rest of my life.

"Well, I have to head back down to Norfolk," she said when she'd gotten all the information she wanted from me. "I want to get through D.C. before rush hour."

I talked to Fahdi that evening and told him my new lawyer was useless and the hope we had of gaining an advocate with her was lost.

"It's okay, Sweetie, we will make it through this," he consoled me. "We will fight. I will fight until my last breath for us, even if there is no one else on this planet willing to fight with me."

"I know," I said, choking back tears. "Can we talk about something else? I get so depressed over this crap. So what have you been up to? How are the guys at work? Have you seen Mohammad or Waleed lately?"

"Well, actually…" he hesitated and my caution flag went up.

"What?" I asked bracing for something horrible.

"I don't work there anymore."

"Son of a bitch, they kicked you out didn't they?" I was so mad my face felt like it had been lit on fire. "I'm sure the Americans had to say just one word and that's all it took for them to boot you out of the agency."

"Calm down," he said in a calm tone that made me even more pissed. "I wasn't fired. As a matter of fact, I was technically promoted."

"Excuse me," I retorted, not sure I'd heard properly. "You were *promoted*? Explain."

"Last week, I arrived to work and Abu Zaid came into my office and told me to start packing up my stuff. Like you, I figured I was getting kicked out, but then he told me I was moving down to the first floor to work in the director general's wing. He told me I'd been promoted to work as one of the Director's private linguists. But I know this was something arranged by the Americans to keep a closer eye on me. I'm right under everyone's nose now."

"So you are now working directly for the INIS Director General *himself*?"

"Yep," he answered nonchalantly. "Talk about a steely and intimidating individual."

"Yeah, I bet. I've heard a lot about that guy. He's no joke. So what have you been doing down there? Or can you not tell me?"

"A whole lot of nothing. I come to work and sit in an office surfing the Internet. I haven't really been asked to do anything yet. That's why I think this was all just a set up to get me under the DG's nose so everyone can keep an eye on me until their investigation into us is over. I'm pretty much completely isolated from all the other INIS employees here, and I know they are intercepting every phone conversation and Internet communication I have from here."

"Well at least they didn't kick you out–not yet anyway," I added.

"I wouldn't even care, Mandy. You know I'd give it all up for you. I'd walk away from everything I have and everyone I know if it meant being with you. I swear I would."

"I know, I would, too," I said, choking down tears. "All right, enough of that. I'm going to get off here now. I figure I better start researching civilian lawyers since the stellar one the Navy provided me with is about as useful as a cock-flavored lollipop. Yeah, I stole that from the movie *Dodgeball*."

After we hung up, I began browsing law offices in the D.C. area on the Internet. I researched several promising-looking attorneys with experience in national security cases similar to mine, sent out a few emails with a brief synopsis of my case, and was contacted by a couple of lawyers that same evening. Of course, they all gave me the same advice: don't talk to NCIS or anyone else for that matter. Oops. They also said that there was really nothing that could be done for the time being because I had not been charged with anything yet. It was all a waiting game until the investigation was officially closed and it had been decided whether or not to charge me with anything.

Chapter 20

**Saturday, 1 October–Monday, 31 October
2005**

As summer turned into fall, the days dragged by like sludge. Every minute felt like an hour and every day seemed to take an eternity. I'd heard nothing from the NCIS agents in nearly three weeks and I was desperate to find out anything regarding my case. I didn't care if it was good or bad; I just needed to be told *something* to satisfy my brain. I sat glued to my cell phone when I was home, and I did my best to stay within earshot of Chief Viraez's phone conversations at work so that I could pick up on any news right away. The suspense was driving me mad and I was a nervous wreck every morning when I woke up, worrying if something bad had happened to Fahdi while I slept. I quickly discovered it was a lot rougher to have to worry about someone you love being in a dangerous place than it was actually being there yourself.

One morning in early October, I awoke just as the sun was cresting the horizon and proceeded with what had become my morning ritual. I grabbed my laptop and jumped on instant messenger to talk to Fahdi.

"Good morning, *habibi*."

I gave him a few minutes to answer while I ran to the bathroom to pee and brush my teeth. When I returned to the computer, a reply was waiting for me.

"Good morning back at ya', *haiati*."

These were the typical greetings we opened each instant messenger conversation with so that we knew for sure we were talking to each other and not an imposter of some kind on the other end. After we'd determined we were both who we said we were, we usually switched over to Skype, a new program which we used to talk to each other using headsets with microphones.

"How's it going over there?" I asked once we were successfully connected and could hear each other.

"Bad."

"Normal bad or different bad?"

"Pretty much just the same, but the neighborhood where my family lives is getting more dangerous. There was a pretty big firefight near my mom's house last night."

"Are they okay?"

"Yeah, they're fine, but my little sister was pretty shaken up. She was walking home from her friend's house when the shooting started. She and her friend crouched behind a wall in one of the neighbor's yards until the shooting stopped and then they made a run for the house. One of the guys who was shot during the firefight was lying dead on the sidewalk and my sister and her friend had to step right by him to get out of there. It was actually the first time she's seen a dead person up close, so she was kind of freaked out."

"Poor girl. I'm so sorry, Fahdi."

"I've done my best to keep her shielded from these things, but it's getting harder and harder to do that here. I'm sending her next week to stay with some of our extended family in Amman for a while. I want my mom and brother to go, too, but they won't leave Iraq. My brother doesn't want to leave his job here at the INIS and my mom won't go without us. I've at least convinced her to get out of Baghdad and stay with her sister up in Mosul. It's not completely safe up there, but it's quieter than it is here in Baghdad right now."

"Oh, I do have some other bad news," Fahdi added in a solemn tone. "Hajji Haitham was found."

"He's dead, isn't he?" I said.

"Yes."

Fahdi went on to tell me that Hajji Haitham's body was found dumped in a field outside Baghdad and displayed signs of severe torture. The corpse was covered in bruises and riddled with small holes made by a power drill. A single gunshot wound to the back of the head was the ultimate cause of death. It was all the signature style of the Badr Force.

"How is Abu Zaid holding up?" I asked.

"He's torn up over it but he's still here. He knows this is ground zero for fighting the corruption in the government and that's what he wants to do more than anything–rebuild our country and have a decent, successful government that will be able to handle things when the Americans leave. We should be helping your military and ours fight the terrorists and insurgents out in the desert, but we're having to fight the evil idiots you guys put in charge of our country instead."

All I could do was apologize. No doubt, we'd made a mess of things over there. Things were better for some people, but worse for others. All we seemed to do was reverse the flow of the river. Iraqis were now technically free, but free to do what? Free to starve since the country's economy was devastated? Free to stay locked in their homes because the insurgency was free to loot, murder, and kidnap people at will? Free to watch their country crumble around them? These were the only freedoms realized with the U.S. liberation of Iraq.

I was scared to death Fahdi would meet the same fate as Hajji Haitham, so I begged him again to not leave the INIS building. He said they still would not allow him to remain there 24/7, but he promised to be as careful as possible. He drove straight home from work and back again, and he remained locked in his house whenever he was home. For better protection, he and a few of his new friends from work now traveled to and from work together fully-armed. Fahdi even invited them to be his roommates since his family was now living up in Mosul and he had the house to himself. A couple of them were Kurds who were on the security detail at the INIS, so they were handy with their AK-47s. And since Fahdi was now working directly for the boss, he was a valuable ally to stick close to. The other two were Sunnis whose home neighborhoods were now too dangerous for them to return to, due to the numerous Shi'ite death squads combing every alley in Baghdad.

Omar was one of the Sunnis. He was the one Fahdi was closest to, his best friend at the INIS. He and Fahdi met when Fahdi was reassigned to the DG's office. Omar was a couple of years older than Fahdi and had graduated from Baghdad University with a degree in computer science. He was hired as an IT guy for the INIS and worked directly for the DG's private computer guys. The DG knew Omar's father, an ambassador under Saddam. Unfortunately, Omar's father had been on Saddam's bad side and Saddam executed him in the mid-90s when Omar was a teenager. He was a bear of a man, standing about six-and-a-half feet tall with broad shoulders and weighing close to 300 pounds., all muscle.

Since it was now clear that INIS employees were being specifically targeted, they slept in shifts at the house with someone always on guard with an AK-47 in hand. Two Kurds, two Sunnis, and an Arab Catholic banded together and holed up in a house in central Baghdad for protection. I'm not sure if this was a sign of progress or regression.

"So what have you been doing while you're locked up in the house?" I asked before we signed off for the evening.

"I'm on the computer most of the time talking to you. I've also been working out when you're not around to chat with."

"Oh really?" I asked playfully. "You're getting all buff and gorgeous while I'm not around to enjoy it? That's so unfair!"

"I'm not doing it to get buff, just to keep from going crazy. An old friend of mine has been coming over, and he and I and my roommates have been working out together and doing some training. He and I trained under the same kickboxing coach together, so we've been doing some sparring and stuff like that."

"I didn't know you used to do kickboxing. When was that?" I asked intrigued at learning something new about Fahdi's past.

"I started at around age fifteen and did it for about five years. I actually won a couple of national championships for my weight class. My mom still has all of my trophies and medals."

"That's really neat! I did Tae-Kwon-Do when I was in middle school. Since I was so small, my mom wanted me to have some self-defense training before going into high school. I earned my black belt and took second and third places at some tournaments, but I never could get a first place trophy."

"My long ape arms helped me a lot," he joked.

"Well, I like your long ape arms and I really miss them being around me now. God, I miss you so much." I felt the depression smack me in the face once again and hot tears stung my eyes.

"I miss you, too, my love," he answered.

"Let's talk about something else, anything else to keep my mind off this," I begged.

"Well, I adopted a kitten," he said to change the subject and it did perk me up a little.

"That's so sweet. A boy or girl?"

"A boy, I think. He's only a few weeks old. I named him Leo. He is yellow and white and so fluffy and cute. I'll send you some pictures of him."

"Please do. I can't wait to see him."

A few weeks later, Fahdi's kickboxing friend stopped by for their usual afternoon workout and brought a letter he'd found taped to his front door. It was a death threat stating that they knew he was hanging out with Fahdi and that if he didn't cease all contact with the infidel traitor, they would kill both of them.

"I'm guessing this is from some old friends of yours?" his friend asked after Fahdi read the letter.

"Very old friends," Fahdi answered.

He figured it was a group still after him from when he worked with the Marines in either Ramadii or Fallujah since the threat mentioned only him and not his roommates as well.

"You should leave. Don't take any chances, man, these bastards are serious."

"Screw them! No one's going to tell me who I can and can't hang out with. I'm sick of living in fear. It's no life. You're my friend, Fahdi," he said, putting a hand on Fahdi's shoulder. "Let's go get the other guys and workout."

A few more weeks later, the kickboxing friend was leaving his house to head over to Fahdi's when several gunmen drove by and opened fire. He was killed instantly. Fahdi and his roommates took a huge risk and attended the funeral. His friend's mother spotted Fahdi at the funeral and recognized him. She marched over to him and slapped him right across the face. She obviously knew about the death threat.

"How dare you show your face here!" she screamed through tears and anger. "My son is *dead* because of *you!*"

"I am so sorry, I…" Fahdi tried to get out the small apology, but she cut him off.

"Shut up! You aren't sorry. You don't care about anything or anyone but yourself. You just walk on and over people to get where you want to be. You've done it your entire life. You didn't care whose life you put in jeopardy when you started working for Uday Hussein, and you don't care who gets killed because of who you are a slave for now."

Fahdi's eyes widened at her mention of Saddam's infamous, ruthless son, Uday.

"Oh, you thought I didn't know about that?" she said with an evil chuckle. "Everyone in the neighborhood knew you were one of his dogs. Your poor mother was scared to death. But you didn't even care about her. You didn't care about her or your sister and brother then, you didn't care about the danger you put them in when you decided to jump sides and started working for the Americans, and you obviously still don't care about them now that you've worked your way to the top at the grand INIS–nothing but an American CIA puppet agency! Your family even had to leave their home behind because of your selfish decisions. Your poor mother. And to think my son looked up to you. He idolized you. But he got run over by the bulldozer of destruction and misery that you just keep plowing through people's lives with. Enjoy your time at the top, but I'm sure you'll find it very lonely and cold up there. Now get out of my sight and leave my son's funeral."

When Fahdi relayed the incident at the funeral to me I felt bad for him, but all I could focus on was the mention of Uday Hussein, so I had to dig deeper.

"So what was that about Uday Hussein?" I asked hoping for more details. "You actually worked for him?"

"Yes, but not directly," Fahdi answered willingly. "I worked within one of his many organizations. I was recruited at a young age as part of Uday's youth program. They offered me a good job and at the time, it was a very good opportunity."

"But he was such a monster!" I protested, feeling sick to my stomach at thinking Fahdi as one of Uday Hussein's foot soldiers and a part of his evil business empire built on drug trafficking, smuggling, murder, and rape. "He picked young girls up off the streets and raped them! He killed innocent people just for the hell of it!"

"I was just a kid, Mandy," Fahdi said in defense. "And yes, he was smuggling things in and out of the country and he threw lavish parties and he was a crazy son-of-a-bitch and completely out of control when he was drunk, but as far as some of the more depraved things you've heard of, well, I can't promise things like that didn't happen, but I can promise you I never saw any such things. Girls fell over each other for a shot at being his mistress."

"I cannot believe I'm hearing this. I can't believe you're defending this guy!"

"I'm not defending him, I'm just telling you what I did and didn't personally witness."

"Well, did you enjoy working for him?"

"Honestly, yes. I made good money. I was given privileges and benefits that were really pretty awesome. It was a good time. I got to go to awesome parties and do a lot of cool stuff."

"So what exactly did you do? What was your job?"

"I worked in shipping and transportation for a while. I made sure his international shipments coming into and out of the country were properly routed and made it to their destinations. Usually stuff like beer and hard liquor which was technically smuggled, but when your daddy's the president, it's not like anyone's going to stop you. Then, because of my kickboxing background, I was offered a position on the security detail. They put me through pretty intense special forces-type security and survival training courses, and then I got to accompany Uday to a few soccer matches and to some clubs as part of his personal security detachment."

"Are you fucking *kidding* me?! You were, like, one of Uday Hussein's personal body guards?" I asked with my jaw practically on the floor by now.

"Well, I did it for a little while, but I preferred doing the smuggling thing, so I pretty much stuck to that."

"So I'm guessing you quit when the war started."

"Well, I was actually at one of Uday's palaces in Tikrit when you guys started bombing the hell out of Baghdad."

"Was Uday there, too?" I asked now, genuinely intrigued and putting my disgust to the side for a minute.

"No, he and Qusay and Saddam had already gone into hiding–I don't know where, probably somewhere in the north of the country. Most of Uday's people scattered, too. A few guys and I stayed at the palace until we knew it was a lost cause. I went home to my mom's house in Baghdad when the Americans started bombing Tikrit. I knew it was only a matter of time before they targeted the palace I was at."

"Wow, there are so many questions whirling around in my head right now, but I don't want to discuss this here, not over the Internet, especially considering we don't know who all is listening."

I still felt nauseated over what Fahdi had just told me, but I quickly became angry as I realized the implications.

"I don't believe this. The simple fact that you're a native Iraqi has us in deep enough trouble already. The fact that you used to *fucking work for Uday Hussein does not help our situation at all!*"

"Please calm down. I'm so sorry but this is the plain truth. We promised to always tell each other the truth and that's what I'm doing. It was just a job. It provided well for my family and me. I didn't hurt people or do any of the horrible things I know you have in your mind. I'm not ashamed and I'm not going to hide it."

"Like I said," I interjected. "I don't want to discuss this now. I want to get back to my original request: for you to get permission to start living in the building so you aren't risking your life every day when you leave and go home."

"I'm sick of hiding and I'm sick of running, Mandy. This is why I don't want to live in the building–it might as well be a prison. I can't stay there forever and who knows how long it will take for all of this to clear up. You won't be out of the Navy for almost a year and the case against us most likely won't be closed before then."

"Fahdi, this is exactly why I am asking, begging, you to do this. I've already got all of my problems to worry about; please don't make me worry about you, too. I am scared to death every day, that something horrible is going to happen to you. I wake up every morning wondering if something happened to you while I slept. I don't know how much more of this I can take Fahdi. I–I'm going crazy. I'm a nervous wreck every minute I'm awake and I have horrible dreams when I sleep. It's a relentless worry that is literally sucking the life out of me."

"Okay, okay, okay...shhhh," he soothed in an attempt to calm me down. "I'm so sorry. God, I wish I could take you away from all this and wrap my arms around you and make you smile. I would do anything to see you smile. I'll talk to the DG tomorrow and ask about moving into the building."

"Oh, thank God. Thank you. You have no idea how much of a relief this is to me."

As promised, the very next morning, Fahdi requested to meet with the DG. The DG's private secretary told Fahdi the DG would squeeze in a quick meeting with him later that evening, but he'd have to make it quick. Fahdi waited until 8 p.m. that evening when someone finally came to his office and said he had five minutes to talk to the DG. When Fahdi entered the director's office, the DG barely glanced up from his position behind his giant, dark mahogany executive desk. He shot him an icy glare and motioned for Fahdi to approach his desk with a flick of his hand.

"Good evening, Sir, I am sorry to bother you…"

"What do you want?" The general said in a deep, irritated voice, cutting off Fahdi's introduction.

"Sir, I was just wondering if it would be possible for me to start staying in the building overnight. Just during the week. I'll return home on the weekends, but if I could stay here at least during the week I'd greatly appreciate it."

The general continued to glare at Fahdi and showed no sign of answering his request, so Fahdi shifted his weight and continued.

"It's getting pretty rough in my neighborhood and I've already sent my family up north. I really don't have any reason to go home during the week. I'll sleep in my office and stay cloistered in there at all times after hours. No one will even know I'm here."

"You're asking me for a favor?" The DG asked with a hint of condescension in his tone.

"Yes, Sir," Fahdi answered sticking to his position.

"How on God's great Earth can you expect any favors from me? Do you even grasp the seriousness of the situation your little stunt with the American girl has placed this entire agency in? You have embarrassed us. You have embarrassed me, personally. You have threatened our relationship with the United States intelligence agencies. Do you even realize that you singlehandedly have shaken international relations between two nations who were at goddamn war two years ago, one of which just so happens to be the most powerful military power on the entire planet! No. You don't. You have *no* idea the damage you have caused. All you can think about is that cute little American girl and how she makes your dick perk up at just the thought of her. You have jeopardized *everything* we have been working for over the past two years because you couldn't keep it in your pants! The trust the INIS has built with the U.S. military and government agencies is now under complete scrutiny. The Americans are investigating this from every angle. They suspect you were pumping her for information. They suspect you may have been put up to it by one of your supervisors. They are investigating this thing all the way from the top to the bottom. They aren't sure this entire thing isn't a complete conspiracy with connections leading all the way to the top–to *me*! They are investigating the possibility that you're working for a group on the outside with ties to God knows who, meaning the INIS is *still* implicated for not sniffing you out. You should feel quite important, Fahdi. A good portion of the C.I.A.'s Baghdad manpower is focused on you right now. You better pray there's nothing even remotely shady in your past, present, or possible future that they could catch wind of, or the instability in your neighborhood right now will no longer be an issue because you just might wind up in a prison cell.

"So, the answer to your request is *no*! You may not stay here after working hours. *Hell no* to be more precise. If I had my way, you wouldn't step foot in this building ever again. You'd have been gone the second this thing exploded. I wanted to kick your ass out the day all this crap landed on my desk, but the Americans wanted to keep you close so they could keep an eye on you until they get to the bottom of this issue. Let me make this clear to you: once the Americans are through with you, you no longer work for the INIS. You will be gone so fast your head will spin. It would actually make my life a lot easier if you were dead. You're lucky I haven't killed you myself."

Fahdi wasn't too stunned by the general's reaction. He half expected to get such a speech, but he did it for me. He knew how much it meant to me that he at least try to make things safer for himself, so he knowingly walked right into that browbeating because he loved me.

Chapter 21

Tuesday, 1 November–Monday, 14 November 2005

In the early hours of November 1, a loud pounding on the front door ripped Fahdi and the other guys in the house from their sleep. By the time the guy on watch made it into the room Fahdi was sleeping in, everyone in the house was awake and staring wide-eyed at each other.

"What the hell is going on?" Fahdi asked.

"It's the Iraqi National Guard and Army," the guy on watch replied in a breathless tone. "They entered the neighborhood about an hour ago."

"An hour ago?" Fahdi snapped. "Why didn't you wake us up?!"

"I've been up on the roof watching them since they arrived," he responded in defense. "It appeared they were just conducting some random joint home visits. They didn't seem like they had any interest in your house, so I thought they'd pass us by. As soon as I noticed several of them heading this way, I got down here as fast as I could to get you."

Fahdi put his hand on the man's shoulder reassuringly, but before he could say anything, the pounding on the front door continued incessantly. Fahdi responded to the screaming from the other side of the door and said he was opening the door. Before he got the door half way open, three uniformed Iraqi National Guard members and two Iraqi Army soldiers pushed their way into the house. All were armed and had their weapons at the ready. The apparent leader of the group stepped forward and demanded to see the IDs of every person in the house. Since the numbers were dead even, the eyes and weapons of a security forces member tracked each of the guys in the house as they retrieved their identifications.

"Quite a motley crew, aren't you?" the leader said with a sadistic chuckle after perusing the highlights of each of the men's IDs. "Did we interrupt your party?" he asked with mock consideration.

"Screw you!" one of the guys spat back. "You assholes are nothing but murderers and Iranian puppets! Doing their dirty work like little bitches. I'm curious, when you're sucking their dicks, do you cradle their balls or do they prefer you to finger their assholes?"

"Shut the hell up," one of the National Guard guys snapped back, pushing the barrel of his gun into the chest of Fahdi's roommate.

"I hope they taught you how to use that thing at the cub scout summer camp the Americans put you through for training," Omar threatened as he pushed his chest hard against the rifle.

"Back off," Fahdi said to his friend in a calm tone. "It's not worth it."

"You need to keep your dogs on shorter leashes," the soldier in the altercation said to Fahdi.

"Well, we're very hurt we weren't invited to your little get together," the National Guard officer said, continuing his cynicism but obviously wanting to neutralize a volatile situation. "We'll just make sure you boys aren't hiding anything you're not supposed to have before we let you get back to your little homo-orgy."

He snapped his fingers and his men swiftly upended everything in the house. Their main mission was obviously to destroy as much as they could; searching for illegal contraband was a very secondary task.

Fahdi and his buddies made it through the National Guard harassment unscathed, but their luck didn't last. About a week later, their car was fired upon while they were on their way to work. Fahdi called me as soon as he could after the attack and I bit my fingernails until they bled as he recanted the incident. He explained that when they turned a corner after leaving the neighborhood but before they made it into Baghdad proper, they drove straight into an ambush.

"Was it the National Guard again?" I asked angry enough to chew metal.

"No," Fahdi answered. "These were just street thugs. Probably just trying to kidnap us."

"Kidnap you because you work for the INIS?"

"No, I don't think so. I think they were probably just thugs looking for easy targets to nab for ransom from families. It's the quickest and easiest way to make money around here right now."

He went on to describe the ambush. Omar was driving and when they turned the corner, he heard AK fire coming from both sides of the car. He suspected it was a routine kidnapping, because they didn't try to shoot inside the car but did their best to disable the vehicle by taking out the front tires. Unfortunately, a stray bullet did shatter the passenger side window and caught one of the guys in the neck. The round entered through the back of his neck and exited out the front. Fahdi was in the backseat and when he saw the blood gushing, he told Omar to floor it and head for the hospital. Fortunately, the car wasn't disabled, and they were able to escape.

"The doctors worked on him for three hours," Fahdi continued. "When they sent a nurse out, I completely expected her to tell us he was dead. But she said they were able to stop the bleeding, get him a transfusion, and stabilize him. The bullet passed through just the fleshy part of his neck and didn't hit anything significant. She said he was still unconscious, but would most likely pull through and wake up in the next forty-eight hours."

"Were you injured at all?"

"Just a few scratches from the broken glass of the windows."

*****

I was technically due for leave to go visit my family since I'd returned from Iraq, but NCIS made sure I was denied any leave requests because they considered me a flight risk and didn't want me traveling outside the immediate area. When I told my lawyer they were denying all my leave requests, she acted outraged and said it was bullshit. Not surprisingly, she did nothing to challenge it. I wasn't particularly desperate to visit my family. I mainly just wanted to get away from what I was dealing with daily. I reported to the base every day for eight hours and then returned home and sat alone in my apartment the rest of the time. I had a roommate, but she was deployed to Qatar at the time, so it was just her cat, Paris, and I. I was lacking in relaxed human interaction.

Since I wasn't allowed to go anywhere, my dad and step-mom came up from Florida to visit me, but the visit was anything but relaxed. My dad called me every week since my return from Iraq to tell me in one way or another how I was throwing my life away and making a horrible mistake by choosing to maintain my relationship with Fahdi. I guess he figured a face-to-face discussion would be more persuasive.

They took me out to dinner at Olive Garden their first night in town. I was tense in anticipation of the inevitable speech I knew was coming.

"The government doesn't play around with stuff like this, Mandy," my dad finally said as we all began eating our salad and breadsticks. "They don't want you to associate with this guy and, quite frankly, neither do I. They can put you in prison. Do you understand that? Ever heard of a place called Leavenworth? If you don't cut him out of your life, they will do it for you. You're playing with fire and you're going to get burned. This man is not right for you. He is from a completely different culture and he will never accept or understand who you are. I know you think you're in love but, trust me, you're not; there's no way. You spent less than four months together. You two hardly know anything about each other. You're from two opposite worlds and the odds are stacked against you. A successful marriage is an impossibility."

I didn't argue or defend my position. I didn't even look up from my salad. I simply let him say what he felt he needed to say.

"You're not even listening to what I'm saying are you?" he asked with a huff. "It's going in one ear and out the other."

"Look, Dad, I can't even begin to explain, so I'm not going to try. I know what I've gotten myself into, but I'm already in it, so I'm not going to get anywhere by trying to dig myself out. And I refuse to give up. So I'm just going to keep digging until I either bury myself or make it through to the other side and hopefully be able to just walk away from all of this. Abandoning him right now would be the easiest route, but I know if I do, for the rest of my life, I'll wonder 'what if.' I'd rather end up in prison than give up and refuse to fight for what I want."

"You're like a pit-bull, Mandy," my dad said mostly to himself. "Once you get a hold of something, you don't let go. You're hard-headed like your old man. I just hope you realize that you're on a sinking ship before you drown."

Chapter 22

Tuesday, 15 November–Saturday, 17 December 2005

In mid-November, I received a call from my lawyer, Lt. Marons. She informed me that she was transferring to the naval airbase in Pensacola, Florida. I perked up at the news, hoping this meant I'd be assigned a new lawyer.

"So who will be taking over my case?" I asked, trying my best not to sound too enthusiastic.

"Oh don't worry, I'm still your lawyer," she replied cheerily.

I felt my face flush with frustration. Because of the sensitive nature of my case and all the classified aspects, we were not allowed to discuss details over the phone or via the Internet. Whenever I wanted to speak with my lawyer, we had to physically meet in an approved location, usually a special room approved for the verbal discussion of classified information.

"Well, how is this supposed to work with you being over 1,000 miles away?" I asked with sharp indignation in my voice.

"Well, the Navy will just fly me up there whenever we need to meet," she answered as if I was making a big deal out of nothing.

"Okay, whatever," I replied derisively.

"Look, I really don't think anything is going to happen with your case anyway," she continued. "I've discussed the details of your case with my bosses at JAG headquarters in Norfolk and everyone agrees that at most, you will receive an NJP and be released from the Navy when your contract is up next summer."

What she was saying was such music to my ears I forgot what an annoying snob she was–for a minute.

"Ultimately, your commanding officer is the one that decides whether or not to send you to a court martial, but the agencies you worked for here and over in Iraq do not want the classified details of this case coming out in a trial, and their opinions far outweigh your C.O.'s. Even if NCIS conducts a closed trial, a lot of the documents, evidence, and court records would still, by law, have to be released to the public. So, unless they come across undeniable proof that you committed something as serious as espionage, then they're probably just going to let it go. Of course, you will still most likely be busted in rank, lose some money, and probably serve some restriction time but it's better than a court martial."

I was incredibly relieved by what she was telling me and I desperately hoped this would be the outcome, but I knew better than to get my hopes up too high. I hoped for the best, but expected the worse.

By mid-November, I was going stir crazy. I felt trapped, I felt like I was suffocating, and my nerves and patience were both shot. Since meeting with the lawyer in D.C., both NCIS and NSA were giving me the silent treatment. I hadn't been given any updates on the status of the investigation, and I didn't know if anyone was even working on my case or if it was just lying on a desk somewhere.

With my stress level pushed to the edge, I couldn't eat, I couldn't sleep, and every time the phone rang, I felt nauseated because I knew it could be news that I was either being arrested or that Fahdi had been killed.

I went to the base and sat in the Master-at-Arms's office, staring blankly out the window for hours on end, praying every time the phone rang it was news of some kind about my case. I was startled out of one of my blank stupors by the boom of Chief Viraez's voice a couple of days before Thanksgiving.

"McEwen...McEwen!" the chief shouted to break me from my trance.

I jerked my head and looked at him, but I merely responded with a, "Hmm?"

"Look, McEwen," the chief began in a sympathizing tone, "why don't you go ahead and get out of here for the day." I continued my blank stare, not catching on. "You have a medical appointment to get to don't you?" he asked in a hint-hint-nudge-nudge tone.

I caught on. "Uh, yes? Yes, I do. Roger that, Chief."

Viraez played this scene more often as we progressed through the holiday season. He'd let me cut out early to go home, where I could at least be alone and not have to endure the scornful looks from others on the base— all of whom seemed to know my story. People would catch a glimpse of my nametag and stiffen in recognition. Usually, a look of disdain would flash across their faces, followed by their apparent disgust at having to breath the same air as me. The tales of my escapades spread like wildfire within Fort Meade and soon, throughout the fleet. I was an internal military celebrity of sorts. I received emails from Navy buddies I'd known from boot camp and language school in California asking me if I was the McEwen that had the affair with an Iraqi.

At least this was the basic truth. Several variations of rumors were also circulating, they included: 1) I'd been raped by an Iraqi, 2) I was working for the Iraqi resistance, and 3) I'd secretly married an Iraqi on the terrorist watch-list. I was known on military bases from California to Qatar. Navy personnel transferring to Ft. Mead who had to stop in at the Master-at-Arms's office as part of their check-in process, recognized me on a regular basis. (The check-in for the Master-at-Arms's office simply meant someone added your name to the urinalysis list so you could participate in the monthly lottery that selected 25% of the luckiest members of the command for a random drug test.) Since I was often the one processing the new arrivals' paperwork for our office, I got to meet face-to-face with everyone coming in from bases around the globe. It was the same scene over and over again: they would see my nametag, cock their head, and start off with, "Heeeeey, are you..."

"Yep," I'd answer curtly without even looking up from their paperwork. "That's me."

One day, a young kid fresh out of tech-school came in and handed me his check-in paperwork. His name was Nick and he seemed timid and uneasy. After I got him signed up for the pee lottery, he asked me if I could tell him how to get to the next office on his list, which, ironically, was the legal office. When new people arrived at the command they usually had a sponsor assigned to them to show them around and help them get checked-in everywhere. I asked him where his sponsor was, and he said the guy never showed up to meet him and he couldn't get a hold of him, so he was roaming around on his own trying to find his way to all of the offices on the check-in sheet. I told him I'd help him out and walked him to every building and office he needed to check-in at and gave him a tour of the base so he could find his way around on his own. I also told him to call me if he needed anything or had any questions. He thanked me over and over and it made me feel really good to be a savior in someone's eyes instead of a worthless maggot.

*****

By late November, the unyielding monotony of my daily life as I played the waiting game became too much for me to endure. I was sick of hearing the same old song from everyone. Any time I asked my lawyer or Chief Viraez if there was any news about my case, I got the same answer, "All we can do is wait." I wanted to claw my own eyes out. I had to do something proactive or I was going to go crazy.

I started researching immigrant visas for Fahdi on the Internet. I knew how well our government doesn't communicate with each other so I had a feeling I could probably go ahead and submit a visa application for Fahdi and the folks at immigration would be clueless as to who we were. I spent several days studying the application process, the paperwork needed, the documents needed, etc. I could have been an immigration lawyer by the time I was done. Once my research was complete, I decided a fiancé visa was our best route and downloaded all the paperwork I needed off the immigration website. When an immigrant came to the U.S. on a fiancé visa, they were given a 90-day visitor visa and had to legally marry the U.S. citizen who sponsored them within that 90 days or they would be deported back to their home country. The bad news was that it typically took a year to get through the entire process and actually get a visa in hand. It took even longer if the immigrant was coming from the Middle East. But it was a start, and it was something I could do on my own.

I decided not to tell Fahdi about my attempt to apply for a fiancé visa because I knew it was a long shot and I didn't want to get his hopes up just to shatter them again. It took me nearly three weeks to fill out the application forms and gather all of the necessary documents to include in the visa petition packet. It became clear to me very quickly why people were coming into the U.S. illegally. I consider myself pretty sharp and fairly-well educated, and getting the visa packet completed and filed properly was a definitive pain in the ass for me. I can't imagine what it's like for someone who struggles with English and doesn't have a college education. And aside from the daunting mound of paperwork, they charged an arm and a leg just to submit your application: over $300 when I filed in 2005. And that was just to get the ball rolling. When all was said and done, legal immigrants could count on spending upwards of $5,000 on fees and immigration-related expenses along their path to U.S. citizenship. Another thing I noticed was the fact that there really wasn't a legal way to immigrate to the U.S. unless you were immediately related or engaged to a U.S. citizen or legal permanent resident. Everyone always complained, "Well I wouldn't be so mad if all the illegal aliens would just come here the right and legal way..."

Well, newsflash, there *isn't* a legal way to immigrate to the U.S. if you just decide one day you want to move here.

On December 6, I received a less than relieving phone call. I answered my cell phone and a heavily accented young woman's voice asked, "Is this Mandy?" From the accent and horrible connection, I knew the call was coming from Iraq.

"Yes. Who is this?"

"This is Dina, Fahdi's sister."

I was immediately nauseated and feared the worst. I'd never spoken to his mother or sister, and I didn't even know his sister could speak English–albeit very broken English.

"Hello? Are you still there?"

My fear had rendered me speechless, but I managed to squeak out a "Yes, I'm here," to let her know I was still on the line. I closed my eyes and said a small prayer as she continued.

"Fahdi is in the hospital."

I squeezed my eyes shut as the tears came in a stinging frenzy. I did my best to control my breathing to mask my breakdown.

"He is okay."

"Oh thank God," I blurted, noticeably sobbing at this point. "You scared the hell out of me! What happened? Why is he in the hospital?"

"He passed out at work. They took him to the American military hospital in the Green Zone. The doctor said it was just exhaustion and stress. His blood pressure was really high."

"Well, can I call him?" I asked once I was able to speak again.

"He is sleeping right now. They gave him some medicine for his blood pressure and to help him sleep, but he asked me to call you."

"Wait, are you in Baghdad?" I asked, confused. "I thought you and your mom were up north?"

"We came back a few days ago to visit family for Christmas," she answered.

I was pissed because I had a feeling Fahdi's worrying about his mom and sister's safety again while they were back in Baghdad may have led to his collapse, but I bit my tongue and just let it go. "So he's going to be okay?"

"Yes, they said they will let him leave in the morning if his blood pressure is down. He has lost weight too–probably about ten kilos since we left for Mosul."

On Fahdi's already lean frame, ten kilos (approximately twenty-two pounds) was drastic, making him now about 140 pounds at 5'10". "We are going to stay with him. My mom said she won't go back to Mosul and will stay here and force feed him if she has to."

I wanted to tell her she and her mom were only making things worse by returning to Baghdad because I knew how much Fahdi stressed and worried about them, but I again held my tongue. Looking back, I wish I'd have been my usual brash self and said what was on my mind. How could I have known then what would happen?

Two days later, Dina and her mother were attacked in almost an exact replica of the attack Fahdi escaped from just weeks before. They were in Fahdi's car on their way to visit some family on the other side of Baghdad when they were ambushed. Again, Omar was driving, and again managed to escape and get the women to safety. Luckily, no one was seriously injured in this latest escapade. But the true terror was in the similarity of the situation–it was too coincidental.

"Omar is sure it was the same group of assholes," Fahdi said when we talked via Skype the night following the attack. "He said he even recognized some of the gunmen as the same mouth breathers who attacked us before."

"So what does this mean?" I asked, already knowing the answer.

"This means someone is after me personally. That's all I know."

"Well, do you know who?"

"Ha! Name a group and I've pissed them off," he said jokingly, but I could hear the fear and anger in his voice. "Hell, for all I know it could be *your* people trying to get rid of me for what happened between you and me. It could be the group kidnapping the INIS people. It could be resistance fighters still after me from when that asshole sold the list I was on of locals working for the U.S. It could be any one of 100 damn groups!"

"Okay, okay, calm down," I said, trying my best to soothe him. "Getting hysterical isn't going to solve anything."

"Yeah, well I am hysterical! The assholes almost killed my mother and my little sister!" he screamed.

I knew his anger wasn't directed at me, so I remained silent and let him get it out.

"Look, I'm sorry," he said, returning his voice to a normal level. "I just miss you so much and I'm so sick of all this. You guys shouldn't have ever come here–well, not you–you know what I mean. I'm glad the U.S. invaded because it brought me you, but that's the *only* good thing that came out of this whole ridiculous mess."

"I'm sorry." It was all I could say. But I wasn't sorry. Going to Iraq and meeting Fahdi was the best thing that ever happened to me. "Are they okay?" I asked, referring to his mom and sister.

"They were scared to death. My poor sister peed herself, which I think traumatized her more than the AK-47 bullets whizzing past her head. When Omar got to a safe area, he pulled over to make sure everyone was okay. My mom stepped out of the car to brush the broken glass off her clothes, but Dina refused to leave the car. She was balled up in the backseat with a death grip on the seatbelt. Omar tried to pull her out, thinking she was hurt, but she screamed at him to leave her there and not to touch her. My mom knew she was okay and what had happened so she told him to just take them home."

"Are they going to stay in Baghdad?"

"Hell no! My uncle is driving them back up to Mosul tomorrow morning and I told them they're not to come back until I say it's okay."

"Good," I breathed a sigh of relief. One less thing Fahdi would have to worry about. "How about you? Are you okay? Are you taking your blood pressure medication?"

"I'm doing fine. And yes, Mom, I'm taking my medicine," he added sarcastically.

"Final question: how's the car?"

"Oh man, my poor car," he lamented. "I just got the damn thing fixed from the last attack. I've got three busted windows again, but at least the front and back windows are still intact–those are the expensive ones. And it's fine mechanically, which is all that really matters. It looks like hell, but it can still get me to and from work."

"So what are you going to do about the issue of someone trying to hunt you down?"

"I don't know. I'll try and get the DG to let me stay in the building again. There's really nothing else I can do."

I groaned, knowing the DG would most likely again deny Fahdi refuge in the building.

*****

The timing of the December 15th, 2005, Iraqi parliamentary general elections played very much into Fahdi's favor. With the ratification of the Iraqi Constitution finally taking place in October, it was time for voters to elect a permanent 275-member Iraqi Council of Representatives. This made December an extremely busy month for the INIS, and especially its director general. Fahdi was needed in the building nearly 24/7 in the two weeks leading up to the elections, to translate mountains of government documents and serve in other duties as well. He pulled twenty-hour shifts and only took time away to shower and catch a couple hours of sleep here and there. The extra work spawned from the elections kept Fahdi in the Green Zone and safe from any more attacks.

*****

As the director general's and his deputies' plates filled with more and more official engagements to attend, odd jobs began to trickle down to Fahdi since he officially worked in the DG's office. On several occasions, he was assigned to attend government meetings and conferences as an official representative of the INIS. He didn't make any decisions or speak on behalf of the DG, but took notes and reported the gist of the events to the DG's private secretary or sometimes even to the DG himself.

One day, the DG and his deputy were scheduled to attend an important convention hosted by the U.S. State Department. The heads of all official Iraqi agencies were to be in attendance, but the deputy was suffering from the flu and feared he wouldn't be able to sit through the entire affair without vomiting. Everyone else in the DG's office was out on assignments elsewhere, so the DG told Fahdi he'd be accompanying him to the convention so he'd better find a suit to wear.

Fahdi was summoned to the DG's office and stood before the general's desk the morning of the convention.

The DG eyeballed Fahdi in silence for several uncomfortable minutes and then finally spoke. "You're going to come with me to this dog and pony show, but you're going to keep your head down and only open your mouth to translate for me when I tell you to. Do you understand?" The DG said in a commanding tone.

"Yes, Sir, I understand," Fahdi responded. "But I don't understand why you even need me. Your English is probably better than mine. Why do you need a translator?"

The DG smiled and rose from his desk. He walked around and stood in front of Fahdi, towering a good six inches above him. "Never reveal everything about yourself to anyone," he said. "Remember that. Knowledge is power. If someone knows everything about you, they'll always have power over you."

The State Department Convention was indeed the muddled spectacle the DG warned Fahdi it would be. It was a lot of freshly appointed Iraqi government officials in newly-purchased, expensive, western-style, Italian-made business suits accessorized with five-hundred-dollar shoes and thousand-dollar Rolex watches shouting at each other and squabbling like children in a schoolyard. The only thing a majority of the separate factions did agree on was that the INIS should be dissolved entirely. This issue took center stage for a brief few minutes during the convention, and the DG and Fahdi were suddenly in the spotlight. Not surprisingly, one of the individuals spearheading the topic of disbanding the INIS was an official representing the Interior Ministry.

"The INIS has no legal authorization to even exist," the ministry official argued before the council. They function outside the legal realm of the Iraqi Constitution and are nothing more than a rogue agency operating as an arm of the American CIA."

(Even Fahdi and I agree that the INIS was one of the few outfits maintaining some semblance of balance within the new Iraqi power structure. The INIS was the

Amanda Matti

main counterweight to the heavily Shi'a dominated Iraqi government that was very much in bed with Iran.)

Fahdi looked to the DG expecting him to vehemently defend himself and his agency, but the DG remained closed-mouth and appeared surprisingly calm.

"Even the INIS Director, General Al-Shawani is nothing but a U.S.-paid mercenary," one of the representatives from the Prime Minister's office piped in. "He stabbed his leadership in the back and ran many years ago. True, he was against Saddam, but he has a traitor's heart. Who's to say he won't jump sides again and turn against Iraq's current government?"

By this point, the DG was still relaxed, but Fahdi was fuming. He quickly lifted himself out of his seat and did exactly what the DG had instructed him not to: opened his mouth.

"We are *all* traitors are we not?" he exclaimed, prompting a shocked-eyeballing from the DG. "I mean, none of us would be in this room right now if we weren't technically traitors to the old regime. How about you all take a good look in the mirror and use your heads before you open your mouths and let your ignorance roll out."

At this, the DG reached up and put a firm hand on Fahdi's arm, signaling that it was time to return his ass to his seat. The DG still remained silent but the tension quickly died down, and a State Department ambassador redirected the meeting to a discussion regarding the training of the new Iraqi Army.

"You've spent too much time in U.S. Marine camps," the DG leaned over and whispered into Fahdi's ear. "You're too hot in the head and too vulgar in the tongue for such events," he said in a berating tone, but cracked a sly smile.

When they arrived back at the INIS building, the DG told Fahdi to join him in his office. Once in the office, the DG pulled out a bottle of Johnny Walker Blue Label Whiskey and two glasses. He poured the drinks and handed

- 236 -

Fahdi one of the glasses. They both remained silent and took simultaneous swigs of their drinks. Finally, Fahdi broke the silence.

"Look, Sir, I apologize for…"

The DG held up his hand and cut Fahdi off with a gesture. "My fault," the DG said. "I should have known better than to take you into a place like that. You are too passionate for politics," he added with a genuine smile. "You let your heart lead you instead of your head, which is why you're in the mess you're in right now with that American girl."

Fahdi remained silent and just stared down at his drink.

"Speaking of the American girl, how is she doing?"

Fahdi gave a shrug and tried to act surprised by the question as if he wasn't communicating with me, but the DG saw right through his feeble attempt at nonchalance.

"The threats of every government and army on this planet couldn't keep you from following your heart," the DG said cocking his head to the side. "That much I do know."

All Fahdi said was, "She's doing okay, Sir."

"Good. Please tell her I said hello," the general said as he took his seat in the giant leather executive chair at his desk.

"Why didn't you defend yourself today?" Fahdi asked no longer able to hold it back.

"What good would it have done?" The general answered. "There is nothing you can say to fix what is broken in this government, in this country, right now. You can only fight and work to make it better through actions. Save your words and save your energy–that's my advice. There is nothing these men could ever say to wound me in any way. I have scars that run deeper than any tongue, no matter how sharp, could ever slice." He took another swig of his whiskey. "Besides, the essence of what they said today is the truth. I staged a coup against Saddam, and the

Americans, at least the CIA, were in favor of the idea. When I failed, they offered me a pat on the back and asylum. Then Saddam tracked down all three of my sons and had them slaughtered."

"How do you keep going?" Fahdi asked, unable to fathom how the DG found the will to live after the murder of all of his children.

"You keep moving forward. You keep fighting. You keep *acting* in hopes that something you do will have an effect on this world. I maintain faith that of all the little pebbles I throw into the water, at least one will make a lasting ripple and justify the decisions I made that snatched my sons from this world and left my wife crying into her pillow every night for three years, screaming in her sleep." He looked up from his drink and directly at Fahdi. "This world is a cruel place for passionate souls, Fahdi. But it's better to feel pain than to feel nothing at all. This is why I sympathize with you and truly hope you are reunited with this girl you obviously love so much."

Chapter 23

Sunday, 18 December–Saturday, 31 December 2005

A week before Christmas, Fahdi and Omar once again found themselves in the middle of it. This time, they were attacked inside Fahdi's house. It was just the two of them because the other guys had been granted permission to remain in the INIS building full time and were taking full advantage of that privilege. Four gunmen opened fire on the front of Fahdi's home from the street. Omar and Fahdi were in the living room when blazing AK fire ripped them from sleep. Both guys rolled off their respective couches and hit the floor for cover. Luckily, most houses in Baghdad are built of solid concrete so the walls shielded them well, and rounds only made their way inside the house through the windows and front door. Omar and Fahdi got a hold of their weapons and returned blind fire in the direction they were being fired upon. Fahdi spent the entire clip of his Browning pistol and began crawling across the room to get to his AK-47 that was propped against the far wall.

When Omar was out of ammo, he, too, began crawling for his bag that had two more loaded pistol clips in it. The fire from the street ceased while Fahdi and Omar scrambled to reload. They hoped they had successfully scared off the gunmen, but no such luck. As soon as Fahdi reached his AK, he pulled out his cell phone and frantically dialed the hotline the INIS had recently established for its employees. The hotline was about ten times more useless than 9-1-1 when it came to situations like this. It was simply a line that was manned 24/7 by a watchman who took notes on the situation and passed them up the chain of command. By the time anyone was dispatched to check out the incident–that is even *if* anyone was sent at all–whoever made the call was most likely already kidnapped or dead. Fahdi gave his name, address, and a brief synopsis of what was happening to the guy on the hotline. A couple of minutes into the call, they heard someone break through the back kitchen door and enter the house. Fahdi didn't hang up the phone, but he threw it to the floor and readied his AK. He and Omar exchanged glances, but remained silent and braced themselves for a hand-to-hand fight.

They heard two voices in the kitchen but weren't sure how many gunmen were in the house. Fahdi gestured to Omar to find out if he was reloaded. Omar nodded and Fahdi gestured that he, too, was locked and loaded. The intruders made their way through the kitchen then started firing again as they entered the main living area where Fahdi and Omar were located. Fahdi returned fire from his position on the floor while Omar fired from behind the couch he was using for cover. They just hoped to get lucky and hit something. They heard one of the guys cry out in pain so they knew they at least injured one of them. They heard the injured gunman stumble back into the kitchen and out the back door, but they continued to receive fire from two more men.

Fahdi scrambled down the hallway and into one of the bedrooms, but Omar was pinned between the couch and a wall with no exit route. Knowing he was trapped, Omar laid flat on the floor and aimed his pistol from under the couch. He shot and hit another gunman in the ankle. The man fell to the floor in agony and screamed to his buddy that he'd been hit. Fahdi seized this opportunity to jump back on the offensive, and sprang from the bedroom back into the hall. He began shooting as he ran back up the hall and into the main area. He grazed the final gunman in the shoulder, which was enough to knock him to the ground. Omar emerged from his position behind the couch ready to blow each of their heads off, but Fahdi shouted, "Don't kill them!" The guy that was struck in the shoulder scrambled out of the house before Omar could get to him but the one with the shattered ankle wasn't going anywhere.

"Don't leave me here!" The wounded gunman screamed, but his accomplices were all long gone. "You assholes!"

Fahdi and Omar heard a car screech away and figured they only faced three gunmen in the house because the fourth had waited to drive the getaway car.

"Holy crap, Fahdi!" Omar said, breathless and feeling his body for bullet holes. "We shouldn't be alive! We should be dead man! What the hell just happened?"

"Shut up!" Fahdi screamed to both Omar and the man on the floor writhing in pain and still cursing his fellow gunmen who left him behind. "Who the hell are you?" He yelled, shoving his AK in the wounded man's face. The man was older than Fahdi, probably in his fourties, in good shape with an athletic build. "Who do you work for?"

The man only snarled and spit in Fahdi's face.

"I'm going to ask one more time before I shoot you in the eye and watch it come out the back of your skull," Fahdi said slowly through clenched teeth. "Who are you with and why are you after us?"

But the man just stared at Fahdi and tightened his lips in defiance.

"Fine, I have a better idea," Fahdi said, pulling the gun away from the man's face. "If you don't want to talk, I'll make you talk."

Fahdi and Omar got some rope and bound the man's arms behind his back, then Fahdi and Omar each grabbed one of the man's legs and dragged him to the backyard, making sure to pull most of his weight by his freshly-shattered ankle. The man screamed in pain, so Omar removed one of his own sweaty socks and shoved it in the man's mouth. They tied some more rope around the man's injured leg and looped the other end around a metal bar that ran along the top of the rear yard wall of Fahdi's house. Together, Omar and Fahdi pulled on the rope and began hoisting the man upside down and let him dangle from his wounded foot. They let him hang for a minute until they were afraid he would pass out from the pain. Then they released the rope and watched him slam to the ground, knocking the wind out of his lungs. He nearly choked on Omar's sock, but Fahdi graciously removed it from his mouth to see if he was ready to talk. He was.

"You, scumbags!" he spat out when Fahdi removed the sock. "I'll *kill* you! I'm going to cut off your balls and feed them to you!"

"Yeah, yeah…now who do you work for?" Fahdi asked again.

"I am on *official* business for the Interior Ministry! I am with the Badr Brigade and reinforcements from our unit are probably on their way here right now! You both are going to be so screwed when they get a hold of you," he said with an evil giggle. "If you let me live, they might only feed you one of your nuts instead of both of them!"

"So, you're a Badr reject," Fahdi asked half to himself. "And why are you after me?"

"You traitors are nothing but the American CIA's dogs! You lick their boots while they bend Iraq over and rape us!" The hostage spat back.

"The only reason you and your other Shi'ite buddies even have any power in the IM right now is *because* of the Americans!" Omar shot back, smacking him across the cheek with the butt of his pistol. "They pushed Saddam and the Sunnis down for you! Something you could never do on your own!"

The man spit blood onto the ground before he answered. "Yes, the American military did help, but not the

CIA. They want things back the way they were and even put all of Saddam's old henchmen back in power at the INIS. The same monsters who oversaw the gassing of children and the slaughter of thousands of innocent Shi'ites in Southern Iraq are back at the top over there! Running secret operations and spying on us like Saddam's regime never left. It is a new day in Iraq, a day for the Shi'ite people to take back what is rightfully ours and lead our country to greatness. Saddam's former dogs are simply now the CIA's dogs and you should all be put down! You're murderers and torturers! The CIA taught the generation before you how to torture and murder and now they are teaching you! Look at you! Look at what you are doing now!"

Fahdi was about to bash the hostage in the teeth with the butt of his AK when they heard pounding coming from the house. Someone was at Fahdi's bullet-hole-riddled front door, pounding and shouting for someone to open up. Omar stayed with the hostage in the backyard while Fahdi stepped inside the kitchen door pistol in hand.

"Who's there?" Fahdi shouted out in Arabic.

"We're here in response to a call made to the hotline. This address was given," an Iraqi male voice called back from the other side of the front door. Fahdi shoved his pistol into the back of his Adidas tracksuit pants and went to the front door. When he opened it, he recognized the two men as members of the INIS security squad and each was armed with an AK-47.

"Are you the one who made the call?" one of the men asked Fahdi.

Fahdi nodded.

"May we see your badge?"

No one had yet mentioned the INIS by name, but Fahdi knew what badge they wanted to see. He led the men inside and retrieved his badge to prove his identity.

"Who else is here with you? Is anyone in need of medical attention?" he asked in a tone that made it obvious to Fahdi he already knew there was an injured person on the property.

"Omar, also an agency employee, is in the backyard with one of the gunmen who attacked us. We injured him in the shootout," Fahdi replied and led the men to the backyard.

"Ah, the cavalry's here," Omar announced sarcastically as the group made their way into the backyard. "You guys missed all the fun!"

The INIS security guys untied the gunman and surveyed his injuries. "We will take him with us," one of the men declared, and the two security guards carried the man out front to their vehicle.

The following afternoon, Fahdi and Omar were both summoned to the INIS security office. Upon arrival, two U.S. officials, who were obviously awaiting their arrival, greeted them. The two men politely introduced themselves as Max and Steve and gave no indication as to exactly *who* they were.

"We wanted to ask you gentlemen about the incident last night. Can you tell us what exactly occurred at, I believe it was, your home, Fahdi?" one of the men asked.

Fahdi and Omar reiterated the prior evening's incident, but did their best to keep the details to a minimum, knowing the fact these guys now knew their names and faces was not a good thing.

"Well, we want you gentlemen to know that we sympathize with you regarding the attack, but we cannot condone the unwarranted abuse you subjected the wounded IM official to following the incident," Steve declared. "The Interior Ministry has reported this case all the way up to the Prime Minister's office and is calling for your dismissal from the INIS and even your arrest for cruel and unusual punishment under the crimes against humanity act."

"You've got to be fucking kidding!" Fahdi said.

"*They* attacked *us*!" Omar declared excitedly. "They shot up his house and broke in to come after *us*!"

"And this isn't the first time they've come after us," Fahdi added. "My car's been shot up twice–they almost killed my mom and little sister just last week! This is bullshit."

"Look, we understand," Max interrupted. "The relationships between separate factions of the Iraqi government, particularly between the INIS and the Interior Ministry, are very shaky right now. We are well aware of the kidnappings of INIS employees and have a strong suspicion the Interior Ministry and perhaps even the Prime Minister's office is involved."

"Oh really?" Omar said mockingly. "Are you geniuses just now figuring this out?"

"So what's going to happen to us?" Fahdi asked as calmly as possible.

"Well, on the upside, the director general and I spent the morning on the phone with officials over at the IM regarding this situation, and we reached an agreement to basically call everything even," Max informed them.

"I think the general likes you," Max said to Fahdi with a half-smile. "He's definitely got a soft spot for you, and I know the man pretty well. He's a hard old bastard with soft spots for no one. But I believe you would have been safe anyway," Max added with a hint of derision. "The U.S. isn't going to let you go anywhere until another matter that I'm sure you're familiar with is cleared up first."

"All we're asking is that you refrain from engaging in armed conflict with anyone," Steve advised. "Seek cover, try to get out of the area, and call the hotline–that's what it's for." At the mention of the hotline, Fahdi and Omar just rolled their eyes.

"Well, the best way to avoid all this is to allow us to stay here in the building permanently," Fahdi suggested.

"I'm sorry, but that's not our call," Max answered. "That's a matter you'll have to take up with the director general's office."

"Yeah, been there, done that, was told to fuck off," Omar replied fuming. "While you dickwads sit all secure and cozy on your bases within the Green Zone, we're the ones out there fighting the war you assholes started! So I apologize if we're not performing to your standards and liking, but tough shit! Until we start getting some real support from you assholes, I'll hang whoever the hell I want by their balls from my goddamn front porch."

*****

I requested leave to visit my family in Ohio for Christmas, but was once again emphatically denied permission to leave the area. I wasn't surprised and I really wasn't even that disappointed. I was just sick of being confined and feeling trapped. I had no desire to face my entire family for the holidays; it would have just been a firing squad of questions and judgments that would have made a court martial look like a Girl Scout picnic.

They shut down all the non-essential offices on base for a week, so I didn't have to report to the Master-at-Arms's office. I just sat in my room in my townhouse and spent most of the week on instant messenger with Fahdi. The excess time alone and the first snowfall of the season plunged me into a deeper depression. A few days before Christmas, I went for a routine check-up at the military medical office on base. Unsurprisingly, they informed me that my blood pressure was pretty high, giving me hypertension. I immediately thought of Fahdi and his elevated blood pressure and felt oddly comforted by the fact that at least we were sharing something. My loss of appetite from the stress had also taken its toll and was evident when I stepped on the scale and realized I'd lost more than ten pounds since coming home from Iraq. On my petite 5'1" frame, ten pounds was like twenty or more on the average person. (Which depressingly works the same both ways. If I gain five pounds, I go up an entire clothing size.)

The constant fear that I could receive a knock on my door at any time and be arrested and hauled off to the brig, coupled with the terror that shot through me every time the phone rang fearing it was news that Fahdi was either dead or seriously injured was not conducive to a healthy lifestyle. To top everything off, I had another phone meeting with my lawyer, who cheerily reminded me that investigations like mine could take years to complete, and even though my contract with the Navy was up the following summer, I could be placed on a legal hold and forced to remain on active duty until my investigation was closed.

I was at rock bottom when I checked my mailbox the Tuesday after Christmas and saw an envelope from the USCIS–United States Immigration and Citizenship Services. I held my breath and ran inside my house. I bounded up the stairs two at a time until I reached the third floor. Once I was in my room, I threw the rest of the mail on my desk and ripped into the envelope from immigration. Inside was a single official looking piece of paper. I merely glanced at the header and tears of joy filled my eyes. "NOTICE OF APPROVAL" was written across the top of the paper. When I was able to focus my vision again, I learned that Fahdi's fiancé visa application had been reviewed and approved by the U.S. validation center and had been forwarded to the U.S. embassy in Amman, Jordan for processing. It was a small victory! We still had months of paperwork and interviews ahead of us before Fahdi had a visa in hand, but considering the circumstances at the time, I was elated by any ounce of good news that came my way. I immediately jumped on the phone to pass the good news on to Fahdi.

"Hey, guess what I just got in the mail," I said as soon as Fahdi answered.

"What?"

I then remembered that he still had no idea about the application to begin with, so I started from the beginning. "Six weeks ago, I filed a petition with U.S. Immigration for you to get a fiancé visa to come to the U.S."

"What?!? Are you serious?"

I immediately deflated. He sounded pissed.

"You're going to get yourself deeper into trouble, Mandy. You shouldn't have done that."

"Well, I was going to tell you that I received a response from them. They *approved* the petition. They sent your file to the U.S. embassy in Amman to start processing your visa."

His tone immediately changed. "Seriously?"

"Seriously," I confirmed.

"So what happens now?" he asked.

"Well, I'm going to call the embassy in Amman as soon as I get off the phone with you and see what I can find out from them."

"Oh my God, this is the best news I've heard in months," he said with a shaky voice. "Do you really think they'll give me a visa? I mean, considering everything we're dealing with right now?"

"Well, they have no grounds to deny us," I replied. "Neither of us has been charged with anything, and U.S. Government agencies are so disconnected from each other, we'll probably be married with three kids before the Navy, NSA, or CIA could get around to blocking a visa from immigration. If I've learned anything while working for the government, it's that agencies don't like to communicate with one another. They all think they're better than each other and don't want to share their secrets. And considering the sensitivity of our case, I'm sure no one wants to pick up the phone and explain to immigration why they should shelf our visa application."

As soon as I hung up with Fahdi, I called the U.S. embassy in Amman. They confirmed their receipt of our application and said the consulate was processing the package. I knew getting a visa still didn't solve all of our problems, but my main goal at the time was to get Fahdi out of Iraq and into the U.S. Even if I wasn't free from the Navy or locked up in a brig somewhere when Fahdi made it here. As long as he was on U.S. soil, I knew he could claim asylum. All he had to do was prove that returning to his native country would be an imminent risk to his life– obviously not an issue. I just wanted him safe. I'd worry about fighting the Navy and NSA and whomever else later. As long as he survived, everything else could be fixed.

Over the next couple of weeks, Fahdi continued to work for the general as his private translator. In spite of his less-than-professional outburst at the Department of State convention, the general assigned Fahdi to attend several more meetings and conferences as the INIS's unofficial representative/messenger boy at various locations within the Green Zone and throughout Baghdad. When Fahdi asked the DG why he was sending him on all these errands that individuals much higher up than he should have been conducting, the DG replied with a smile, "Because you and your friend smacked around four of the Interior Ministry's henchmen. My sending you to meetings with them rubs it in their faces and that gives me pleasure."

Chapter 24

Sunday, 1 January–Saturday, 21 January 2006

Like Christmas, I rang in the New Year alone in my room talking to Fahdi via instant messenger. My roommate had returned from her TDY in Qatar, but she was off at a New Year's bash somewhere in the city. She'd invited me to go with her, but I had no desire to be surrounded by a sweaty crowd of drunken people. Fahdi and I sullenly observed the fact that we had now been apart longer than we were actually together. But we took it as a good sign because we were both still as determined as ever to fight to be together.

I was anxiously anticipating word from Amman regarding Fahdi's visa application, but instead, I received a call on January 5th from NCIS. They wanted to meet with me again. Busted. I knew they were calling me in to discuss the little stunt I pulled in applying for Fahdi's visa.

When I arrived at the familiar interrogation room, Agent Argyle and Agent Foster greeted me with their phony smiling faces. "Amanda!" Argyle said happily, rising from his seat and extending his hand for me to shake. "How have you been?"

I gave their BS right back to them and eagerly shook their hands, flashing them back a broad, fake smile of my own. "I've been great, guys," I said with mock enthusiasm. "How's life been treating you both? Or I guess I should ask how *my* life's been treating you since that's what you spend your days rooting around in for evidence of my treachery that will no doubt make you both heroes."

I'd recently discovered that my case was anything but cold. The NCIS was covering all their bases and digging deeply. Rumors on a military base spread faster than within a middle school cheerleading squad. I'd caught wind of reports that every U.S. person who had been stationed at the base in Baghdad during the time I was there had been questioned about me. The NCIS couldn't get to Iraq to question them, so they were waiting to grab each person individually as their TDYs ended and they trickled back into the U.S. Everyone I worked directly with at the building had been questioned at length, as well as my roommates back at the Baghdad base. Even all of my friends and anyone who worked with me at NSA prior to my Iraq deployment were rounded up for questioning. My roommate came back home from Qatar only to discover the NCIS had confiscated her computer from our townhouse to go through it and see if I'd been using it to communicate with Fahdi or plot terrorist activities. I felt horrible and did my best to apologize to her. She was really cool and told me not to worry about it. Thankfully, unlike my laptop, which I hadn't seen since the NCIS carted it off upon my return and didn't really expect to see ever again, they returned my roommate's computer within a few days–having copied the entire hard drive I'm sure.

"We wanted to bring you in today to talk to you about the immigration visa you applied for several weeks ago," Agent Argyle said, getting to the point.

"Did I break any laws or violate any orders by applying for a visa?" I asked, feigning naiveté as I already knew the answer.

Argyle and Foster looked at each other, both seeming at a loss for words. "Well, no not technically," Foster answered. "But it doesn't help your situation either. It just doesn't look good, that's all."

"Guys, I think we're beyond 'looking good,'" I retorted, trying my best to look relaxed even though I was anything but. "You people are trying to nail me to the wall for espionage. We're talking a crime that carries the *death penalty*. Once you threaten a person with something like that, it's hard to ask them to think rationally before doing something that may make them 'look bad.'"

"Amanda, we are on your side," Argyle said, leaning across the table and sounding almost convincing with his plea. "We want you to be able to go back to your old life, to continue your career in the Navy. You're so young with so much potential. You've got your whole life ahead of you. Don't throw it away."

"I have no desire to return to my old life," I said coldly. "I have a new mission now and an entirely clearer understanding of this world. I'll never be able to go back and I wouldn't ever want to."

Foster tried to get through to me from another angle. "Woman to woman, Amanda," she said in a friendly tone. "I feel for you. I honestly do, and I don't want to see you get hurt. You're a good person, Amanda, and I know how awful you'd feel if you were responsible for helping a person with bad intentions get into this country. But even putting that aside, you have to at least acknowledge the possibility that you are at least being used. Fahdi could very well simply be using you to get to the U.S. And I'm not even saying he's a terrorist mastermind or anything even close to that–chances are, he isn't. But that doesn't mean he's not still using you just for a green card. I've never been to Iraq myself, but I can only imagine isn't a very nice place to be living right now. Can you at least think about that? Please, for me?"

"For yourself, too," Argyle added to send the point home.

Their distressed pleas made me realize one thing: they were desperate. I knew then and there that they were scraping the bottom of the barrel in my investigation and had found nothing to pin me with. If they were resorting to an attack on my emotions to drive Fahdi and me apart, then they were standing on their last leg.

"Amanda, we don't think you're a spy," Argyle added. "In fact, we're sure of that. Your investigation is wrapping up and should be closed soon. We're here because we truly care about you and we want you to be safe."

"Thanks for your concern, but I can take care of myself," I replied bitterly.

*****

One morning in mid-January, the general summoned Fahdi to his office. Fahdi figured he was going to be given another assignment to attend some meeting, but the DG had bad news, very bad news. When Fahdi entered the office the DG was seated behind his massive desk signing documents.

"It appears our *friends* over at the Interior Ministry have plenty of friends of their own in the new parliament," the DG said without even looking up from his work. He laid his pen down and looked at Fahdi. "The Badr Brigade has been granted official status to operate as a police squad within the Baghdad city limits and are now authorized to function legally as an arm of the Interior Ministry."

Fahdi just shook his head in disbelief.

"Oh, but I have even better news," the DG continued. "Along with this new status comes the power to issue arrest warrants through the Iraqi courts. They submitted their first list today. You'll never guess who's on it."

Fahdi's heart sank into his stomach. "No way," were the only words he managed to get out.

The DG nodded. "It appears you really stepped in it when you shot up that squad that came after you and smacked around one of their injured men. Turns out, he's the son of an IM bureaucrat who doesn't like that you nearly crippled his son."

"So what happens to Omar and me?" Fahdi asked now, visibly shaking.

"Actually, just you," the DG corrected. "No mention of Omar. They came to *your* house, they probably don't even know who Omar is. He got lucky. But you are not alone; there are several other employees here at the INIS whom the IM would like to *speak* with. I was kindly asked via court order to turn you over to the custody of the IM when you and the others reported to work today." Fahdi remained silent. "And I am going to kindly ignore this request." Fahdi breathed a sigh of relief. "But we can't ignore them forever. I do not have the authority to overrule a court order, and our American friends have told me they are taking a neutral stance on this issue. I suggest you remain within the walls of this building and keep your head down. All we can do is hope this blows over."

The IM's determination to arrest Fahdi did not blow over, however. Three days later, two Badr Force officers arrived at the INIS with Fahdi's arrest warrant in hand. They were escorted to the DG's office where the general and Max were awaiting them. They showed the DG the warrant and told him to release Fahdi into their custody by order of the Iraqi courts.

"I'd be happy to let you gentlemen haul him off, but he's not here," the DG lied. "He hasn't shown up for work the past three days and no one seems to know where he's gone. Rumor has it, he went to Jordan."

"I hear he's got family up in Turkey," Max chimed in.

"No, I think it's Syria," the general corrected, carrying on the charade.

The Badr officers huffed, knowing they were getting the runaround. "Well, I think I'll just call a squad to come in and search every inch of this building just to make sure he hasn't been hiding out under your nose."

"You gentlemen may have an arrest warrant, but unless you have a search warrant as well, you will be seeing no more of this building than the inside of this office," the DG informed them in a calm tone.

The lead Badr officer scowled. "We will be back," he confidently informed the DG and then left with his men.

"You know you can't hide him away in here forever," Max said to the general after the Badr Officers had gone. "If they keep pushing for this and you keep stonewalling, we're going to end up with a very public incident on our hands that neither one of us can afford right now."

"Yes, yes, I know," the DG replied with a wave of his hand.

"It'll be good if you can babysit him for the time being to keep the clowns over at NCIS happy while they conduct their little witch hunt into him and his girlfriend, but if they decided not to pursue any charges against him, you're going to have to hand him over to the IM…unless you have any better ideas."

The DG thought for a minute. "I wish your government would arrest him. Even if you throw him in Abu Ghraib, it'll be a million times safer than a secret IM prison."

The DG brainstormed for a couple of hours and finally came up with an idea. Although he knew it would only be another temporary solution, it would buy Fahdi some more time. He made his way to Fahdi's office to tell him the plan. The DG rapped lightly on Fahdi's office door and, almost immediately, the door opened a few inches. Fahdi peered through the small opening to see who was at his door.

"Sir!" Fahdi gasped in surprise at seeing the DG on the other side. He swung the door open the rest of the way and invited the general inside. "I wasn't sure who to expect," Fahdi said, offering the DG a chair. "One of the security guys came by this morning and told me to not leave my office on your orders. What's going on?"

"Your friends at the Interior Ministry sent their henchmen here for you this morning," the DG explained. "Don't worry, I told them I hadn't seen you in several days and was unaware of your whereabouts."

"Thank you, Sir."

The general rolled his eyes. "Don't thank me yet. Go ahead and have a seat," he said and motioned Fahdi to a chair. "Look, you can't hide forever," the general replied solemnly. "We already know there are employees here at the INIS leaking information to the Interior Ministry. If they don't already know for sure that I'm keeping you in a closet, they will soon. I've decided to assign you to another remote operations site, similar to the one you and Mandy were deployed to on the Syrian border last month. It's not going to hold them off forever, but it'll put some ground between you and Baghdad and hopefully, buy you some time. With any luck, the Americans will arrest you before the IM. I know this is a grim hope, but trust me, an American prison is far better than the alternative."

Fahdi nodded his head. "I understand, Sir. I'd rather stay here in Baghdad where I'm able to better keep up with Mandy's case, but I appreciate your help. I'll go."

"There is one more thing," the general added in a solemn tone. "You will not be able to have any communication with Mandy while you are out there."

"What? This was their idea wasn't it?"

The DG knew by "their idea" Fahdi meant the American government.

"Jesus Christ," Fahdi continued. "These people are fighting two wars around the globe and they're wasting this much energy on us? Just to keep us apart!"

"I'm not shipping you off because the Americans are pulling my strings or because I want to break up you and your girlfriend," the DG retorted sternly. "I'm doing this to keep your ass alive! I know the only thing that matters to you in this world right now is Mandy, but everything you two are fighting for won't be worth shit if you're dead! And, believe it or not, the fact the Americans are still interested in you *is* what's keeping you out of the IM's hands right now. The only reason I even have the ability to keep you employed here at the INIS and am able to ship you off is because the Americans sure as hell don't want you in the hands of the IM. So, if I were you, I'd pray the Americans' interest in you outlasts the IM's or you're very well a dead man."

Fahdi knew the DG had a point and backed off.

"Now, the next time you communicate with Mandy tell her you're going to lay low for a while someplace safe and you'll be out of touch until further notice. Trust me, she'll understand. She already knows about the attacks and that Badr is after you." Fahdi shot the general an awkward glance. "What? Like you didn't know we were listening to your phone calls and reading your mail? If you two truly love each other the way you profess, this will be nothing. Now get some sleep," he barked in a commanding tone. "You fly out tomorrow night."

*****

The next morning, Fahdi did as instructed and called to tell me he would be hiding out for a few weeks at a satellite base. He didn't tell me where and I didn't ask. He just told me to trust him and I did. I was just relieved he was getting out of Baghdad, but I dreaded being out of contact with him for so long.

Chapter 25

Sunday, 22 January–Tuesday, 14 March 2006

Fahdi spent the next six weeks in exile somewhere in the Iraqi desert working as a bottom-of-the-rung INIS operative. Unfortunately, the Interior Ministry continued its push to round up everyone on their wanted list–a list that seemed to grow by the hundreds every week. Arresting officers were dispatched to the INIS several more times throughout the month of February to collect Fahdi as well as several other INIS employees. The DG maintained his story that he had no idea where Fahdi was, but he was discouraged by the IM's persistence and began to worry that the satellite base Fahdi was at still wouldn't be far enough to keep him safe.

Meanwhile, I passed the six weeks in slow agony. There was still no news regarding my case and not a word from Fahdi. I felt like I was in a vacuum. Then finally, on March 7, 2006, I received the news I'd been hoping to hear for the last six months. I was called to the JAG office on base to meet with Lt. Klitch. When I arrived, he informed me that the joint NCIS/NSA criminal investigation against me had been closed as no substantial evidence was found to merit the pursuit of any espionage charges in a federal court. He spoke these words to me with such bitterness, he looked as if he was in physical pain. But I was so overwhelmed with a rush of emotional relief I didn't give a shit how much he hated me at that moment. I just sank to the floor of his office and began sobbing with joy.

"This does *not*, however, mean the Navy will not be pursuing internal punishment for your offenses," Lt. Klitch announced loudly in order to rise above the sound of my jubilant weeping. "The Commanding Officer has decided you will receive a non-judicial punishment for violating the written no-contact order, as we have a pile of evidence that proves you have been in continuous communication with the Iraqi man since you returned."

I regained my composure, got to my feet, and looked that asshole dead in his eyes. "I don't give a shit what you do to me," I said with acid in my tone. "There's nothing within your pathetic power that could even make me bat an eye after the hell I've been through. I apologize that you missed out on the pleasure of court-martialing me and watching me sent off to rot in prison, or worse. So sorry to disappoint you," I finished with disdain.

"Your disciplinary review board will convene Mach 15th at 1 p.m. in the conference room down the hall," Lt. Klitch said, choosing not to respond to my statement. "You are to arrive fifteen minutes early in your dress blue uniform."

"Yes, Sir," I said, fighting to suppress a smile.

I returned to the Master-at-Arms's office and informed Chief Viraez of the good news. To anyone else in the military, finding out they were to receive an NJP would have been a serious downer, but for me, it meant victory.

"I'm really happy for you, McEwen," Viraez said with a smile and a pat on the back. "As you know, we typically force those awaiting a DRB to remain in the barracks the night before to ensure they don't try to leave the area, but something tells me I don't have to worry about you not showing up for yours."

"Oh, I'll be there," I stated assuredly. "With a goddamn smile on my face!"

"Good. Now go home and get some rest. I'll be marching you into a room tomorrow full of a lot of angry sailors."

"Roger that, Chief."

The fact that my DRB date was scheduled for the Ides of March should have warned me that our war wasn't yet over, but I was so elated at this point in time, I couldn't have even imagined the horrors that were about to occur in Fahdi's world.

The day after I received my glorious news, Fahdi received a satellite phone call from the DG. All he told him was that he was sending two of his personal security guards to come get Fahdi and escort him back the INIS building in Baghdad. Fahdi tried to find out what was going on, but he knew from the sound of the DG's voice that it couldn't be good. The fact that the DG was sending two of his private security guards meant one thing: the DG or *someone* was worried that he was going to try and run.

When Fahdi arrived at the INIS building the next day, the guards walked him straight to the DG's office.

"Welcome back," the DG said as Fahdi entered the office.

"What's going on?" Fahdi demanded trying to get right to the point. "Why did you bring me back?"

"I'm afraid I have good news and bad news." He went on to inform Fahdi that I was in the clear. He told him my investigation had been closed and no criminal charges would be filed against me. Unfortunately, this also meant the Americans had no interest in keeping him around anymore.

"So what does this mean?" Fahdi asked, waiting for the blow.

"The IM found out where we had you stashed. They would have been out there to pick you up themselves, but I convinced them to allow me to bring you back myself and promised to turn you over to them tomorrow morning."

"But how did they know?"

"I'm not sure. We're looking into that right now," the DG answered, but Fahdi could tell he was holding something back. "Fahdi, I promise you I'll do everything in my power to get you released."

"If anything happens to me, I want *you* to be the one to call Mandy," Fahdi said, staring the general down. "I don't want her hearing it from anyone else." The DG nodded.

As Fahdi was leaving the DG's office, he practically ran into Max. Upon seeing Max, everything suddenly made sense to Fahdi.

"This you *your* doing isn't it?" Fahdi said with venom in his voice. "You told the IM where the DG sent me, didn't you! You finally figured out that I'm not some sort of double agent and Mandy didn't commit any espionage so you're burning me. How nice for you that the IM was ready to step in and do your dirty work for you."

Max, of course, completely maintained his calm demeanor. "I am sorry how things worked out for you, Fahdi. At least you can rest easy knowing Mandy's problems will soon be over."

Fahdi wasn't sure if by "problems", Max was referring to him or my investigation–probably both.

Just as Fahdi turned to storm away Max reached out and firmly grasped Fahdi's shoulder to keep him right where he was. Fahdi shot him an icy glare, then Max leaned in and spoke in a low voice near Fahdi's ear.

"Keep your eyes and ears open. If I happen to come and *get* you, I'll be expecting to gain something useful in return," Max relayed in a cryptic tone, but Fahdi understood perfectly. Max was hoping to use him for recon on the inside of the IM prison. "Are we clear?" Max asked.

"Crystal," Fahdi replied and walked away. He knew he was now nothing but a puppet and Max held all the strings.

That night, Fahdi climbed up to the roof of the INIS and sat in the same spot where we'd had our first kiss. He remained on the roof chain-smoking his way through nearly a carton of cigarettes to counter the urge to contact me. He figured it was better if I continued to believe he was simply holed up at some obscure base in the desert than rotting in an IM prison cell. He reminisced of our short time together and came to terms with the idea that we may never see each other again.

Fahdi awoke in the morning to a large hand gently shaking his shoulder. He opened his eyes and realized he'd fallen asleep on the rooftop and slept through the night. The sun was just breaking over the horizon when he rolled over to see who had awoken him and looked up into the face of Abu Zaid.

The burly man smiled and said, "I thought I might find you up here."

Fahdi sat up and rubbed the sleep from his eyes.

"They are looking for you," Abu Zaid continued. "The Americans came to our department thinking you were there perhaps with your brother. When they said you should be in the building but they couldn't find you anywhere I had a good idea of where you were."

"How *did* you know where to find me?" Fahdi asked.

Abu Zaid smiled knowingly. "I've been in love. And I've also been an intelligence officer my entire adult life. You think I didn't know where you and Mandy sneaked off to all those nights?"

"I may never see her again," Fahdi said in a dazed tone staring out at the rising sun.

"Yes, you will. God would not have brought you together from separate ends of the world just to tear you apart. There would be no reasoning in that, and above all, He is reasonable."

"From what I can tell, I don't think God likes me very much anyway," Fahdi replied, standing up and brushing the sand and dust from the roof off his clothing.

"If He didn't like you, you wouldn't still be here, and He wouldn't have placed Mandy in your path. He's given you his greatest gift of all: love. And no true love in this world comes without a battle of some kind. The harder the battle, the truer the love."

Fahdi just prayed Abu Zaid's words were the truth.

"Now come, they are waiting for you."

Abu Zaid walked with Fahdi back inside and to the elevators. They rode in silence down to the main floor of the building. When the doors of the elevator opened, Abu Zaid looked at Fahdi.

"Stay strong, my friend. And *Inshallah*, you will be reunited with her soon."

Fahdi nodded, exited the elevator, and headed for the general's office.

In the DG's office an IM official and two Iraqi Police officers were awaiting his arrival. "Here he is, gentlemen," the DG announced with a heaviness in his voice that probably only Fahdi heard.

"Is there anything else?"

"That will be all, Sir. We appreciate your cooperation in this matter..." the IM official started to say, but the general cut him off.

"Get out of my office. And get out of my building," the DG said through clenched teeth, fighting to subdue the fury in his voice.

Chapter 26

"Mandy"
Wednesday, 15 March–Sunday, 19 March
2006

On the afternoon of March 15, 2006, I stood at attention in my dress blues outside the Ft. Meade JAG building conference room with Chief Viraez at my side waiting to escort me into my disciplinary review board. When I was called to enter, I realized how popular my case really was. NJP hearings and the DRBs that typically preceded them were open for any sailor in the command to attend. By allowing these open brow beatings, sailors saw firsthand the consequences of screwing up and hopefully learned from their shipmate's mistakes. The relatively small conference room my DRB was held in was completely packed. Five khaki-clad upper-enlisted sailors sat at a rectangular table in the center of the room and all four walls of the room were lined with sailors five or six deep. I'd been to a couple of DRBs in my six years, but the most spectators I'd ever seen in attendance were maybe ten or fifteen people aside from the five members on the board. There were at least fifty onlookers at my DRB and more crowded outside the conference room door straining for a peek at the action. I felt like a medieval criminal headed for the guillotine, and I was kicking myself for not thinking to sell tickets to the celebration. Damn.

Once I was in the middle of the room standing at attention before the board, the Command Master Chief read my charges aloud.

"Petty Officer McEwen, you are being charged with a violation of Uniform Code of Military Justice article 92, 'Disobeying a lawful written order' for failure to adhere to a no-contact order issued by the Commanding Officer of Naval Information and Operations Command, Ft. Meade, Maryland. Do you understand this charge?"

"Yes, Master Chief."

"Do you deny this charge?"

"No, Master Chief."

"Do you understand that when your CO issues an order you are to follow it without question?" one of the other chiefs on the board barked.

"Yes, Chief," I replied.

"Well, obviously you don't," the same chief spat back.

"There were extenuating circumstances, Chief," I declared.

"Yes, we understand you've become romantically involved with an Iraqi citizen you met while on deployment in Baghdad," a third member of the board piped in. "Do you have any idea what kind of negative light this sheds on the Navy? On the entire U.S. military? You were sent over there to do a job and you spent your time fooling around like you were on vacation in Vegas!"

I remained silent. There was nothing I could have said to change the views and ideas they already had firmed up in their heads, so I didn't even try.

"I am embarrassed and disgusted to even see you in a Navy uniform," the same chief continued. "I wish I could have brought parents who have lost sons and daughters fighting in the war over there into this DRB and made you look them in the eye and explain how you treated it as if it were some kind of frat party."

I continued to bite my tongue and stared straight ahead, looking right through them. I succeeded in maintaining this posture until a comment rocked me from my poise and I bit back in defense.

"Here's what I want to know, Petty Officer," the senior chief seated on the far right end of the table said. "Out of 400-some-million Americans to choose from, why do you have to be with an Iraqi man?"

At that question even several people in the room, all of whom had been careful to barely breathe much less make a sound, let out audible gasps. Even the Master Chief heading the board visibly stiffened at the outlandish question.

"Excuse me?" I asked, intonating in my voice that I'd heard him but was giving him a chance to recant what he'd just said.

"Seriously, I'm sure everyone in this room wants to know why a pretty girl like you feels she simply *has* to be with someone like him?"

"I shouldn't even validate this atrocious question with a response, but just for the sake of argument, I'm going to go out on a limb here and bet that more than a couple of people in this room have spouses who are originally from a different country. I know for a fact that Chief Porter's wife is from the Philippines, where he met her on assignment," I pointed out about one of the chiefs at the table. "And how many other Navy and other military members have spouses from Japan, Korea, Vietnam, Taiwan, and numerous European countries. Granted, in most cases the military member is male and the spouse is female, so I guess that's the factor here. When a male U.S. military member marries a foreigner it's an acceptable happening–she's a war prize. But if a female military member falls in love with a foreigner, red flags immediately shoot up. She's obviously being tricked. Someone's using her female emotions against her. She just can't see past her naïve little nose and realize that a foreign man is only using her for what he can get out of her. And oh shit!" I exclaimed putting my hand over my mouth in mock alarm, "she is an intelligence analyst with a security clearance! If she's emotionally involved with someone, chances are she's sharing national secrets every time she spreads her legs because that's just the reality of how it works, you know. Screw you!" I shouted at the asshole chief. "Why don't you just tie me to a stake and light a fire?"

"I think we've covered everything we needed to," the Master Chief said, stepping in to neutralize the situation. He was smart enough to know the last question was completely out of line, so he decided to go ahead and adjourn the DRB before things got completely out of hand.

Chief Viraez escorted me back out of the room and we walked in silence across the compound back to the Master-at-Arms building. My face was still red and I was fuming on the inside.

"Just let it go, McEwen," Chief Viraez finally broke the silence as the climbed the stairs of the building. "I can't believe they took it that far, but it's not worth getting all worked up over. Four more months and you'll be leaving all this crap behind and you won't give a damn what they think or say."

"Ignorant jerks," I muttered. "It's no wonder practically everything our military touches turns to crap considering we've got dicks like that at the helm."

"They're still your superiors, and even if they don't believe it, I know you still have respect for that uniform you're wearing and what it stands for."

"Respect the uniform, even if the man in it deserves none," I said reciting a popular phrase most military members learned early on in their careers.

"Exactly," Chief Viraez said with a nod.

I spent the next week preparing for my NJP, which we call a Captain's Mast in the Navy.

It's basically a mock court trial where the judge is your commanding officer. He or she will read you your charges, decide what you will be convicted guilty of, and then hand down a punishment. There's a list of punishments that the CO is authorized to give you according to Article 15 of the UCMJ, which governs the rules and regulations of non-judicial punishment. These punishments can be 1-60 days of restriction, a fine of up to two half-month's pay, reduction in rank, extra duty, or any combination of these.

Restriction was basically like being grounded by your CO. You were given a bare room in the barracks (which you would most likely share with one or two other restrictees) that had nothing in it but beds and wall lockers with an iron. You must wear your uniform or PT gear, which was just military workout clothing (typically a Navy brand t-shirt and matching sweatpants), for the entire duration of the restriction. You could only leave the restriction room for your three daily meals at the galley and use the gym once a day for an hour. You could also leave to perform your extra duties usually assigned along with your restriction, which were typically things like scrubbing the floors and bathrooms in the barracks. You would also leave to report to whatever office you already worked in for your usual duties, but you wore a special badge that identified you as a restrictee so your supervisors knew to keep an eye on you, not allow you to interact with others, or leave the work area. Aside from these exceptions, you only left the restricted room to report to the quarterdeck, the main entrance to the barracks that was manned 24/7 by two watchmen, every morning at 6 a.m., again at noon, and finally at 8 p.m. At these times the officer on duty inspected your uniform (it better be wrinkle free and your boots better shine) and your restriction room and bathroom for cleanliness and to ensure you hadn't smuggled in any contraband. It was pretty much like being in boot camp again: no TV, no phones, no Internet, no communication with the outside world, no interacting with anyone.

Since it was highly likely I'd be serving some time on restriction, I made arrangements in case I wouldn't be home for the next two months. I paid up all of my bills for the next two months, arranged for one of my friends to babysit my cat, and called my parents to let them know what was going on. I wasn't really even dreading restriction. They allowed us to have books (military-related of course) and keep a journal. Two months of peaceful, distraction-free time to do nothing but read and write–not exactly punishment for me.

The day of my Mast, I stood outside the same conference room decked out in my dress blue uniform with Chief Viraez by my side, exactly as I had the week before. Inside the conference room, my Commanding Officer and Executive Officer stood behind a podium at the far end of the room. Again, there was a roomful of attendees (Masts were also open invitation affairs) lining both sides of the room, leaving just a narrow aisle down the room from the door to the podium.

It was procedure for the Command Master-at-Arms to escort the sailor receiving the Mast into the room and stand shoulder-to-shoulder with him or her during the proceeding in case they snap and try to physically attack the CO or XO (Executive Officer) at some point. Typically, the sailor being Masted didn't work in the Master-at-Arms's office for seven months prior to their Mast and closely knew the Master-at-Arms the way I did. So I felt fortunate to be escorted into my Mast by Chief Viraez, whom I now considered an ally and friend.

My Captain's Mast was a pretty cut and dry affair. My CO told me I'd been found guilty of violating UCMJ article 92, "Failure to obey a lawful written order," by disobeying the no contact order issued to me by my CO. I was lucky in that the commanding officer who'd actually issued the order was no longer our CO. The CO changed almost every four years and we'd just gotten a new one in December. I could tell the current CO wasn't really that angry over the whole thing; he never even used a stern tone during the proceeding. It was basically just a yeah-you-did-this-after-you-were-told-not-to,   here's-your-slap-on-the-wrist affair He didn't even give me the harshest punishment he could have. He just busted me in rank and gave me forty-five days of restriction. He could have given me sixty days of restriction, or forty-five days of restriction with two hours a day of extra duty (scrubbing toilets and floors), and fined me half of my pay for two months, so I got off pretty easy.

When the Mast was over, Chief Viraez and I were waiting outside the conference room for the captain to finish signing all the legal paperwork when the XO approached me.

"I heard about some of the less-than-acceptable comments that were made at your DRB last week," he said quietly.

Neither he nor the CO were present for the DRB as it was ceremoniously just a chance for the upper-enlisted members of the command to chew you out.

"For what it's worth, I want you to know that I sincerely apologize for what was said and I wish you the best of luck with everything," he concluded, offering his hand for me to shake.

I simply said, "Thank you, Sir."

Since the punishment began immediately following the Mast, Chief Viraez walked me to my car so I could retrieve my packed sea bag and then escorted me to my restriction room in the barracks. "I'm truly sorry about this, McEwen."

"It's really okay, Chief," I replied, forcing a smile. "You can't imagine how relieved I am that this is the worst punishment I ended up with. I could be preparing for a court martial right now."

"I know, but you still don't deserve this." I just shrugged. "I'll see you tomorrow morning at the office. I requested that you still work for me on your usual schedule throughout your restriction."

"Thank you, Chief. I'm sure it'll be a welcomed change of scenery from staring at the same four walls of the restriction room."

Conveniently, the building that housed the Master-at-Arms's office was right next door to the barracks, making my commute to work for the next month and a half all of about 100 yards from door to door.

"If there's anything you need tonight, call me. I'll leave a message for tonight's CDO that you are under my supervision and authorized to call me from the quarterdeck phone whenever you need to."

CDO stood for Chief Duty Officer, which was typically an upper-enlisted member (E-7 or above) or a lower level officer who worked a 24-hour watch shift babysitting the barracks and keeping an eye on the Navy buildings after hours. They worked with and were in charge of the lower-enlisted people who had watch duty. There were typically four or five individuals working the watch at a time. Below the CDO was the OOD (Officer of the Deck), who was usually a middle-enlisted rank (E5-E6), and then there were a couple lower-enlisted individuals (E1-E4) who did the grunt work of making rounds inside and out, checking that doors were locked and that no one weird was creeping around outside. The OOD and the lower-enlisted watch personnel only worked twelve-hour shifts.

"Thank you again, Chief, I really appreciate it–everything."

"Keep your chin up, McEwen. You're almost out of the shit," he concluded with a wink and then left me alone to settle into my new home for the next forty-five days.

The restriction quarters were two rooms joined in the middle by a small hall with a door to a shared bathroom on one side and a door to the main hallway of the barracks on the other. Both rooms were approximately 12'x12' with three twin racks and three wall lockers in each room. Since I was the only person in the command on restriction at the time, I had the whole place to myself.

I claimed the first rack closest to the door and threw my sea bag on it. I emptied the contents of my bag and organized everything into my wall locker. Once everything was in place, I pulled out one of ten new books I purchased for my imminent restriction, plopped down on my rack, and read until it was time to head to the quarterdeck for my 8 p.m. evening roll call. One of the biggest aspects of my restriction that I was dreading was eating every meal at the base chow hall. I had an emotionally horrid relationship with military chow halls ever since I gained twenty pounds of pure flab in boot camp from eating the fatty and calorie packed galley food. I have an extremely slow metabolism and live on things like cereal and salad to keep my weight under control. Being force fed greasy, protein packed meals three times a day turned me into the bizarre anomaly who gained weight in boot camp while everyone else lost it. I have a fairly athletic body and the boot camp workouts didn't faze me enough to offset my greatly increased caloric intake, so I packed on the pounds like a piggy getting ready for market. When I arrived at the Language School after boot camp, I had to crash diet and even became bulimic for a period to shed the extra weight. At school we had mini refrigerators in our room, so I stocked up on my trusty cereal and salads and swore I'd never eat in a galley again. Never say never, right?

On my way up to the quarterdeck, I walked by the barracks kitchen where two guys were cooking up some dinner for themselves. When I got closer I recognized one of the guys, and after a minute of trying to place him, I realized it was Nick, the nervous young kid I'd helped find his way around the base when he arrived back in December. As soon as it hit me who he was, he glanced up from his cooking and noticed me, too. He recognized me right away and waved.

"Hey, Petty Officer McEwen, would you like to join us for dinner? This is my roommate, Jeremy. We're cooking up some spaghetti and garlic bread if you're interested.

I pointed to my restrictee badge and said, "Wish I could, but thanks anyway."

"Oh man, that sucks," he said seeing the badge. "What did you do?"

"It's a long story."

"Well, maybe some other time."

I nodded and continued on to the quarterdeck to see what kind of treatment I'd receive from the people on watch. I just hoped they weren't going to be complete dicks to me. I reported to the quarterdeck and surprised the officer on duty, he had no idea he even had a person in the restriction room. I told him I'd just arrived that afternoon and my restriction folder should be on his desk somewhere. He flipped through the folder and said I was good to go. I was a little confused because I knew I was supposed to have my uniform and room inspected, but I didn't argue and promptly headed back to my room before he could change his mind. The restriction folder was a guide for the watchmen on the quarterdeck that told them what to do with me each day. I later learned that Chief Viraez conveniently forgot to add the inspection instructions and checklists to my restriction folder. A huge score for me that meant I'd be relatively left alone and not hassled by any power-tripping people on watch who would want to screw with me.

When I passed back by the kitchen, I waved at Nick who waved back and I continued on back to my room. Their dinner smelled delicious and for the first time all day, I noticed the emptiness in my stomach. I had not eaten since the day before due to nerves and stress. I would have greatly preferred Nick's spaghetti to any of the chow hall's cardiac arrest specials. I changed out of my uniform and into my PT clothes and was about to head to the chow hall when I heard a light knock on my door. I groaned and figured I hadn't dodged a room inspection after all. I was genuinely surprised when I opened the door and saw Nick on the other side.

"What are you doing?" I whispered. "You're going to get me in trouble."

"Don't worry, your jailors are off on rounds at the other end of the building," he said with a wink. "I made you a plate of spaghetti." He shoved a paper plate covered with a paper towel into my arms. "There's a plastic fork in there, too. Just shove everything to the bottom of your bathroom garbage can when you're done and no one will notice. I got busted for underage drinking at A-School, so I know firsthand how much restriction sucks. Galley food every day for two months is the crux of the entire punishment."

"Thanks, Nick, you're a lifesaver."

"Hey, you helped me out once, too."

When I was finished with my dinner, I pulled out my book and continued to read. I'd always wanted to read Cervantes' *Don Quixote* but hadn't had the time to devote to a 1,000 plus page book. Here was my shining opportunity. I justified it as military-related; it's about a knight, somewhat. I cracked Cervantes' masterpiece and lost myself in his epic tale until sleep finally found me around 1 a.m.

I awoke to the alarm on my wristwatch signaling that it was half an hour before I was to report to the quarterdeck for my morning roll call. After I checked in, I continued my evasion of chow hall food and skipped breakfast. I then went ahead and walked over to the Master-at-Arms's to report for my workday. Considering I was about forty-five minutes early, I'd beaten everyone else to the office and busied myself with some of the daily menial paperwork.

"McEwen, you're in quite early today," Chief Viraez said when he arrived to the office about twenty minutes later.

"Yeah, traffic was pretty light this morning," I joked.

"Well, I'm glad you still have your sense of humor," he said with a smile. "How are you holding up?" he asked more serious.

"I'm fine," I answered with a shrug.

"Did anyone give you any bullshit at all yesterday or this morning?"

I shook my head. "Not at all, Chief."

"Okay, well you let me know if anyone does."

As the day progressed, the other people in the office kept flashing me commiserate looks and seemed almost afraid to speak to me. When they talked to me, it was, "How are you doing?" or "Are you okay?" in a pitying tone. Every time Chief called out for something to be done, someone jumped in ahead of me with, "I'll do it, McEwen" or "Don't worry about it, McEwen. I got it." When lunchtime rolled around, everyone in the office offered to bring me lunch from somewhere off base and Chief said he wouldn't know anything about it. A couple of the girls were going to Subway and they happily brought me back a sub.

When I stepped back in the office from a trip to the restroom, a few of my coworkers were having a lively discussion about their weekend plans and immediately silenced themselves and returned to their work. At that point, I finally said something to break up the pity-party.

"Guys, I really appreciate all the sympathy," I said, addressing the entire office, "but, honestly, I'm fine. It's a month and a half in a barracks room, not a cell in Gitmo with daily waterboarding. A barracks room I have to myself for crying out loud. That makes my restriction conditions better than the year I spent at tech school with my neurotic roommate who was less than fond of showering on a regular basis."

"We just feel bad for you," Allison, my closest friend in the Master-at-Arms's office, said.

"Well, again, I appreciate it. But you guys are making me feel like I should be more depressed than I actually am. You can ease up a bit."

By evening number two of my sentence, I figured there just was no getting around it any longer. I'd have to procure my dinner from the chow hall. Again, I was on the verge of giving in when there was another soft knock on the outside door to my restriction suite. I shoved my journal under my pillow and threw *Don Quixote* in my wall locker just in case it was a pop inspection. I was pleasantly surprised when I opened the door and saw another young sailor who worked at the Master-at-Arms's office.

Her name was Danielle, she was nineteen, and she also lived in the barracks. I'd met her after she'd failed to report to work on time over at the NSA building on several occasions and was sent to the Master-at-Arms's office by her superiors. She wasn't a bad kid, just not a morning person. They didn't NJP her, so she didn't have to serve any restriction, but to resolve her issue of being late, Chief Viraez punished her by making her work every command urinalysis for six months, and, since she lived in the barracks, having the guys on watch up on the quarterdeck go into her room every morning (even on the weekends) and wake her up every morning boot-camp-style for the entire six months. From what I heard, Danielle became the most punctual member of her office. She and I had gotten to know each other well since we usually worked together at all the urinalysis screenings. Nothing forges a stronger friendship than working side-by-side while you deal with cups of pee all day long. I hadn't seen her in a few weeks, but she was familiar with my issues and what had gone down with me.

Danielle had a Domino's Pizza box in her hands with two pieces lying on top wrapped in paper towels.

"I brought you some pizza for dinner," she whispered. "Figured it'd be better than chow hall food."

I smiled and thanked her for the pizza as I slid it off the top of the box and put it under my sweatshirt.

"I heard what happened, I'm sorry."

"It's really okay. If living for forty-five days with no phone or TV and eating smuggled pizza to avoid chow hall food is the worst of my problems, then I'm doing great," I replied with a smile.

I wolfed the pizza down and hid the evidence at the bottom of my bathroom trashcan again. Then I retrieved *Don Quixote* from my wall locker and settled back in on my rack to continue reading. I realized I was already nearly halfway through *Don Quixote* and doubted the ten books I packed would be enough to get me through the duration of my restriction. I had an entire weekend of confinement ahead of me with no work at the Master-at-Arms's office to occupy any of part of my day. I was confident *Don Quixote* wouldn't even last until Monday.

My fear of running out of reading material and getting bored became the least of my problems when the chief duty officer showed up at 8 p.m. to conduct my evening room inspection. He turned out to be a real asshole. (Which I guess I was due for considering the two CDOs I'd dealt with up to that point had been fairly lenient.) He literally white-gloved my restriction room and decided it was unacceptably dusty and ordered me to wipe the entire room and its contents down, starting with the lights covers and working my way down to the baseboards. He also decided that since the restriction room tandem to mine was unoccupied, I was to clean it as well. Luckily, there wasn't a lot of furniture to work around, but I still spent the next three hours making both rooms spotless. When I was confident my work would pass the CDO's white-glove test, I went to the quarterdeck and informed the watch that I was ready for the CDO to return to my restriction room to re-inspect it. As the CDO went over everything again, I could tell he was brought down by the fact that he couldn't find anything else to haggle me over and reluctantly said I was good for the night, but that he would be back for another inspection at 8 a.m.

"I'll be here, Sir," I said cheerily in response. "Looking forward to seeing you in the morning." There was nothing that pissed off a miserable military superior more than happy subordinates, especially subordinates on restriction who were in high spirits. I showered him with flawless military bearing and enthusiastic responses, followed by bright smiles at every question and comment just to be annoying in a completely permissible manner.

The next morning, asshole conducted another inspection and found a few extra tasks for me to attend to that only took about an hour of my time. True, I would have preferred lounging on my rack reading a book or writing in my journal, but there was still an ample amount of restriction time to do that. When he completed my morning inspection, he closed out his time as my CDO with a lecture.

"I don't know why you're on restriction and I don't particularly care," he said in a callous tone, "but obviously you need to shape up and start taking your life and your Navy career more seriously. You're probably what, eighteen or nineteen?" he asked half rhetorically. "You need to get yourself some education and start walking a straight line. Go to college and make something of yourself and don't end up back here," he finished, gesturing at the restriction room. I had to bite my tongue until it bled to keep from snapping back and telling him he was right, he didn't know why I was on restriction and he didn't know me. But, as I'd learned from my life experience, the universe tended to balance things out and the next CDO I had was quite pleasant and laid back.

My new CDO stopped by and politely introduced himself as Lieutenant Gray when he assumed his shift Saturday afternoon. I still had a bitter taste in my mouth from my previous CDO, so I remained reserved and gave short one or two word answers. When I asked him what time he would be conducting my evening inspection he looked around my room and said everything appeared to be tip-top so he saw no need for a formal inspection. I thanked him and breathed a sigh of relief, realizing he wasn't going to be another asshole.

Aside from my daily reports for roll call on the quarterdeck, I had the remainder of the weekend to myself. I did some laundry and ironing, went to the gym, gave in and started eating at the chow hall, which really wasn't half as bad as I had it built up in my head, and finished reading *Don Quixote*. On Sunday afternoon, Lieutenant Gray stopped by to inform me that his twenty-four-hour watch was up and a Senior Chief McDonald would be assuming the CDO watch for the following twenty-four hours. In no uncertain terms, I thanked him for not picking on me during his time as CDO.

He smiled and said, "If you don't mind my asking, why are you on restriction?"

I gladly gave him the short version of the chronicle, after which he said it was a very interesting story.

He then said, "Just remember the Navy is simply a small chapter in your life and won't be around forever. Just put your head down, face the storm, and you'll be through it and on the other side before you know it."

Chapter 27

"Fahdi"
Tuesday, 14 March–Thursday, 23 March
2006

The two Iraqi policemen each had a hand on one of Fahdi's arms and led him from the INIS building behind the IM official. They took him to a white four-door sedan which was already running with a driver waiting inside. They placed Fahdi in the middle of the back seat, flanked by the two policemen. As soon as the car exited the INIS compound, the men in the backseat with Fahdi bound his hands with large, black zip-ties, similar to what the U.S. military used on detainees, and covered his head with a dark hood to prevent him from seeing where he was going. The fact that they did this actually made Fahdi feel somewhat relieved. He figured if they were worried about him knowing where they were taking him, it meant they weren't planning on killing him as soon as they arrived at their destination.

In his hooded blindness, Fahdi tried to keep track of the car's direction by noting every turn and approximately how long they traveled between each of them. But he soon realized from the visual map he was plotting in his head, that his captors were a step ahead and were conducting purposeful double-back maneuvers and circling blocks here and there to throw him off. After about an hour of driving, the vehicle came to a stop and the engine was cut off. They could have been right back at the INIS parking lot for all

Fahdi knew, and he was disheartened at his failure of the first task of his captivity.

In a less-than-gentle manner, Fahdi's escorts removed him from the car and dragged him up a set of steps and inside a building. Fahdi strained his ears, listening for anything to give him an idea of his surroundings. He noticed that it was fairly quiet outside, so he had a good idea they weren't in a busy area of Baghdad. When people spoke, their voices echoed a little, so Fahdi knew he was either in some type of commercial warehouse building or a very large house. He heard footsteps walking toward and past him and counted at least twenty people.

"Take him to holding unit number six," he heard a voice he didn't recognize announce.

With a man still on each arm, Fahdi was dragged about twenty-five yards in one direction and then down two flights of stairs; he counted twenty-eight steps in total. Once at the bottom of the stairs, he heard the distinctive sound of barred prison doors open and slam shut behind him. He was then pushed into a concrete wall and told he could now remove his hood. He reached up and ripped off the hood, feeling like he was about to suffocate. His face was dripping with perspiration and he reached up with his still bound hands to wipe the sweat from his eyes so he could focus and get a look at his surroundings.

He was alone in a small 6'x6' prison-like cell. The back wall and floor were bare concrete, but the sidewalls were made of thick plywood. The door of the cell looked like a typical jail cell door with vertical metal bars. The only light was what managed to filter in through the bars of the cell door from the dimly lit hallway on the opposite side. Aside from Fahdi, the only thing in the room was a small plastic bucket in the corner, his latrine. The bucket was empty but had an obvious residue and a putrid smell emanating from it.

Over the next three days, Fahdi languished in the tiny cell, hearing the muffled screams and cries of other captives. He heard guards shouting at prisoners and the apparent sound of people being beaten and tortured. The specific nature of the torture, Fahdi could only imagine. Max's words echoed in his head. *Keep your eyes and ears open.* Knowing that feeding Max useful information would be his only way out of this hell, he listened closely when the guards shouted. He noted that they spoke in Arabic, but there were evident traces of Persian accents in several of the captors' voices, meaning they were either Iraqis who'd spent a great deal of time in Iran or were native Iranians.

Every twelve hours or so, someone threw a small piece of flatbread and two or three dates through the cell door. Although the temperature inside the room wasn't sweltering, there was relatively no air circulation, so Fahdi became extremely thirsty. He used most of the water to quench his thirst but always saved a little from each bottle to rinse his face and wash himself as best he could over the small bucket that was quickly becoming full. He used the last bit of water to pour over the areas on his wrists that had been rubbed raw by the plastic ties that his captors never offered to remove.

He had no means for keeping time, but he guessed it was near the end of the third day of his confinement when the door to his cell opened and two men with scarves masking their faces from the nose down came in and forcefully pulled him from his cell. They dragged him down the hallway, which was lined on either side with more cells and detainees. He counted eighteen prisoners, but figured there was at least double that amount just in the area of the building he was being held. They took him into a room about twice the size of his cell with a solid metal door, and slammed him down in a metal folding chair. They left him alone in the room for a few minutes. He surveyed his surroundings and noticed dried blood on the concrete floor and some more splattered on one of the sidewalls. The room stunk of sweat and urine. Aside from the metal chair he was sitting in, the only other object in the room was a small metal table pushed into the far corner.

After about ten minutes, three men Fahdi hadn't seen before entered the room. Two were big guys in their mid-twenties, carrying black wooden batons and dressed commando-style. The third was older, probably about fifty, with salt and pepper hair. He was carrying a manila file folder. He was dressed more professionally in lightweight gray slacks and a blue oxford shirt. The older man placed the manila folder on the small metal table, then stepped in front of Fahdi and crossed his arms. He stared at Fahdi for several seconds before he finally spoke.

"Do you know why you are here?" The older man asked in Arabic using the Iraqi dialect.

Fahdi expected to hear at least an Iranian accent, but this man was obviously Iraqi, born and raised. Fahdi returned the man's gaze but didn't speak or move.

"You are a lawful detainee of the Iraqi Interior Ministry. We have solid evidence and eyewitness accounts stating that you forcefully resisted an official arrest and injured four members of an Interior Ministry security team and also captured and committed bodily torture on one of the arresting officers. Do you deny these charges?"

"Do I have an option?" Fahdi asked with contempt. "I'm guessing requesting a lawyer is out of the question."

"I don't appreciate his attitude, Laith."

One of the men with the batons stepped forward and gave Fahdi a forceful, open-handed smack across the side of his head that nearly knocked Fahdi out of the metal chair.

"You actually do have an option, my friend. Unfortunately," the ringleader continued, "if it were up to me, you'd hang right now for what you did to those men. The one whose ankle you shattered happens to be my nephew and will now probably walk with a noticeable limp for the rest of his life because of what you and your friend did to him."

"Well, it's nice to see the asshole doesn't fall far from the tree," Fahdi replied with a wicked smile.

Half-shocked at Fahdi's continued brazenness, the older man gave him a quick backhand of his own across Fahdi's left cheek.

"We have a proposition for you," the older man stated once Fahdi recovered from the last blow. "We know you are an employee for the illegitimate Iraqi National Intelligence Service that serves no one but the American CIA and operates against the new Iraqi government. Making you not only a rebel who's committed attempted murder on government security officials, but also a traitor guilty of espionage. These crimes carry the death penalty, as I'm sure you're already aware. We are willing to offer you your life in return for your cooperation. You will answer our questions and make a recorded confession. If we are satisfied you may live to see daylight again. If not, we are more than happy for you to die here. Are you willing to cooperate?"

Fahdi nodded his head, knowing that resisting would only result in more beating that wasn't going to get him anywhere.

"Good, I'll be right back."

The man left Fahdi alone with the two guards for a few minutes and then returned with another man approximately the same age and dressed similarly. The new man entered the room with a notepad, pen, and a small digital voice recorder. He put everything down on the metal table and picked up the manila file folder. While absently flipping through the contents of the folder, he told Fahdi that they were going to ask him some questions and everything would be recorded.

He spoke fairly fluent Arabic but with a distinct Persian accent. Fahdi had a good idea that he was one of the many Iranian Intelligence officers covertly operating within the Iraqi Interior Ministry.

"According to your file here, you worked directly with the U.S. military for the first couple years of the war and you've been at the INIS now for about eighteen months," the Iranian officer stated.

Fahdi nodded.

"Tell us about your time with the U.S. military."

"I was just a translator," Fahdi replied.

"And at the INIS?" the Iranian asked. "I'm guessing you're just a translator over there, too."

"Yes."

"Well, even if you are just a simple translator, you know a great deal more than you even realize. And if you're something more than just a lowly translator, you're going to tell us what we want to know or you'll be begging for us to kill you by the time we get done with you."

Over the next three hours, Fahdi was brutally interrogated about his history working with the U.S. military and the INIS. Fahdi told half-truths and gave his captors just enough information to satisfy them but not anything particularly critical. The Iranian officer conducted the interrogation and asked most of the questions while the older Iraqi man took notes and operated the recording device. When they believed he was withholding information or suppressing details, the Iranian had the guards beat Fahdi with their batons and bare knuckles, whichever they preferred at the time.

They asked Fahdi about U.S. military tactics, maneuvers, training, inside operations of the bases, etc. Then they moved on and drilled him on any and all inside information he could give them on the inner workings of the INIS.

By the time they were done with him for the day, Fahdi had a busted lip, a fractured cheekbone, a possible broken nose, a couple of bruised if not fractured, ribs, and numerous bruises and contusions up and down his arms and legs. He considered himself to be in good shape for what he'd just been subjected to, a full-fledged Iranian Secret

Service interrogation. But his celebratory assessment was short lived.

"We are not stupid," the Iranian said to Fahdi before the guards dragged him back to his cell. "I know there is a lot you're not telling us. But I will get it out of you. You're just making things harder on yourself. What you experienced today was a kindergarten picnic compared to what I've got planned for you. We'll see you tomorrow," he finished with an evil smile.

When Fahdi was deposited back in his cell, he curled up in the fetal position in the corner and tried to figure out how he was going to make it through another round of interrogations. He knew that being beaten and bloodied at the hands of Badr Brigade torturers was not going to get him out of the hellhole he was in, and it definitely wasn't providing him with any useful information that he could pass on to Max or the DG if he did manage to survive. He had to come up with a plan, and fast.

When a guard came around with Fahdi's evening meal of flatbread, dates, and a bottle of warm water, Fahdi called out, "Hey," as the guard reached through the bars with the food.

"What?" The guard barked back at Fahdi.

"Do you think I could get someone to empty my piss bucket?" Fahdi asked.

"Shut up," the guard snarled and dropped the contents on the floor.

"Wait, what's your name?" Fahdi persisted, trying a different approach. The guard ignored him and turned to leave. "Do you have a minute to talk," Fahdi asked grasping the bars on the door.

"If I were you, I'd be talking to God and making my peace, traitor," the guard answered. "It's only a matter of time before they put a bullet in your head for working against your own country!"

At that, Fahdi gave up and hoped the next guard on duty would be less ideological and more interested in money.

For the next three days, Fahdi was dragged from his cell to the interrogation room. They asked the same questions over and over in different forms and doled out a beating here and there for good measure. At the end of each session, his captors would try to get him to recite a pre-written confession denouncing the American CIA and the INIS Director General for utilizing illegal militias and spying on the new Iraqi Government to keep it under U.S. control. When Fahdi refused to make the confession, the guards would double-team him and beat him with the batons until he nearly passed out.

After being in the detention center for a week, Fahdi noticed the guard who brought him his evening meal one night was a new guy. He approached this guard as he had the last one and hoped for a better reaction. He asked the man his name and actually got a response. The guy didn't answer until his arms were safely on the outside of the cell door, but then said his name was Rami. Fahdi struggled to his feet and moved closer to the door. He noticed the guard appeared to be barely beyond his teens and Fahdi pushed to strike up a conversation with him.

"Where are you from, Rami?" Fahdi asked.

Rami pulled out a cigarette and leaned against the wall next to Fahdi's cell door. He told him he was from the Al-Dora area of Baghdad. The neighborhood wasn't far from where Fahdi grew up, so Fahdi jumped on the opportunity to keep the conversation going with some familiar references. Fahdi reminisced with Rami for a few minutes about places around Dora and the good times before the war while Rami smoked his cigarette.

"So how did you come to work here?" Fahdi finally asked, attempting to get to the purpose of his scheme.

"It's a job," Rami replied curtly with a shrug. "My older brother was killed near the beginning of the war, and my dad has been disabled since I was a little kid. I was in the army for about a year until the war, but when the U.S. disbanded the military, I didn't know when or if I'd be able to rejoin the new army, so I started looking for alternatives to make money. Some of my buddies told me the IM was recruiting former military members, so we came and checked it out and got hired on. I make enough to take care of my parents and little sister, so that's all I care about."

"I have a little sister, too," Fahdi said. "She's sixteen. How old is your sister?"

Rami stubbed out his cigarette and told Fahdi he had to continue his evening rounds. Fahdi was discouraged that he hadn't gotten any further with Rami, but resolved to try again next time he saw the young guard.

Fahdi curled up on the floor of his cell and closed his eyes. The pain throughout his body was relentless and made sleep difficult to find. He was relieved, however, that the screaming of his fellow inmates had stopped for the night. Their captors typically ended interrogations around dinnertime, but Fahdi knew he'd wake to more screams of men being tortured before the sun came up the next morning.

Fahdi finally slipped into a dreamless sleep sometime in the predawn hours, only to be ripped back into consciousness when one of the morning guards dumped a bucket of freezing cold water on him before shoving a piece of bread and handful of shriveled dates in his face.

"Rise and shine, princess," the guard taunted as Fahdi gasped to catch his breath and recover from the shock of the cold water.

Fahdi hadn't seen the sun or outside world since he'd arrived, but by his calculations, this was the ninth morning he'd awoken in this hellhole so he figured the date as Wednesday, March 15. He wasn't hungry, but reached for the bread and dates and nibbled on them. He was weak and knew he had to do what he could to keep his strength up. As he worked on his breakfast, he thought of me. What was I doing at that very minute? Was I thinking of him? Was I missing him the way he was missing me? Little did he know, I, myself, was mere hours away from receiving my own sentence of confinement–albeit a rather charmed incarceration that couldn't even compare to his in brutality.

Fahdi finished his breakfast and then sat and waited. He waited and waited, sure that every time he heard footsteps approaching his cell, it was men coming to get him and drag him into the interrogation room for another round of torture. But an hour passed and no one came. Then another hour went by, and another, until Fahdi figured it had to be late afternoon and no one had so much as looked at him when they passed his cell. Finally, Fahdi rested his head back down on the cold concrete floor, wishing he'd have known they were going to give him the day off. He would have utilized the time to better relax and concentrate more on resting his injured body. He stared at one of the plywood sidewalls of his cell, dreaming of the day we would see each other again and be able to hold one another in our arms.

"Fourteen," Fahdi heard a voice say behind him.

He lifted his head and saw Rami standing outside his cell. Rami knelt and placed Fahdi's evening serving of bread and dates with a water bottle on the cell floor just inside the door.

"You asked me last night how old my sister is," Rami clarified. "She just turned fourteen last month. Her name is Ameenah."

That was all Rami said. Then he left to continue his rounds, but Fahdi smiled to himself as he ripped off a piece of the flatbread, rolled one of the dates up inside, and ate it.

Rami returned to Fahdi's cell for his smoke break. The detention center cleared out at night, and, from what Fahdi could tell, Rami was one of only two guards who pulled the night watch. Rami and Fahdi chitchatted for most of the night. Fahdi was exhausted and desperately wanted to sleep, but he knew he needed to keep talking with Rami to forge any kind of bond possible.

When Rami's shift was over at 6 a.m., he went home and Fahdi grabbed about an hour of sleep before he was again abruptly awoken. He regretted his lack of sleep when the masked guards showed up to drag him from his cell and deposit him in the interrogation room. Over the next four hours, he endured a barrage of the same questions that he'd been asked over and over for the past week. In between questions, two men would beat Fahdi. He was sure they weren't there to get information out of him, but to just let off steam and have a good time beating the shit out of him.

When Fahdi was returned to his cell that afternoon, the right side of his face was so swollen he couldn't open his eye, and he had heard a distinct crack when he absorbed an especially hard blow to the ribs on his left side. Several hours of daily questioning and abuse continued for another solid week. They beat him with batons, cables, and their fists. He received numerous bare knuckle blows to the face, they sprawled him out stomach-down across the small metal table and whipped his bare back with cables, and used the wooden batons to hit him in the muscled parts of his thighs and shoulders leaving massive knots and bruises.

At night, Fahdi mustered all his strength to continue his chats with Rami, who was fond of spending his smoke breaks hanging out around Fahdi's cell. During the day, while Fahdi lay sprawled on the floor of his cell, he was forced to listen to the agonizing cries of pain from other detainees as they, too, were subjected to brutal interrogation tactics. But it was the continuous sobs of desperate grown men he heard echoing from the cells around him that affected him more deeply than the screams of torture. When he was alone on the floor of his cell, drifting in and out of consciousness, he reminisced of the few short months we were able to spend with each other. We met and were together a mere fourteen weeks in the summer of 2005, but those days were the most wonderful of either of our lives. The hope of seeing me again and fantasizing of the future life we would have together gave him strength and kept him going.

Chapter 28

"Mandy"
Monday 20 March–Monday 10 April
2006

On the afternoon of my fifth full day of restriction, I was lying on my rack staring out through the large window over the head of my bed. It was a beautiful day and the sky was a perfect blue with only a few fluffy, white clouds. I desperately wished to be anywhere but there. A passing airliner at a very high altitude caught my eye, and I watched as it slowly made its way across the sky. I wondered where it was headed. I imagined the ultimate destinations of the 100+ passengers inside its belly. It was traveling north, probably a flight from D.C. to New York, or perhaps Boston. It was too high to be preparing for a landing at Baltimore. It made me think about how desperately I wanted to fly away from that place. I wanted so badly to be on a plane just like that one, bound for the Middle East to return to Fahdi again. *Someday soon*, I told myself. *I will board another plane and return to him again. And it will be the happiest day of my life.* I felt completely detached from my heart and soul. My body was in that restriction room, but my heart and soul were 7,000 miles away. I also dreamed of the day I'd be able to bring Fahdi back to the U.S. with me where he'd be safe. I imagined us having a little house somewhere out in the country and curling up together on the front porch swing, watching the sunset with maybe a kid or two playing in the yard. That was my ultimate dream: a quiet life next to Fahdi.

I finished *Don Quixote* that night. Who's got two thumbs and read *Don Quixote* in its entirety in less than a week? This girl right here. I returned *DQ* to my sea bag in my wall locker and selected my next book. I decided on *The Kite Runner*. It was a current bestseller and strongly recommended by Oprah. I figured, *hey, if Oprah says it's good might as well give it a shot.*

The next day, I learned that I would be getting a roommate that afternoon as another female sailor was standing a Captain's Mast and would most likely receive restriction as part of her punishment. I wasn't happy to hear this. Restriction was for the bad kids. Those who received restriction were typically not the highest caliber of individuals. I was confident I wouldn't be sharing my room with a murderer or rapist, but I knew my easy days of blowing through my restriction sentence relatively unnoticed and under the radar were over.

I met Shivonne when she showed up at the Master-at-Arms's office an hour prior to her Captain's Mast. My first impression of her was not a good one. She was loud, obnoxious, and had the crappy *I-don't-give-a-damn* attitude that made life in the military impossible. She was only nineteen years old, rude, disrespectful, and back-talked everyone, which I figured was the reason why she ended up with an NJP in the first place. She just couldn't control her mouth and do the proper kowtowing required to make it in the military.

When I was released from work and reported back to the restriction room at 1630, Shivonne was already there unpacking and arranging her stuff in her wall locker. Since I had claimed the bed closest to the doorway and the corresponding wall locker, she decided to take the rack on the far wall, leaving an empty bed between us. I was amiable enough and said hello, but after the pleasantries, I remained silent and did my best to keep to myself. I changed out of my uniform and into my PT gear, then settled down on my rack to continue reading *The Kite Runner* until it was time to get some dinner from the chow hall. She asked me a few questions but was relatively quiet and respectful of my reading time.

When 1830 rolled around, I told Shivonne I was heading to the chow hall for dinner and asked if she wanted to come with me. She agreed and we both headed out to dinner dressed in our PT clothes. We went to the quarterdeck and signed the log, identifying the time we left for dinner. Per restriction rules, we were due back in one hour. It was at this time that I realized how easy I'd had it when I was on my own.

Before we could make it to the door, a male voice from the watch office called out in an arrogant tone, "Uh, excuse me."

Shivonne and I both stopped and turned around, knowing he was talking to us.

"You two are my restrictees, right?"

It was the OOD for the night and he was a guy I'd never seen before. We nodded and told him yes.

"And why are you out of uniform? You signed the log and marked that you're going to dinner not to the gym."

Technically, we were supposed to be in uniform at all times between the hours of 0600 and 2200 unless we were going to the gym, but I had been going to the chow hall in my PT gear since starting my restriction the week before and no one had said a word about it. Now that there were two of us, I had a feeling shit like this was going to start happening. He made us return to our room and change into our uniforms. As a punishment for trying to slide past the rules, he told us to be ready for him to conduct a uniform and room inspection at 2000. I was thoroughly bummed. Aside from that one dickhead chief, the CDOs and OODs had left me alone and I hadn't had to put up with any uniform or room inspections. I had a feeling this was just a shade of things to come.

We started getting inspections every night because Shivonne's restriction folder, unlike mine, had the room and uniform inspection instructions for the CDO and OOD in it. When I returned from work in the afternoons, I started cleaning so everything would be inspection-ready. I did most of the work while Shivonne lounged on her rack, playing on her cell phone that she managed to smuggle into the room with her.

I asked her once if she was going to help me clean but she plainly replied, "No. I don't care if we fail," in her usual I-don't-give-a-crap tone.

I didn't want to fight with her and I didn't want to bring unwanted attention and ramifications down on us by failing inspections, so I just bit the bullet and did everything myself. I could have screwed her over by telling Chief Viraez about her cell phone, but I hate tattlers. Since it was her phone, if it was discovered I'd just claim ignorance.

The next morning, Shivonne and I went to our 0630 roll call on the quarterdeck and, since the OOD watch hadn't changed hands yet, had to deal with the same asshole OOD who'd given us a hard time the night before about going to the chow hall in our PT clothes. When we signed in, just to be a dick, he told us he needed to see our military ID cards. I huffed under my breath at the bullshit. I turned to return to the room to retrieve my ID, but before I could get two steps away, Shivonne was opening her mouth yet again.

"Whatch'ya need to see our cards for? You know who we are!" she blurted in her typical *Ms. Thang* tone of voice.

"According to restriction regulations, restrictees are to present their military ID cards at all roll calls so the OOD knows they are the actual restricted individuals and not someone else just signing them in," Mr. By-the-book OOD explained.

"Exactly, but you already know who we are," Shivonne argued. "Or did you forget?"

All I could think was *Jesus, just shut up* please*!*

"Do I need to have the CDO come up here," the OOD threatened.

"No, I'll go get you the damn ID," Shivonne relented. "I just didn't realize you were such an idiot."

About fifteen minutes after resolving the roll call ID card issue, we were back in our room when someone started pounding on the door. When I opened the door, the asshole OOD was standing there with the CDO and they were not happy campers. The CDO explained they were there to discuss the disrespectful attitude we displayed on the quarterdeck at the morning roll call. Lucky for me, the OOD stepped in and clarified that I had been cooperative and it was my roommate who'd been the issue, so they left me out of it.

I hoped the subsequent tongue lashing Shivonne received from the CDO would rein in her attitude a little and keep us both out of hot water for the remainder of our restriction time, but that was just wishful thinking. She sucked her teeth and rolled her eyes at both the CDO and OOD, and everything they said went in one ear and out the other. Over the next week, she continued to backtalk OODs and assert her attitude, and we continued to be punished with double the inspections and even hourly roll calls on the weekend, which really cut into my reading time.

On my way back from one of the roll calls, I was walking past the kitchen area to return to the restriction room when a news report on the kitchen TV caught my attention. I stopped and stood in the doorway to catch a glimpse of the CNN news report.

The bodies of over thirty Iraqi civilian males were discovered yesterday in a Baghdad parking lot. Some were beheaded and others had their hands bound and had been shot execution-style in the head. U.S. forces issued a press release this morning stating that military medical examiners found that some of the bodies were already in a state of decomposition, while others appeared to have only been deceased for perhaps two to three days. The press release went on to state that U.S. officials believe this is the result of sectarian strife that has become increasingly violent throughout Iraq over the past few months.

My heart sank into my stomach and I said a silent prayer for Fahdi. I missed him so much. I hadn't heard his voice in over two months and the only news I'd gotten from him was the short email he sent me the week before I went on restriction letting me know he was still alive. I desperately wished I had some way of getting online to see if he'd sent me any more emails. I just wanted to know if he was okay.

Before I turned to continue back to the restriction room, I noticed a deck of playing cards lying on the kitchen counter. I took it as a sign. I was missing Fahdi so much at that specific moment and there was a symbol of some of the good times we'd had together. Fahdi and I had a lot of fun playing marathon rounds of rummy while waiting for flights during our forward deployment or killing time when we were completely bored. Seeing those cards made me feel better. It was like someone was saying, "Here, take your mind off all the crap worrying you and go play some cards." No one was in the kitchen and after I did a quick look around, I saw the lounge was empty, too, so I popped into the kitchen, grabbed the deck of cards, and slipped them into my undershirt.

When I was safely in the restriction room, I pulled the cards out of my shirt and started shuffling them while sitting on my rack. I shuffled and shuffled and started to cry. Shivonne had left after roll call to go to the chow hall and I was glad she wasn't there to witness my tears. I wanted so much just to play a game of cards with Fahdi, but I had no idea if I'd even see him again. I finally stopped shuffling and started playing Solitaire, but I couldn't stop sobbing.

I heard the outer door open so I quickly wiped my face with my shirtsleeve and shoved the cards under my pillow in case it was the OOD or CDO. When Shivonne entered the room, I relaxed and pulled the cards back out. She was concealing her cell phone in the restriction room, so I was confident she wasn't going to rat me out over the cards and risk losing her cell phone.

"Hey, where'd you get those?" she asked seeing the cards.

"Someone left them in the kitchen."

"What, did you run out of books?" she joked.

"No, I brought plenty. I just figured something different would be nice. Do you want to play?"

"Sure, but I only know how to play one game," she said coming over and sitting on my bed.

"And what's that?"

"Rummy. Do you know how to play that one?"

I felt a calm come over me and I smiled. "Yeah, I know that one."

And for the first time, I was happy to have Shivonne around. We spent a lot of our dead time playing rummy and talking about what we would do when we got off restriction.

"I'm going to a bar and getting drunk!" Shivonne declared with a laugh.

"I just want to be free to walk around Wal-Mart at 2 a.m. in my flip flops and pajama pants," I said.

We ended up with another OOD on a power trip later that week. He announced at the evening roll call that he would be conducting a full dress uniform inspection, as well as a room inspection, and boot-camp-style wall locker inspection. We'd have to organize everything in our locker according to boot camp standards and fold everything from our uniforms to our underwear military style. This was new for us.

I saw Shivonne's face tighten up and I knew she was seconds away from exploding and letting her mouth go wild, but I stared her down and pleaded with my eyes for her to just let it go. Luckily, she noticed me and got the message. She deflated like a popped balloon and kept her mouth shut. I mouthed the words *thank you* to her and she gave me a half smile that let me know she was going to be cool, but she wasn't happy about it.

Chapter 29

"Fahdi"
Friday, 24 March–Monday, 10 April
2006

On the eighteenth day of his captivity, Fahdi was once again dragged from his cell and taken to the interrogation room. This time, however, he was thrown down on a sturdier chair and they cut the black plastic ties from his hands that had been put on the day he was arrested. By now, his raw wrists had scabbed over, but it felt so good just to be able to separate his arms for the first time in over two weeks. Unfortunately, they didn't remove the ties to be nice.

"I am going to give you one last chance to give us something useful because, quite frankly, you haven't proven to be worth the breadcrumbs we throw you every day," the main interrogator stated as two guards strapped Fahdi to the wooden chair.

Once Fahdi was tied down, one of the guards left the room and returned a few seconds later wheeling a small electric generator behind him. Fahdi noted the wires coiled up around the top of the generator and knew what his captors were planning to do with them.

"I'm tired of dicking around with you. I've got better shit to do. You *will* sign your confession today and you *will* sign and make a recorded statement regarding the illegal activities being conducted over at the INIS at the command of the director general and the American CIA. If you do not do this willingly, I will inflict so much pain on you you'll wish you were dead. Are you ready to make your statements?"

Fahdi remained silent.

The man bent over with his hands on his knees and put his face within inches of Fahdi's. "I'm going to ask you one last time. Are you going to sign your confession?"

Fahdi took a swift deep breath and then spat in the man's face. He stumbled back in rage and wiped his face with his shirtsleeve, cursing Fahdi.

"You son of a bitch!" he roared. "Wire him up!" he shouted to the guards.

The guards wheeled the generator next to Fahdi's chair and uncoiled the wires. Small jumper-cable alligator clips were at the ends of the wires, and one of the guards held Fahdi's head still between his arms while the other grabbed his jaw and forced his mouth open. He shoved the wire into Fahdi's mouth and clamped it to Fahdi's tongue. Fahdi did his best to work the clip off with his teeth, but it was so tight it bit into his tongue hard enough to draw blood, and he was unable to get it off. The guards attached a second clip to one of Fahdi's fingers and then backed away. The main interrogator opened a bottle of water that was sitting on the table and dumped the entire contents over Fahdi's head.

"Last chance," he said as he stepped next to the generator. Fahdi remained silent and his torturer flipped a switch on the generator.

An excruciating blast of electricity entered Fahdi's body and caused him to convulse uncontrollably. He let out an animal-like scream and realized it was the same type of scream he'd heard numerous times coming from other prisoners while he sat in his cell. A few seconds after his torturer flipped the switch again to cut off the electricity, Fahdi regained his senses and noticed the unmistakable stench of searing flesh. He knew it was coming from his own body, most likely his tongue, which felt like it was on fire.

"Are you ready to confess?" The man asked.

Again, Fahdi did not respond.

"Have it your way."

He flipped the switch back on.

Fahdi awoke several hours later on the floor of his cell. The second blast of electricity had rendered him unconscious. Aside from the pain in his swollen tongue and finger where the electricity entered his body, he noted several knew injuries to his face where the guards had obviously punched him a couple of times to try and revive him after he passed out from the pain.

Fahdi remained as motionless as possible, afraid that if it was discovered he'd regained consciousness, they'd haul him back into the torture room. Luckily, he was lying with his back to his cell door. He opened his eyes and did his best to try and focus his vision by staring at a spot on the back wall of his cell. He had no idea how long he'd been out, but judging from the relative quiet throughout the prison, he guessed it was evening or already night.

After about thirty minutes of exercising his vision, Fahdi heard footsteps coming down the hall toward his cell. He held his breath in fear, but relaxed when he recognized Rami's voice. Assuming Rami was just arriving to work, Fahdi guessed the time to be around 8 p.m., which was when Rami's shift usually started.

The sound of Rami's voice grew louder as he neared Fahdi's cell and Fahdi realized he was talking on a cell phone. Fahdi mustered all of his strength and managed to roll over so he could get a look at Rami when he walked past the cell door. When Rami breezed by, Fahdi did indeed notice Rami was holding a small flip-phone to his ear. Fahdi realized they must not have been that far beneath the ground level if Rami was able to get a signal. *Five minutes with that phone–that's all I need*, Fahdi thought.

Rami's footsteps halted a few paces past Fahdi's cell and he heard him turn and start to come back.

"Hey, let me call you back later," Rami said into the phone and then flipped it closed. Rami stepped in front of Fahdi's cell door and then bent down.

"Damn dude, you look like shit," Rami said once he got a closer look at Fahdi. "I see they started shocking your ass. I was wondering when they'd get to that."

"Yeah, thanks for the warning," Fahdi replied meekly around his swollen tongue.

"I figured you knew it was on the menu at some point. Why don't you spare yourself a lot of pain and just tell them whatever the hell it is they want to hear. Give them the info they want so you can get out of here."

"And go where? Into a body bag?" Fahdi asked with a forced chuckle that sent pain shooting through his cracked ribs. "The only stop after this is a back alley somewhere with a bullet in the head."

"No, man," Rami said shaking his head and smiling like Fahdi was making a joke. "You'll either end up at Abu Graib where the Americans run the place like a hotel or they may even just let you go."

"You honestly believe that, don't you?" Fahdi said half-shocked at Rami's naiveté. "They're torturing people. You think they just let us walk away after this?"

"I don't like it, but desperate times call for desperate measures," Rami replied. "If there's no other way and it's for the greater good, you do what you gotta do."

"The greater good, huh? I thought you were just here for the paycheck?" Fahdi retorted.

"Yeah well, I'd still like to live in a country better than the prison we had under Saddam."

"Look around you, man! You think this is better?" Fahdi spat as he scooted himself up into a sitting position against the sidewall of his cell. "We went from being under Saddam's thumb to being under Iran's whacked out thumb. What's the difference?"

"Last time I checked, it was the Americans who rolled in and took over. They're the ones running the show," Rami said.

"They took out Saddam and then handed the reins over to Iran without even realizing it," Fahdi argued. "You think the Americans even know about places like this, much less condone them? You don't work for the Americans, Rami. You're an Iranian junkyard dog."

"I think the electricity got to your head, man. I'd get some sleep if I were you. In case they plan on *talking* to you some more tomorrow," Rami said standing up to leave. "And I really don't give a shit who's paying me at the end of the week, as long as I'm getting paid."

Fahdi knew it was time to make his move. "Wait. I saw you talking on a cell phone," Fahdi blurted before Rami could walk away.

"You gonna report me?" Rami asked smugly.

"No. But since you're mainly here for the money, I have a business proposal for you."

"You don't seem to be in much of a position to be making business deals."

"You might be surprised," Fahdi replied in an effort to sound as intriguing as possible. "How much will it cost me to use your phone for five minutes?"

"Gee, I don't know. How much you got on you?" Rami asked jokingly, knowing full well Fahdi's pockets were empty.

"I can get you the money. Just name a drop point and time and I'll make sure it's delivered."

Rami thought about it for a minute. "Fifty dollars–U.S."

"Done." Fahdi replied immediately. Rami fully expected a negotiation and at Fahdi's quick response, realized he should have asked for more money.

"When and where do you want it delivered?"

"My uncle owns a shop in the Dora neighborhood," Rami explained. "The Al-Hassan Bakery and Grocery.

Have the money delivered there tomorrow by 4 p.m. Have it given to my uncle directly. His name is Abu Khalid."

Fahdi nodded and reached out his hand for the phone, but Rami shook his head.

"No, not now. We'll wait a couple of hours until everyone's asleep. By 2 a.m., the other guards on duty are usually passed out in the office, too. I will come back then."

Fahdi wasn't happy about having to make his call in the middle of the night, but he didn't want to push the issue and risk Rami changing his mind about the whole deal. He'd just have to pray the DG would answer his phone at 2 a.m. In the meantime, he returned to the floor of his cell to try and get some much-needed sleep.

Before he knew it, Rami's voice was waking Fahdi from a shallow sleep.

"Hey! It's time," Rami said in a loud whisper.

Fahdi sat up and rubbed his eyes.

"You have five minutes, and that includes the time it takes you to make whatever arrangements you have to in order to get me my money," Rami said sternly.

"Don't worry, you'll get your money," Fahdi said plainly.

Rami took a quick look up and down the hall, and then swiftly passed the phone to Fahdi through the bars of the cell door. As soon as Fahdi flipped the phone open Rami looked down at his watch. Fahdi managed to steady his shaking hands enough to punch in the DG's cell phone number. Then he closed his eyes and prayed the DG would pick up. On the third ring, a groggy voice answered the phone and Fahdi fought back tears of joy and relief.

"Sir? This is Fahdi," he managed to squeak out in a wavering voice.

"You're still alive," the DG responded in a tone that Fahdi wasn't sure reflected relief or aggravation.

"You've got to get me out of here," Fahdi said, getting to the point before his time was up.

"I'm working on it, but I'm not going to get any help from Max until you have something for him. Did you get any information? Anything at all I can pass on to him?"

"I don't know much. I'm in a prison of some sort, located in the basement of a building. I don't know where. They blindfolded me in the car. There are probably twenty or thiery other prisoners. Can't you triangulate the signal from this phone somehow?"

"How long can you talk?"

"I've only got five minutes."

"You know that's not nearly enough time," the DG replied with a hint of an apology in his tone. "Get us more information and I'll have more leverage to get you released."

"How do you all expect me to get any information in this situation?" Fahdi nearly shouted in frustration. "They've been beating and torturing me!"

"You got a hold of a phone didn't you?" The DG responded calmly. "Try to stay focused and help yourself. Get some more information and I'll do what I can on my end to get you out of there. I promise."

Rami looked at Fahdi and tapped his watch with his fingers signaling Fahd's time was running out.

"I need you to get $50 to a bakery in Al-Dora," Fahdi instructed while looking Rami in the eye.

"I'm guessing this is to pay for your phone call."

"Yeah. And if you ever want to hear from me again, you'll get that money delivered by 4 p.m. tomorrow to the owner of the Al-Hassan Grocery. His name is Abu Khalid."

"You know we don't negotiate with terrorists," the DG responded solemnly.

"Then I guess it's a good thing he's a *baker*," Fahdi responded coolly, never breaking his eye contact with Rami and then hung up the phone.

Fahdi spent the remainder of the night curled up on the floor in the corner of his cell unable to sleep. Every time he closed his eyes, he saw the faces of his tormenters as they flipped the switch and sent a burst of agonizing electricity coursing through his bruised and broken body. He relived every beating and every shock from the generator over and over. He dreaded the morning and wondered what tortures he'd face in the new day. A shred of relief came over him when his daily water bottle was tossed into the cell and rolled up near his head. Lately, he'd been receiving his daily meal in the late afternoon, meaning he'd passed the majority of the day on the floor of his cell without being taken into the interrogation room. He was confident he wouldn't be seeing his torturers at all that day. With this realization and the relief it brought, he was finally able to close his eyes and sleep, although a restless one plagued with nightmares.

He awoke several hours later to the sound of someone clanging something metal against the bars of his cell door. He rolled over and saw Rami. "What time is it?" Fahdi asked, disoriented and groggy from sleep.

"Almost eleven o'clock," Rami answered. "I tried waking you when I got here at eight, but you were out cold."

"Considering the fact that you didn't force me awake, I'm guessing you got your money," Fahdi said.

"Your man came through," Rami confirmed. "My uncle said a guy dropped a package off for me at the store today around noon. A full pack of cigarettes with a $50 bill shoved inside. I'm guessing the cigarettes are a gift for you." Rami produced the pack of cigarettes from his pocket and pulled one out. "Let's have a smoke together," he said, offering the cigarette to Fahdi. "I'll keep the pack on me; I wouldn't want you getting caught with contraband in your cell. Just flag me down whenever you want one."

Fahdi took the cigarette and Rami lit the end for him through the bars.

"That $50 was just a taste of what I can offer you," Fahdi said after taking a drag from his cigarette.

"Well, that's good to hear," Rami responded with a smile. "Because if you want to use the phone again, the price just went up to $100. You understand, of course? The risk I'm taking is fairly substantial and I figure this is a reasonable price."

"Yes of course, I understand," Fahdi replied composedly, playing right along with Rami's scheme. "But as I'm sure you noticed from the conversation yesterday, I'm not calling my wife or mother. I have no family here. The people I'm calling aren't paying to hear the sound of my lovely voice. They want information."

"Oh, I don't know about that," Rami said backing off. "You're talking not just getting me fired but getting my ass killed. Five-minutes on the phone is all I..."

"Five-hundred dollars," Fahdi said cutting him off. "Provide me with satisfactorily useful information to relay in a five-minute phone call every day and I will make sure $500 is delivered to your uncle's store every day by 4 p.m. Do we have a deal?"

"I don't know, man. This is some risky shit."

"You said yourself this job is just a means to an end..."

"Yeah, but I don't want that end to be the end of my damn life."

"You're here for the money, Rami. Just think what you could do with that kind of money. Do you want to be a watchdog for the next however many years, working in places like this? You're better than this. Take the money and invest it in something like your uncle's store. Use it to remodel and go into business with him as a partner. Be your own boss. Unless you prefer making two-hundred bucks a week tossing water bottles to condemned men for the next few years."

Rami thought about it for several minutes and finally caved. "What do I have to do?"

"Just answer some questions," Fahdi said. "Come back in an hour. I will ask you five questions, you will answer them to the best of your ability and then you'll let me use your phone for five minutes. It's as simple as that. Five questions, five minutes, five-hundred dollars."

"I'll see you in an hour." Rami agreed and left to complete his watch rounds.

An hour later, Rami returned to Fahdi's cell. "What are your questions?" he asked Fahdi.

"How many prisoners are they keeping here in this facility?"

"Right now there are sixty-two."

Fahdi furrowed his brow in confusion. "I've been dragged down this hall several times. You're telling me there are over sixty cells down here?"

"No, you're obviously one of the V.I.P.s. There are typically two or three men to a cell, but orders from the top are no other prisoners are to be confined with you."

"How many guards and staff are assigned to this facility?"

"There are only four of us here on duty at night. During the day, there are probably about ten to twelve guards and four interrogators."

Fahdi thought about his next question for a few seconds. He desperately wanted to ask the number one question that was burning a hole in his tongue, but knew better than to start off with it. Rami most likely wouldn't answer it and may back away from the whole deal. Fahdi knew it would be best to wait a few days until Rami got attached to the cash flow before he asked his burning question, but curiosity got the better of him and he took a shot in the dark. "Where are we?" he finally asked as nonchalantly as possible. "I need an address."

Rami smiled. "So your friends can come storming in here in the middle of the night to bust you out and most likely put a bullet in my head in the process? I think not. That is an answer that's going to cost you a hell of a lot more than $500, buddy."

"Okay, fine. I understand," Fahdi relented. "Have you worked at any other detention facilities?"

"Yes,"

"How many others have you been assigned to?"

"Five others, aside from this place."

"Will you at least give me the locations of those facilities?"

"I see no reason not to, but you've already asked your five questions. Make your call," Rami said, tossing his cell phone through the bars of the door to Fahdi.

Fahdi flipped the phone open and called the DG. "Get a pen," he said as soon as the DG answered. He passed on the information Rami had provided and then dropped the bomb regarding the $500 payment required.

"Fine," the DG said regarding the money. "But just know that I'm fronting this money out of my pocket. If this information doesn't pan out, I'm taking the repayment out of your ass."

"I honestly hope you get that opportunity," Fahdi said and hung up the phone.

"You think about those locations," Fahdi said to Rami as he handed his phone back. "I want those addresses tomorrow if you want another $500."

Fahdi knew it was too much to hope that he'd have another day off from torture, so he tried to get some sleep before he was dragged back into the interrogation room. Considering his captors had started using electroshock on him, he knew he was on borrowed time. Once a prisoner started being electrocuted, it was usually a week tops before he disappeared from the facility, and Fahdi was fairly sure he wouldn't be peacefully released to go home.

As Fahdi suspected, he was escorted from his cell and back into the interrogation room around mid-morning. He tried to prepare himself both physically and mentally for the shock treatments, but he quickly noted the generator was missing from the room as they sat him down back in a small metal folding chair. The guards gave Fahdi the usual treatment, a couple of punches across the face to soften him up a bit, and then the main interrogator entered the room. Fahdi was asked the same round of questions they'd been asking for weeks and threatened that if he didn't confess to the INIS's crimes, secret dealings with the CIA, and the director general's power hungry ways, he'd face more punishment. Fahdi knew as soon as he signed anything, he was dead, so he took the beatings and hoped Max and the DG would come through for him. He was actually relieved they were simply beating him and not electrocuting him. He had a fleeting thought that this was significant in some way, but it was quickly knocked from his consciousness by another blow to the side of the head from one of the guards.

That night, Rami informed Fahdi that he had received his money and was ready to answer more questions. Fahdi asked where the other Interior Ministry detention facilities were located and approximately how many prisoners and guards were at each. Again, he passed the info along to the DG in a five-minute phone call, and again, $500 found its way into the hands of Rami's uncle at his grocery store.

Over the next few days, Fahdi continued to be interrogated and beaten but not submitted to any more electric shock treatments. Rami continued to provide information on a nightly basis and answered questions about the facilities, specific names of IM guards and officials he knew working in the detention facilities, and various other facts the DG suggested Fahdi try and find out. By the fifth phone call, the DG informed Fahdi that Max was relatively pleased with the info Fahdi was providing and that he was actively working on getting him released. Fahdi had his doubts, but also had a feeling Max's interference may have had something to do with the reason Fahdi was simply being beaten lately and no longer electrocuted.

On April 9, Fahdi was once again taken to the interrogation room. A shot of terror ran down his spine when he recognized the heavy wooden chair and saw the generator in the corner.

"You must have some friends in high places," the interrogator said as the guards strapped Fahdi to the chair. "This tells me you have been holding out on me. I told you if you were completely truthful with me, you'd avoid a lot of pain. I feel betrayed," he said in mock dejection.

One of the guards approached Fahdi and began unbuttoning his jeans.

"What the hell?!" Fahdi screamed in panic.

"I warned you," the interrogator said curtly.

The guard managed to scoot Fahdi's pants down low on his hips while the other guard came over with the wires from the generator. The guard that removed Fahdi's jeans proceeded to hold him against the chair by the hips while the other guard clipped the ends of the wires to Fahdi's genitals. The pain from the bite of the metal clips was enough to make Fahdi nauseated and he had to fight to keep from throwing up. A guard poured a bottle of water onto Fahdi's crotch and then they flipped the switch.

Fahdi writhed in agony for what felt like an eternity. When they cut the power off, he could no longer hold back and he vomited over the side of the chair. He just missed the boot of one of the guards who reacted by delivering a fisted punch to Fahdi's neck for nearly soiling his shoes.

"You bastards!" Fahdi roared once he caught his breath. "I'm going to kill you all! I will rip out your eyes and feed them to you!"

"I don't think you're in any position to be making threats," one of the guards said.

The switch was flipped back on and Fahdi was again submerged into the depths of excruciating pain and felt consciousness slipping from him. He was brought back to the surface by a warm sensation and then the electricity was cut off again.

"It seems you've pissed yourself," the interrogator said without intonation.

"We're going to keep going until you shit your pants!" one of the guards taunted.

When the electricity was turned on for the third time, Fahdi fought to maintain consciousness and focused on channeling his thoughts and anger into dealing with the pain.

I won't let these assholes break me.

When Fahdi was deposited back into his cell, every muscle in his body felt like Jello, and the throbbing pain between his legs was unbearable. He groaned in pain and shook as what felt like residual currents of electricity periodically coursed through his body. His pants were stiff from the dried urine, but he had successfully been able to control his bowels and refused the guards the satisfaction of shitting himself. His hands were bound again with a black zip-tie, but this was the least of Fahdi's worries at that point.

When Rami arrived for their nightly meeting he took one look at Fahdi and said, "Holy shit, dude."

Fahdi managed to roll over so he could look at Rami, but didn't have the strength to even lift himself from the floor into a sitting position. "Did you want to do this tonight or do you want me to just leave so you can rest up?" Rami asked.

"No. Don't leave, please," Fahdi gasped, scooting a little closer to the door. "I have to make the phone call." Rami obliged and handed Fahdi the phone.

"You have to get me out of here now," Fahdi spluttered into the phone when the DG answered. "I don't know how much longer I can hang on."

"Alright, we'll make it happen," the DG answered. "Have you found out where you are?"

Fahdi eyeballed Rami. "No, not exactly."

"We need a precise location," the DG responded. "We've got an idea but not an exact address."

"Rami, please. I need to know where we are," Fahdi begged. "I promise nothing bad will happen to you. You have my word. No one will know."

Rami remained silent for several seconds, but Fahdi knew he had him. He was going to crack.

"Another $500 for this information alone," Rami bargained.

Fahdi nodded. "You got it."

"Sadr City. Two-story office building on Gejara Street, right off Orazdy Square."

Fadi closed his eyes in relief. "Thank you," he said in a whisper more to himself than to Rami.

"I heard him," the DG affirmed. "We're on it. Hang in there. We'll see you soon."

Thirteen hours later, two guards showed up at Fahdi's cell and opened the door. With one on each side of him, they half carried him out of the cell, but instead of turning right in the direction of the interrogation rooms, they went left. They escorted Fahdi up a flight of stairs and out of the basement dungeon he'd been held in for thirty-five days. They took him to a crude empty office with a small table and dropped him down in a chair. Several minutes later, the door to the office opened and in walked a person Fahdi never thought he'd be happy to see: Max.

"You don't know me," Max said brusquely.

A few second later, several Iraqi IM officials entered the office behind Max.

"We really appreciate you transferring this prisoner over to the U.S. Federal Bureau of Investigation," Max announced to the IM men in an official tone. "We've been trying to track this scumbag down for months," he continued redirecting his gaze to Fahdi.

The IM officials muttered something about always being glad to assist the U.S. government, and Max quickly guided Fahdi out of the room. They exited the building without saying a word to each other and climbed into a waiting SUV.

As soon as they were clear from the IM compound, Max produced a small pocketknife from the center console and cut the restraints from Fahdi's wrists.

"So now you're with the FBI?" Fahdi asked in a small voice.

Max chuckled. "Do I *look* like an FBI pussy to you?"

"So where are we going now?" Fahdi asked changing the subject.

"I'm taking you to the hospital to get checked out. You look like you've been roughed up pretty good. If nothing else, hopefully they'll at least give you a bath. You smell like shit."

No, I smell like piss. Fahdi thought to himself. But just one more day and he knew he probably would've smelled like shit.

Chapter 30

"Mandy"
Tuesday, 11 April–Friday, 26 May
2006

The remainder of my restriction sentence passed without incident. On the night of my release, I sat on my rack with my packed sea bag next to me, staring out at a crystal clear night sky filled with stars. I counted the seconds until midnight and thought about Fahdi. He didn't even know I had been on restriction. It had been nearly two months since I'd received the email from him telling me he was still alive, and well over three months since I'd actually heard his voice. It was hard to believe that a little over three months was actually the entire amount of time we had spent together in Iraq. We'd come so far and been through so much. The end was finally in sight, but we still weren't across the finish line. There was still so much that could go wrong before we were together again. Hell, for all I knew, something had happened to him while I was on restriction and he was already dead. I considered this possibility, but in my heart, I knew he was still alive. He was still out there on the other side of the world, fighting and trying just as hard to be reunited with me as I was to be with him.

When my watch struck midnight, I grabbed my sea bag and made my final trip from the restriction room to the quarterdeck. The OOD signed me out and returned my car keys.

"Stay out of trouble, Petty Officer," the OOD said as he handed me my keys.

"Oh, I don't know about that, but I will honestly try," I answered with a smile.

I drove home and, as soon as I made it into my townhouse, I opened my laptop and jumped online. I logged into my email and found one from Fahdi sent just the day before. There was nothing from since the final email I'd received from him prior to starting my restriction. I found that quite coincidental and wondered if he somehow knew I'd been on restriction. He wrote that he was still alive, doing okay, and that he would try to contact me via Skype in a couple of days. I emailed him back and told him I, too, was doing well, and I'd be waiting to hear from him. I didn't know for sure if he knew about my restriction, so I didn't want to mention anything about it in an email.

After finishing up with the email, it dawned on me that I probably had a ton of regular mail to go through as well. My roommate had left my mail piled on the kitchen counter for me, so I went downstairs to sift through it and see if anything important had come while I was away.

About halfway through the stack, I came upon a letter from immigration. My heart rate sped up as I ripped it open. The letter was from the consulate office at the U.S. embassy in Amman, Jordan. Fahdi was scheduled for a visa interview October 13, 2006–over five months away. I was disappointed that it was so far in the future, but relieved that at least things were still progressing. We had a specific time in the future to look forward to. I returned to my room and shot Fahdi another quick email updating him on the news and then called it a night. I'd been released from restriction on Wednesday morning, and I had to report back to work at the Master-at-Arms's office at 0730, so I tried to grab a couple hours of sleep before work.

Once at work, Chief Viraez informed me that I was to report to the Legal Office because Lt. Klitch needed to speak with me. *Joy.* I had no desire to see that man, but I did want to find out if all of my legal issues were cleared and if I would be free to separate from the Navy when my contract was up the beginning of August. I had so many days of leave racked up I could actually be done with the Navy as early as the end of May. The thought that I may be free to return to Jordan and see Fahdi again in as little as thirty days made me swell with happiness and gave me more than enough strength to face Lt. Klitch.

At the JAG office, Lt. Klitch's secretary informed me he'd stepped out for a minute but told me to go ahead and have a seat in his office.

"Sorry to keep you waiting," Lt. Klitch said to me as he entered his office a few minutes later.

I noticed his voice was completely free of the usual bitterness he had when speaking to me, and I immediately felt a pang of dread that I was about to hear bad news.

"It's no problem, Sir," I answered as cordially as possible.

He took his seat behind his desk and pulled my file from a drawer. "Okay, you've served your forty-five days of restriction, so let's discuss what happens next," he said, opening my file and thumbing through the pages. "I've spoken with the commanding officer along with the XO, and we've decided that it would be in everyone's best interest if you and the United States Navy simply parted ways on peaceful terms."

"That's what I was hoping and planning as well, Sir."

"Well, we mean right now," he clarified. "As soon as next week if possible."

My heart nearly leapt from my chest. *I could be completely free in a week!* "That sounds great to me." But I had a feeling there was some kind of catch that came along with this proposal.

"You will be granted a general discharge under honorable conditions. This is primarily just a technicality considering you won't be fully completing your first enlistment," he explained. "But, right now, we feel you are pretty much just a waste of a uniform and taxpayer dollars, and we really have no need for you to be biding your time over at the MA's office for the next three months."

I'm sure he noticed my icy glare, but I remained silent.

"Besides, I know full well you have no more desire to be here than we have for you to be here. Take the deal and move on with your life. You can contest this suggestion if you like, but I wouldn't recommend it. You never know when a zealous NCIS agent may choose to reopen your case. When it comes to national security cases, they often review them periodically and are known to reopen them quite often," he added in a threatening tone. "If you are no longer in the Navy, NCIS can't touch you. They'd have to turn you over to the FBI, and they rarely waste their time doing that."

"So, basically, I'm being kicked out," I stated plainly.

"I wouldn't look at it that way. In fact, I think the CO is being more than generous in granting you a discharge under any kind of honorable conditions. With this type of separation, all you lose is your GI Bill."

I expected some ramifications with this deal for the future, but I decided I'd just have to accept them. The sooner I was free from the Navy's grip, the sooner I'd be able to better help Fahdi get out of Iraq, and that was my main priority. I picked up the pen and signed the agreement.

Over the next week, I went through the military out-processing procedures that included taking a required week-long class intended to assist military personnel in readjusting to civilian life so they can survive on the outside. It was quite similar to the class prisoners had to take prior to being released back into society.

I called my mom and step-dad and arranged to have them come out with a moving trailer, help me pack up my belongings, and move me out of my townhouse. My only plan was to be on a plane to Jordan as soon as possible and stay there however long it took until Fahdi was approved to come to the U.S. My parents offered to let me stay with them at their home in Ohio until I left for Jordan and said they'd keep my stuff as long as I needed. Since Fahdi's visa interview wasn't until October, I probably wouldn't be back before then, and from the research I'd done on visa timelines, it was safe to say it would be at least another three months after Fahdi's interview before he actually had a visa in hand.

My final day of U.S. naval service came on Friday, May 26, 2006. I drove to the personnel department to surrender my military ID card and pick up my official signed and stamped discharge paperwork, known as a DD-214. This was the paper you were supposed to safeguard for the rest of your life because it was proof of your military service. When the clerk at personnel handed me my DD-214, I glanced over it and felt the stab of the knife Lt. Klitch thrust into my back. As he stated, it did indeed list my discharge type as, "General Under Honorable Conditions." However, under reason for separation it was plainly printed, "Misconduct–Commission of a serious offense." Furthermore, under the reason code was a four-digit number that signified I am ineligible to ever rejoin the military and barred me from being able to obtain any form of civilian government employment. I wouldn't be able to so much as get a job at the Post Office. *You son of a bitch.*

"Is everything okay?" the personnel clerk asked me, noticing my reaction after reading over my DD-214. "Has there been a mistake?"

"No," I said, shaking my head. "Everything is just fine," I said through clenched teeth and balled up the paper. The clerk just stared at me in shock as I slid her my ID card across the counter and left the office, depositing my DD-

214 in the trashcan on my way out. Six years of military service down the drain. I'd known since the seventh grade that I was joining the Navy. I was in the Sea Cadet program at fourteen. I joined the Navy Delayed Entry Program as soon as I was eligible at age sixteen. Since my birthday was in the summer, I graduated from high school and shipped off to boot-camp before I was even eighteen years old. At this point, my entire adult life had been spent in military service and now, it meant nothing. Worthless. But, it was still a small price to pay considering the charges I'd faced merely weeks before and for having the freedom to be together with Fahdi.

On my way home, I picked up the phone and called Fahdi. "I'm out," I said as soon as he answered the phone.

"You sound like you regret it," he replied solemnly.

"No. I don't regret it. Don't make me regret it," I added.

"I swear I will do everything in my power for the rest of my life to ensure that you don't, Mandy."

"I know," I said, fighting back tears. They were tears of joy, tears of frustration, tears for the betrayal I felt, and tears of anxiety for the unknown future that lay ahead for both of us. "I love you."

"*Ahabich*. I love you too."

He was still in Iraq and he sounded tired, but he assured me he would be in Jordan to meet me when I arrived. I'd purchased a one-way ticket to Amman and was scheduled to depart from Columbus, Ohio the following Thursday: June 1st. My mom and step-dad had left my townhouse the day before with the majority of my things in tow, and I planned to follow with my residual belongings packed in my Ford Ranger pickup truck as soon as I had my separation paperwork in hand.

When I exited through the gates of Fort Meade for the last time, it felt bittersweet. I caught sight of the massive, mirrored-glass NSA building in my rearview mirror and wished with everything in me that I was leaving under different circumstances. But I'd chosen my path. I made my decision and I knew in my heart it was the right one. As the NSA building faded to a dot in my mirrors, and I drove north up the Baltimore/D.C. Parkway, I found myself smiling. A chapter in my life was closing and I was embarking on a new adventure. I joined the military chasing adventure and, although not exactly how I had imagined, I definitely succeeded in my quest. I was excited (and a little apprehensive) about what the future held for me, but I was sure of one thing: I was headed in the right direction.

Chapter 31

"Fahdi"
Tuesday 11 April–Friday 26 May
2006

A few days into Fahdi's recovery at the hospital, Max stopped by to visit. The doctors determined that Fahdi suffered from three fractured ribs, a broken nose, swollen kidneys, numerous contusions and lacerations across 80% of his body, and moderate to severe malnutrition, including a significant Vitamin D deficiency.

"So, how you feeling?" Max asked, taking a seat beside Fahdi's bed.

"Like I had the shit beat out of me."

"You didn't say anything did you?" Max asked half-jokingly.

"What do you think?"

"I think you and I both know you'd be dead right now if you had."

"So what happens now?" Fahdi asked, eager to not only change the subject but to find out what he was going to have to worry about next.

"Well, quite frankly, you're going to die," Max said plainly.

"Excuse me?"

"Well, you'll be dead on paper at least," Max clarified. "The DG has requested you be returned to the INIS to continue in his employment. Unless you want the IM tracking you down again. You're much better off dead."

"I'm trying to get a visa to the U.S., Max. If I am technically dead, how am I supposed to immigrate to the U.S.? I won't even be able to get a damn passport to leave Iraq!"

"Don't worry about that–we'll take care of it."

Fahdi had a sinking feeling that returning to the INIS didn't mean he'd only be working for the DG, but that he also now belonged to Max as well. But it wasn't like he had any alternative options.

"So, are you in?" Max asked impatiently.

"Yes," Fahdi answered in a dismal tone.

"Good, because you're already dead," Max said and plopped a large manila enveloped on Fahdi's chest.

Fahdi opened the envelope and found a cell phone and his official death certificate signed and stamped by the Iraqi Ministry of Health inside.

"You died the day before yesterday at 1:06 p.m." Max explained. "You committed suicide in your holding cell. When you were discovered by the guard on duty, you were rushed here to this hospital where you were pronounced dead upon arrival. Cause of death: self-inflicted strangulation as a result of hanging yourself by a bootlace in your cell. As soon as I leave, you are to use that cell phone to call your immediate family and explain that they need to have a funeral for you–as large and public a funeral as possible. And, they need to be completely convincing. Do not tell them any more than you have to, but make sure they understand your life, as well as theirs, depends on them carrying this task out successfully. The fact that you are still alive is not to be known by anyone beyond your mother, brother, and sister. If your brother and sister are not 100% reliable when it comes to this matter, I suggest you keep them in the dark as well. Your mother will obviously have to know the truth, but I've become confident in a mother's ability to lie quite convincingly when it comes to protecting the lives of her children.

"You will remain here at the hospital for the next few days until the funeral takes place and continue your recovery. After that, you will return to the INIS. Remember, you are now a ghost and that building is your tomb. You will only leave the building under the cover of darkness to perform missions under my direction. You talk to no one. You visit no one. You *do not* exist. You may resume communication with Mandy, but she is not to know of any of this. As far as she is concerned you are simply biding your time here in Iraq working as the general's coffee bitch until you get your visa to the U.S. Do you understand all of this?"

Fahdi nodded.

"Alright. I'll see you in a few days," Max said and stood to leave. "Oh, and by the way, that cell phone is limited to domestic use. I know you want to talk to Mandy as soon as possible, but you'll just have to wait until you get back to the building. Just a few more days, I promise."

After Max left the hospital, Fahdi did as he was instructed and called his mom and, as weird as it was, helped her arrange his own funeral. They decided his brother and sister were needed to help pull everything off, so they let them in on the scheme. Fahdi's funeral and burial took place the following day in his parents' small home village outside of Mosul in the mountains of northern Iraq. At the end of the day-long event, an ornate casket that Fahdi's brother spent several hours the previous evening filling with rocks to add weight then sealing with super glue, was laid in the family burial plot next to Fahdi's deceased father. A headstone with a photo of Fahdi was even ordered to mark the false grave.

"So, did everything go as planned?" Fahdi asked his brother over the phone the morning after the funeral.

"Yeah, I guess so. At least everyone here is sure you're dead."

"How did Mom handle it?"

"Holy shit, dude–you'd have thought you were really dead. She was screaming and crying the whole time. I even had to take her aside a few times to ask if she was okay and remind her you aren't really dead. She said you may not be physically dead, but she knows you are effectively dead here in Iraq and will be leaving soon for good to go to the U.S., which made her feel almost as bad."

"How about Dina?" Fahdi asked, moving on. It killed him to think of the pain he continued to put his mother through and cursed himself again for ever offering to help the U.S. translate that day in his neighborhood.

"Dina did okay. I had to smack her in the back of the head once, though, when I caught her rolling her eyes while she helped mom walk through the cemetery. But, overall, it was a success. I'll take a picture of your grave when they get the headstone placed and send it to you," his brother added with a chuckle.

"Spare me," Fahdi said and hung up the phone.

After two weeks in the hospital, Fahdi was nearly fully recovered and Max gave the okay for him to return to the INIS building. As soon as he was back in his old office, Fahdi shot me a quick email. The one I received a couple of days before the end of my restriction and read the first night I was back home.

After emailing me, Fahdi went to see the general for the first time since he'd been released from prison. He softly knocked on the door of the DG's office and waited for the general's commanding voice to give him permission to enter. When the DG looked up from his desk and saw Fahdi, his hard face softened a bit and Fahdi even noticed the hint of a smile, albeit a brief one.

"I see you are still alive," the DG said, maintaining his typical harsh tone.

"I guess I have you to thank for that," Fahdi replied.

"I'm glad you are alive and back," the DG said with a smile. "Now, unless you have something urgent you need to discuss, go away," he said, shooing Fahdi with a flick of his hand.

"No, I just wanted to stop by and say hello," Fahdi said lightly. He turned and put his hand on the doorknob. "And thank you...for everything, Sir," he added and then slipped out of the office.

That evening, Fahdi contacted me via Skype. It was the first time we'd heard the sound of each other's voices in over three months. He didn't say a word about his stint in the IM detention center, simply that he was back in Baghdad working for the DG as a translator and was preparing to come to Jordan soon so we could be together.

I relayed the highlights from my DRB, NJP, and subsequent forty-five days of restriction. He was quite upset by my punishment, but I neutralized his fury when I passed along the news that I would be released from the Navy in the next couple of weeks.

"So, it's almost over," he said with a sigh.

"It's almost over," I echoed.

I informed him that my final day in the Navy was tentatively set for May 26 and that I'd be on my way to Jordan as soon as possible after that. I just had to make a brief stop in Ohio first and would be flying out from there. He said to let him know as soon as I had plane tickets and he'd make sure he was in Jordan a couple of days ahead of me to find us a place to stay.

"Oh my God, I can't believe I'm going to get to see you again in just a couple of weeks," he said. "It's like a dream come true."

"Yeah, for me too," I said, feeling tears sting my eyes. "I told you I'd never give up!"

I scanned and emailed him a copy of the letter from immigration informing us of his visa interview date in October, and we discussed trying to remain together in Amman until the interview. Before we hung up, he told me he was going to be pretty busy at work during the day until he left for Jordan, but that he would be buying an international cell phone the next day so that we could call each other whenever we wanted.

Over the next couple of weeks, I progressed through my out-processing with the Navy while Fahdi and the tactical team trained for their upcoming mission. I purchased my plane ticket to Jordan on May 18 and immediately called Fahdi and told him I'd be arriving in Amman at 2 p.m. June 2nd. Fahdi planned on leaving for Jordan a few days before I was scheduled to arrive, giving him some time to find us a place to live prior to my arrival.

The countdown to our long-awaited reunion was on.

The morning after our plans were finalized, Fahdi was summoned to the DG's office to meet with Max and the DG and discuss Fahdi's experiences in the IM prison. Fahdi passed along info and intel that assisted in the planning of a joint U.S. and Iraqi military forces raid on several secret IM prisons. When everything was over, the coalition recovered 136 illegally-detained prisoners and arrested several IM officials. It was only a drop in the bucket, but it was a start.

The night before Fahdi left for Jordan, his friend Omar stopped by his office to wish him well.

"So I guess you're really leaving?" Omar said as more of a statement than a question.

"Yes, Brother, I've got a new life waiting for me. Hopefully a better one."

"Come on!" Omar exclaimed spreading his arms for emphasis. "You're going to walk away from all this?" he said facetiously. "But seriously, admit it, you're going to miss this."

Fahdi shrugged. "I don't think so, man."

"Whatever. Take care of yourself. I wish you and your American girl the best."

"Thanks, my friend."

When Omar left, Fahdi went to see the DG.

"I guess you're here to give me your resignation," the DG said when Fahdi entered his office. Max was also in the office seated in front of the DG's desk.

"Yes, Sir."

"Well I'm not going to accept it," the DG replied harshly.

"Excuse me?" Fahdi asked baffled.

"Don't panic, you can leave to go be with Mandy in Jordan. But as far as the agency is concerned, you are on extended personal leave. Just in case you ever need to come back to work here."

"Well, with all due respect, Sir, I honestly hope not."

The DG smiled and crossed the room to shake hands with Fahdi. Max rose from his chair and also shook Fahdi's hand. "Good luck, Fahdi. Perhaps we'll meet again someday."

"Again, Sir, with all due respect, I hope not," Fahdi replied with a smile.

Chapter 32

**Friday, 2 June
2006**

I hugged my mom and step-dad on the curb of the drop-off area at Columbus Airport. "Are you completely sure about this, Mandy?" my mom asked with a hint of uneasiness in her voice.

"No, Mom, I'm not sure. I'm positive."

I was flying back into the depths of one of the most, if not *the* most, unstable regions on Earth to seek out what I was sure was true love with no idea of when I would return. Yet I felt not a sliver of apprehension and only immense optimism.

"You've always had a sensible head on your shoulders, Kid," my step-dad, Larry, said. "I just hope it doesn't let you down now."

"Don't worry. I know what I'm doing," I assured them both and then pulled up the handle of my large-wheeled suitcase.

I waved goodbye as I made my way into the terminal and then lost sight of them after I turned the corner to head for the Delta ticket counters. I was scheduled to fly from Columbus on a small Delta commuter to Chicago's O'Hare Airport where, after a brief layover, I'd board a non-stop, thirteen-hour Royal Jordanian flight to Amman. I was extremely relieved when the clerk at the Delta check-in counter swiped my passport and promptly issued me my boarding pass. This meant I was obviously not on the no-fly list–a fear I had considering my history.

I made it to Chicago without incident, and as I made my way to the international terminal, I felt the fire of excitement inside me double.

Oh my God, this is really happening. After all this hell, in approximately 15 hours, I will be in Fahdi's arms.

The thought made me feel invincible and I beamed from ear to ear as I boarded that plane to Jordan. I knew I should try to get some rest on the flight that would take me ahead seven time zones, but I was too damned excited to even close my eyes.

Finally, after biting each of my fingernails up to my elbows, my flight touched down right on time at Queen Alia Airport in Amman. I was swallowed by the massive crowd of people from our flight as we all made our way through customs. I stood on my tiptoes and strained my neck to look for Fahdi over the crowd, but I didn't see him anywhere. A Jordanian customs official stamped my passport and I continued with the flow of the crowd toward the baggage claim area still desperately looking for Fahdi.

Suddenly, I felt two arms around me squeezing me in a hug so tight I was unable to breathe. We stood there in the airport holding on to each other as tightly as we could while modest Mid-Eastern onlookers gawked at our blatant public display of affection. We remained that way for several minutes without saying a word, with tears streaming down both our faces.

Finally, Fahdi broke the silence. "There were so many times I thought I'd never see you again," he whispered, still not releasing me from his embrace. "I love you so much."

"I'm here now," I whispered back. "And no government, king, president, evil dictator, secret agency, or *anyone* is ever going to take me from your side again. I promise."

Epilogue

Friday 2 June 2006–Present Day

Prior to my arrival Fahdi had managed to secure us a beautiful, spacious, two-bedroom, two-bathroom furnished apartment for $500 a month in a building owned by an older Palestinian Christian couple who had fled the Palestinian/Israeli turmoil a decade before and settled in Amman. They owned a three-story building in a quiet Amman suburb with five apartments. The older couple and their grown sons, along with their families, occupied four of the apartments and the fifth, they rented out for extra income. Apartments in Amman were an extremely hot commodity and didn't remain vacant for long due to the massive influx of refugees Jordan received from Iraq, Palestine, and Lebanon. It was the safest and calmest major city in that region. A two-bedroom, two-bath apartment in Amman rented for upwards of $1,000 in U.S. currency. We lucked out and our new landlords were generous enough to give us a great deal because they felt it was their Christian duty to offer a helping hand to Fahdi, a fellow Christian Arab fleeing his country. They were happy to have an American tenant as well.

Fahdi and I spent our first two weeks together simply getting to know each other in a relaxed, non-work, non-warzone environment. He told me bits and pieces of what occurred during our nine months apart, but I could tell he harbored some deep and very raw wounds. I didn't press him for details and let him tell me only what he wanted to say. He suffered horrendous nightmares and would often struggle so fiercely in his sleep that I'd have to leave the bed to avoid possible injury. I'd stand or sit against the wall of our bedroom and watch him fight off his tormentors, silently willing him to wake up so I could hold him and tell him everything was going to be fine and that he was safe now. He'd awaken drenched in sweat and panting, but I always allowed him to wake on his own. It was more strenuous on him if I tried to force him awake while in the midst of one of his episodes. In the beginning, I worried about his health, both physically and emotionally. He was still underweight due to his stint in the IM prison, but as the weeks progressed, he steadily gained weight and his nightmares grew fewer and farther between.

During the month of June, we spent our days exploring Amman. We checked out the tourist sites but were just as happy to do the simple things an ordinary couple enjoyed, like going to the mall or catching dinner and a movie. I took Fahdi to see his first movie in a real movie theater. It felt so great to just act like a normal couple that I don't even remember what movie we saw.

The first week of July, we rented a car and took a road trip across Jordan. We visited the Dead Sea for a couple of days, toured the ancient city of Petra (the city carved into the mountainside and where Indiana Jones and the Last Crusade was filmed), and snorkeled in the Red Sea off the coast of Jordan's southernmost tip. We stayed in gorgeous hotels, ordered room service, strolled along beaches, and fell even deeper in love.

While staying in the hotel on the Dead Sea, I discovered a complimentary magazine in our hotel room that was published by a Jordanian company but was completely in English. The magazine was called *Living Well* and was a women's fashion/current affairs magazine similar to *Redbook*. I read it cover to cover and was excited to learn that the publisher was located not far from our apartment in Amman. When we returned from our road trip, I emailed the publisher a resume and cover letter just to see if I'd get a response. Much to my delight and surprise, one of the magazine's associate editors responded and asked me to stop by for a chat. They were always interested in hiring American writers for freelance work.

I attended an interview and was subsequently offered a writing position. My first story, a feature in the upcoming August edition, would detail the brief war between Israel and Lebanon, which began during our road trip. The conflict only lasted a week, but both sides exchanged brutal blows. Israel launched a massive bombing campaign on southern Beirut, reducing numerous areas of the city to smoldering rubble. They already had writers on the ground in Lebanon covering the actual conflict, but refugees from Lebanon were flooding into Amman and the editors wanted me to capture that aspect of the story. I easily found my first refugee, and from recommendations from her, I quickly integrated into the recently-arrived refugee community. I spoke to over a dozen women from every point on the social scale, most of whom were simply trying to protect their children. Several left Beirut as soon as the first Israeli bomb fell, while others endured several days until they finally decided it was time to get out. My article was indeed published in the August edition of *Living Well,* and I was paid enough to convince me to take another assignment for the magazine.

Right after I submitted my first article for *Living Well,* I began feeling slightly abnormal. I thought I was coming down with something, but when I awoke one morning completely nauseated the realization of what was going on hit me square in the face. I knew I was pregnant. I picked up a pregnancy test at the local drug store (complete with illustrated directions featuring a woman in full hijab and abaya urinating on the stick). Sure enough, I was right.

Our landlady recommended a female doctor downtown, so Fahdi and I made an appointment. Ironically, the OBGYN was an Iraqi. Fahdi and I definitely got some weird looks from both the nursing staff and other patients when we were called in to the exam room. Typically, the husband remained in the waiting room while the woman went into the exam room alone, but since the doctor spoke little English and the rest of the staff only spoke Arabic, Fahdi had to be with me the entire time and translate.

Nevertheless, I was very pleased with my landlady's recommendation. I wasn't sure what to expect, feared the worst, but was pleasantly surprised. The office was clean and the staff was very nice. I also noted the office, as far as I could tell, was equipped with up-to-date machinery and technology. They did an ultrasound and confirmed what I already knew. Fahdi and I listened to our baby's heartbeat and the doctor calculated I was already over seven weeks along with an estimated due date of March 16, 2007. I'd gotten pregnant within the first week of my arrival in Jordan. In fact, it was so close I caught Fahdi counting the days on a calendar back at the apartment later that evening and I smacked him.

My pregnancy was a huge surprise. I hadn't menstruated in over eight months, and a military doctor back in the States told me that I had stopped ovulating, most likely due to the stress of the situation I was in. So, I didn't think I'd be able to conceive until I had a period again. We weren't exactly in an ideal situation to be having a child, but Fahdi and I were both excited and happy to be expectant parents.

We wanted to get married but we had already petitioned U.S. immigration for a fiancé visa., If we got married now, we would have to start all over from the beginning with a spousal visa, which would set us back six months or more. So, we continued with our original plan in Jordan and counted down the days to Fahdi's scheduled visa interview. I had no qualms about spending my pregnancy in Jordan and even accepted the possibility of having to give birth there. As long as I had Fahdi by my side, I knew there was nothing I couldn't handle.

In early August, Fahdi took me out for a lovely dinner at a restaurant near downtown Amman that we'd both come to love since arriving in the city two months before. After dinner, we walked along the streets and just enjoyed being together. A few minutes into our stroll, Fahdi finally said what was on his mind. He told me I had to go back to the United States and that he had to return to Iraq. I thought he was joking, but when he stopped and looked at me I saw the seriousness in his face. He told me Jordan just wasn't safe enough for me. He was able to accept the risk when it was just the two of us, but now that I was pregnant, that changed the entire dynamic. I swore nothing on this Earth would keep us from being together, but I never considered a little being the size of a lima bean would have the power to pull us back apart.

In mid-August, Fahdi practically dragged me kicking and screaming to the airport and put me on a flight back to the United States. I cried the entire first leg of the trip from Jordan to Paris. In retrospect, Fahdi made the right decision. Less than a month after I left Jordan a gunman opened fire on three British tourists in Amman, killing one and injuring the other two.

A few days after I flew back to the States, Fahdi returned to Iraq and resumed his position at the INIS, thankful the DG hadn't allowed him to officially resign after all. We both hoped it wouldn't be long after Fahdi's interview in October that he'd have his visa in hand and be able to join me back in the States. But, yet again, what we hoped for and what reality delivered were two different things.

I moved in with my mom and step-dad in Ohio when I returned from Jordan and managed to land a full-time position with a local, small-town newspaper as a staff writer and graphic artist. I loved my job and my pregnancy progressed smoothly. Fahdi and I were depressed to be separated once again, but at least we weren't horribly stressed out from being investigated for espionage. We found peace in knowing that we were free to see each other if we really wanted to.

Fahdi returned to Amman for a couple of days in October to attend his visa interview, and, although they didn't give him confirmation, he believed the interview went well and left confidently. Unfortunately, they didn't give him an estimate of when he could expect to receive his visa should it be approved. They just said it could take anywhere from a few weeks to a few months. Sadly, it ended up being the latter.

We waited for the call from the consulate every day, but Christmas and New Year's came and went and we heard nothing. As my March due date approached, we prayed that Fahdi would make it to the U.S. in time to be present for the birth of our child. But again, we were disappointed.

On March 12, 2007 at 8:06 a.m., I delivered a healthy 7lb. 2oz. baby girl via C-section. We named her Elise Rayne. When it came time for the hospital to make out her birth certificate, they carefully asked me if I knew who the father was and if I wanted his name added to the certificate. I tried to explain the situation, but the hospital staff looked at me skeptically and ultimately refused to put Fahdi's name down as Elise's father. They feared I was either making him up or trying to trap a U.S. military guy into taking responsibility for my baby. When I asked how I could get him on the birth certificate in the future, they told me if he was in fact willing to accept responsibility before her first birthday, he could request to be put on the birth certificate but a paternity test may be required. I asked if they wanted to go ahead and test her for AIDS and make sure she had no residual effects from all the drugs I most likely did while pregnant with her since they had me pegged as a white trash whore.

I took tons of photos and videos and emailed them to Fahdi on a regular basis, but we were both extremely bitter that he missed getting to see her enter the world and was now missing all of her first moments. Her one-week birthday came and went. He missed her first smile, her first bath, her first case of the hiccups, and many other firsts.

Finally, right after Elise turned a month old, Fahdi called me with the glorious news. The embassy finally called and notified him that his visa had been approved. To this day, we don't know if Max had a hand in its delay or approval, but it's not like we could have done anything about it if we had known for sure. Fahdi purchased his plane tickets and was scheduled to arrive at Chicago's O'Hare Airport on April 26, 2007. We'd been apart for eight months, only a couple of weeks shy of how long we'd been separated the first time.

I drove the six hours to Chicago to meet Fahdi when he arrived because I was sure he'd run into issues with customs when he touched down on U.S. soil. Nothing had been easy for us for nearly two years, so I did my best to be prepared and head off trouble. I figured if I was physically in Chicago when he arrived and hit customs, I'd be much better poised to deal with any hassles than if I were waiting for him all the way in Ohio.

I was in O'Hare four hours before Fahdi was due to arrive and camped out in the international terminal. He called me from the plane before he took off from Amman, so I knew he was going to at least land on U.S. soil. I paced the terminal for the entire four hours. My blood pressure was through the roof. I was excited. I was nervous. I was ready for a battle. I was ready to fight. I was prepared to have him claim asylum if, God forbid, they tried to deny or revoke his visa at the last minute and send him back to the Middle East. I was shaking and sweating. My blood sugar bottomed out because I hadn't eaten since the day before.

Once Fahdi's plane landed, my apprehension skyrocketed. I watched all of his fellow passengers emerge from customs, but Fahdi never showed. Thirty minutes went by and still no Fahdi. An hour, no Fahdi. I finally talked to a Delta ticket agent who looked at me sympathetically but said there was nothing he could do to help me. I continued my anxious pacing for another half hour when the same ticket agent finally relented and handed me a small piece of paper with a phone number on it. He told me the number was for the customs office where Fahdi was most likely being held.

I called the number and spoke to a less-than-kind immigration official that refused to give me any information as to why Fahdi was being held up. All he would tell me was that Fahdi was indeed on the plane and with them in the customs office. I waited another hour when two Royal Jordanian Flight attendants came through the double doors and scanned the terminal, obviously looking for someone. I knew they were looking for me, so I approached them and told them who I was. They informed me the customs agents had decided to allow Fahdi to enter the country and he should be coming out soon. I nearly burst into tears but managed to thank them both very much for finding and telling me.

When Fahdi finally emerged, nearly four hours after his plane landed, I ran to him and jumped into his arms. Just like in Amman, we just stood there and held each other for several minutes without saying a word.

I desperately wanted Fahdi to meet his six-week-old daughter, but we'd both had a hellacious day and agreed it was too late to make the six-hour drive home. We spent the night in Chicago at a cheap motel in the outskirts of the city. Once we checked into our room, hunger finally hit us and I decided to baptize Fahdi in true American fashion by taking him for his very first meal in the United States of America at none other than McDonalds. If that wasn't classy enough, he had his first American breakfast the next morning at the Denny's. He actually fell in love with Denny's and said that if someone opened a place like that in Baghdad, they'd be rich.

We arrived to my parents' house in the early afternoon and Fahdi finally got to meet his baby girl. The emotions overwhelmed everyone. There were lots of tears and lots of smiles. It was a culmination of a very long, very arduous battle, but we were finally a family, together and safe.

One of the conditions of Fahdi's fiancé visa was that we had to be married within 90 days of his arrival. I gave Fahdi a week to settle in and then we went to the courthouse, obtained our marriage license, and were married May 15, 2007. For our honeymoon we took a family road trip to Florida to visit my dad, stopping off in the Smokey Mountains near Gatlinburg, Tennessee for a few days. After all the pressure my dad put on me to walk away from Fahdi, he and Fahdi actually ended up getting along really well and have great respect for one another.

Our marriage made Fahdi's presence in the U.S. legal, but he was not yet a permanent resident. Until he obtained a green card, he didn't have the right to work. We desperately wanted our own place, but couldn't afford our everyday bills and an apartment on my salary alone, especially since I'd been on maternity leave and without a paycheck for two months. In the meantime, I returned to my job at the newspaper and Fahdi was a stay-at-home dad.

He loved Elise more than life and was a wonderful father and husband. He got up with her in the night, held her when she screamed for hours on end (she had horrible colic), changed her diapers, bathed her, played with her, fed her, and was completely hands on. He proved to be everything every woman dreams of and more.

When he wasn't directly caring for Elise, Fahdi spent his time studying his new country and learning as much as he could about the American way of life. I spent every night answering a list of questions he'd come up with throughout the day covering a wide range of topics such as how our taxes work (that was interesting because I didn't understand it fully myself, but who does?), traffic laws, how insurance worked, civil laws, and so much more.

In October 2007, he finally received his green card, granting him legal authorization to obtain employment and permanent U.S. residency for two years, as long as we remained married. Ironically, he started receiving correspondences from several companies that were searching for native Arabic speakers to work as civilian contractors for the Department of Defense and deploy with U.S. Military forces to Iraq to work as translators. We laughed when Fahdi received the first few letters and joked that if they knew who we were, they wouldn't be wasting the postage. But, we both vowed neither of us would be returning to the Middle East any time soon and Fahdi continued to apply for simple local jobs at stores and restaurants.

Unfortunately, the economy was on a steep decline and would soon crash and burn. Fahdi had no luck finding a job and we were getting desperate. My parents said we could stay with them as long as we needed, but the three of us were crammed into a 10'x10' bedroom and we wanted so badly to get our own place. Fahdi decided to contact one of the recruiters looking for Arabic linguists and get some more information. The deal was one year in Iraq doing exactly what Fahdi had done before: living and working alongside U.S. Military troops throughout Iraq. He'd be able to come home for two weeks of leave after six months, and the pay was too good for us to turn down. In one year, he'd make enough to give our family a solid foundation, buy us a house, and live comfortably. The *extreme* last thing I wanted was to watch Fahdi get on a plane back to Iraq and for us to suffer through another long separation, but we knew it was an opportunity we couldn't pass up.

The company he signed with flew him from Ohio to Washington D.C. for two weeks in early December for training and indoctrination. He came home a week before Christmas and we spent our first Christmas together. Two days after Christmas, he flew to a U.S. Army base in Georgia and then left for Iraq just after the New Year. I found it comical that the same government that had kicked me out of the military for associating with Fahdi had now hired him directly and was paying him four times as much money as they ever paid me.

Fahdi was stationed with an Army unit in northern Iraq. We settled in for six months of being apart. We were pros by now, and considering our previous lengths of separation, six months was a drop in the bucket for us. Since Fahdi was now a linguist with U.S. permanent residency, he was eligible to work for units that required higher security clearances. Usually, these units were stuck with Middle-Easterners in their forties and fifties who had lived in the U.S. for more than twenty years and were not accustomed to living and working in a war zone. Fahdi's unit was ecstatic to have him: a linguist from the U.S. not only willing to leave the base and go on patrols, but who also knew how to conduct raids and detain prisoners.

Fahdi hated being away from me and Elise, but he truly loved his job. He relished the excitement of working with the military and contributing to his country. He enjoyed the environment and he fit like a round peg in a hole. Of course, I hated him being away, too, but I knew if he'd taken a minimum wage job at Wal-Mart, he would have been miserable.

Fahdi continued to work as a translator in Iraq for the next two years. I maintained my newspaper job, but with Fahdi's income, we were able to build a beautiful house in the Ohio countryside, and I made sure to add the large, covered front porch Fahdi and I dreamed we'd someday sit together on and cuddle. I also returned to college part-time to complete my bachelor's degree in Political Science. So even though I lost my GI Bill, the government still technically ended up paying for my college after all—a little detail that still makes me smile.

In the summer of 2009, Fahdi's mother, brother, and sister arrived in the United States as official refugees. We sponsored them and they lived with us for several months before continuing on to California and settling in a large Iraqi community in an Eastern San Diego suburb.

In October 2009, Fahdi returned from his final deployment to Iraq. We decided it was finally time to start living as a normal family. President Obama and his administration began reducing troops in Iraq, so we knew it was only a matter of time before Fahdi would be without a job anyway. I finally completed my B.A. in Political Science in December 2009, and Fahdi decided to go into real estate and earned his license. He excelled in the real estate business, but the turbulent housing market in rural Ohio struggled to recover from the subprime mortgage crisis and we decided to seek greener pastures elsewhere in the country. In the summer of 2013, we embarked on our own 21st century "Grapes of Wrath" journey and headed for California. We sold nearly everything we owned (including our dream home), packed only what we could fit into our two compact KIA cars, and made the two-day trek to San Diego. We settled in a small apartment just a mile down the street from Fahdi's mom's house and have been living the "California Dream" since. In October of 2014, our family became complete when we welcomed our second daughter, Elaina Reese. As this book goes to print, it's hard for me to believe that eleven years have passed since Fahdi and I shared that fateful first kiss atop the INIS building, surrounded by a world at war yet suspended in a dimension of complete bliss.

CPSIA information can be obtained
at www.ICGtesting.com
Printed in the USA
LVOW13s0852190417
531359LV00019B/646/P